CRIMINAL PROCEDURE

OBJECTIVE

Fifth Edition

Mary M. Cheh
Elyce Zenoff Research Professor
George Washington University Law School

Exam Pro ®

WEST
ACADEMIC
PUBLISHING

Exam Pro Series is a trademark registered in the U.S. Patent and Trademark Office.

© West, a Thomson business, 2001, 2005
© 2012 Thomson Reuters
© 2015 LEG, Inc. d/b/a West Academic
© 2020 LEG, Inc. d/b/a West Academic
     444 Cedar Street, Suite 700
     St. Paul, MN 55101
     1-877-888-1330

West, West Academic Publishing, and West Academic are trademarks of West Publishing Corporation, used under license.

Printed in the United States of America

ISBN: 978-1-64708-094-5

Preface

TO THE STUDENT:

Objective examinations are now common in American law schools. As a result, more students are seeking opportunities to practice and prepare for objective testing. This volume, and indeed the entire Exam Pro Series, answers that need. But that's not all. These books give students a new and enjoyable way to pull together what they have studied, to test themselves on their understanding, and to prepare for any kind of examination, whether essay, short-answer, or objective.

Exam Pro: Criminal Procedure consists of three examinations of forty two questions each. These questions can be used as practice essay questions, hypothetical problems to consider while studying the particular subject in class, or as actual objective questions to be answered under exam-like conditions.

After answering the questions, the innovation (and the fun) lies in assessing how well you did and why. The book contains answers that fully explain why one choice is correct and, as importantly, why the alternatives are wrong. Every answer is a compact consolidation of relevant principles, and these can easily be used as study summaries. If a question is based on an actual case, that is noted and a citation is provided. In addition, each answer includes references to additional sources, namely LaFave, Israel, King & Kerr, Criminal Procedure (6th ed. 2017 & Supp. 2019) and Whitebread & Slobogin, Criminal Procedure: An Analysis of Cases and Concepts (7th ed. 2020), to permit you to pursue topics in greater detail.

Basic courses in criminal procedure do vary, but the subjects covered here are typical of the vast majority. The bulk of the questions address interrogation and confessions, search and seizure, right to counsel, eyewitness identification, and the exclusionary rule. You will also encounter an occasional question in other areas such as entrapment and outrageous police conduct, bail, the grand jury, and harmless error. There is no particular order to the questions, and each exam is meant to include a full cross-section of all of the topics. If you do choose to take any of the tests under exam-like conditions (and that is an excellent idea), allow two hours to complete all forty-two questions.

Professor Mary M. Cheh

George Washington University Law School
August 2020

8qb. x 2 men = 9z writes
= 3 hr exam   1.5 h. + 1h essay + 30 writes essay

Table of Exam Topics

Summary of Contents

CRIMINAL PROCEDURE

OBJECTIVE

Fifth Edition

EXAM I
CRIMINAL PROCEDURE MULTIPLE CHOICE OBJECTIVE QUESTIONS

Raphael Trice was charged with assault with intent to commit robbery and illegal possession of a firearm. The government's evidence at trial showed that, just before 2pm on a Sunday afternoon, Earl Green was shot while walking near his residence. Green testified that Trice approached him and demanded that Green "give it up." Trice then shot Green with a shotgun and ran away. Green, who was only grazed by the shot, immediately called 911 and, within minutes after the incident, identified Trice as the shooter. Green explained that he knew Trice from the neighborhood. He even gave the police the address where he was "pretty sure" Trice lived. Green accompanied the police down to the station to provide further information and, while there, an officer showed him a photograph of Trice and said, "Is this the guy who robbed you?" Green said, "Yes, that's him." A short time later, Detective Truman obtained an arrest warrant for Trice and arrested him in his home. While in the home, Detective Truman saw Trice's mother and several small children who apparently also lived in the home. Detective Truman escorted Trice to his police car where he read Trice the Miranda warnings and asked, "Do you want to answer any questions at this time?" and Trice replied emphatically, "No." Detective Truman then asked Trice for his full name, social security number, and whether he had any serious medical conditions. Truman then asked Trice, "I'd like to know where the shotgun is. There are little kids in your house. I don't want anyone to get hurt." Trice responded, "It's okay, I gave it back to the person I borrowed it from." Truman did not ask any more questions.

[handwritten margin notes: custody; interrogation; rights under 5th Amendment triggered; Booking / Custodial / exception to rights triggered]

QUESTIONS:

[handwritten: Arrest = custody + interrogation → Miranda ✓; → reasonable concern for public safety]

1. **At a suppression hearing prior to trial, Trice moved to exclude his answer to the question about the gun, arguing that Detective Truman did not honor his right to remain silent; the trial court should:**

    [handwritten: → about gun × routine inquiry]

    (a) Deny the motion because the question was part of the routine inquiries that are made of suspects, and Miranda was never meant to apply to such an inquiry.

    (b) Deny the motion because Detective Truman scrupulously honored Trice's invocation of his right to silence and immediately turned from investigative matters to administrative ones.

    (c) Deny the motion because Truman's question was reasonably prompted by concern for public safety and was, therefore, within the "public safety exception" to the Miranda rules.

    [handwritten: Yes that some emergency category / exigent situation]

(d) Grant the motion because, by asking about the gun, Truman failed to honor Trice's right to remain silent, and the public safety exception cannot apply once a suspect is removed from his home.

(e) Grant the motion because no questions may be asked of a suspect if he insists, as Trice did, on his right to keep silent.

too broad

2. **Prior to trial, Trice moved to suppress any testimony related to Mr. Green's identification of his photograph at the police station and any in-court identification of Trice by Mr. Green. The trial court should:** *6th.*

(a) Disallow both the photo identification and the in-court identification because the photo identification was unnecessarily suggestive, and any in-court identification would be impermissibly influenced by the photo identification.

(b) Disallow both the photo identification and the in-court identification because Trice's Sixth Amendment right to counsel was not honored.

(c) Permit Mr. Green to testify as to the photo identification because it was arguably reliable, but disallow any in-court identification because there is some risk of error, and jurors attach too much significance to such identifications.

(d) Permit Mr. Green to testify about the photo identification and to make an in-court identification

(e) Permit Mr. Green to make an in-court identification but not to testify about the photo identification

* * *

Clifford Bogel's brother was murdered in the District of Columbia one day in early June. That very day, Bogel flew from California to the District to make funeral arrangements. Three days later undercover officers saw a man, later identified as Clifford Bogel, run up and shoot a man on the street. Marty, the victim, was shot multiple times and collapsed and died on the sidewalk. The police chased after Bogel, he eluded them briefly, but they eventually captured him and placed him under arrest. At the station house, Detective Gonzalez wanted to question Bogel about Marty's murder and read Bogel the Miranda warnings. Bogel said he did not want to talk "right then." Gonzalez then left the room and did not speak to Bogel again. About one hour later, Detective Parker asked Detective Gonzalez if he could speak to Bogel about the murder of his brother. Gonzalez told Parker that he had read Bogel his Miranda warnings and that Bogel had invoked his right to silence and did not want to talk about the murder case against him. Neither detective had any reason to believe there was a connection between the two murders. Gonzalez then introduced Parker to Bogel, telling Bogel that Parker only wanted to talk to him about the murder of his brother. Gonzalez then left Parker alone with Bogel. Parker told Bogel that he was investigating the murder of his brother and that he wanted to talk to him only about that murder and not the murder that Bogel was charged with. Parker asked Bogel if he had any information

not allowed   not interrogation.
simply investigative interview

about who might have shot his brother. Bogel asked about what others had told the police, and when Parker said no one seemed to know what happened, Bogel then said, "Let me tell you what happened." Bogel then explained his view of who killed his brother, and he went on to make incriminating statements about his involvement in the murder case against him.

QUESTION:

3.   **In the murder case against him, Bogel now seeks to suppress the incriminating statements he made to Detective Parker. Bogel claims the statements were obtained in violation of his Miranda rights. The district court should:**

   (a)   Suppress the statements because Bogel invoked his right to silence and questioning him again within one hour did not scrupulously honor his rights.

   (b)   Suppress the statements because Detective Parker did not rewarn Bogel before he asked him the questions about his brother's murder.

   (c)   Suppress the statements because, once Bogel invoked his Miranda rights, further questioning could only take place with Bogel's lawyer present.

   (d)   Admit the statements because Bogel evinced a willingness and desire to engage in a discussion with Detective Parker.

   (e)   Admit the statements because the questions Detective Parker asked were not interrogation within the meaning of Miranda.

* * *

Sally Johnson was arrested and indicted for the murder of her husband. Counsel was appointed, and she was held in the county jail. Norma Holloway, also awaiting trial for murder, was housed in the same cell block as Johnson. Holloway asked the jail guards if she could talk to Detective Jenner of the homicide squad, whom she knew from some prior brush with the law. Holloway told Detective Jenner that she was on the same cell block as Johnson and offered to report any incriminating statements she might make, "if it could help me with a lighter sentence." Detective Jenner said, "Well, if you bring us something, I'll see what I can do. See what you can find out, but don't get into any interrogation type thing with her. Just listen and pay attention." Over the next two days, Holloway engaged Johnson in conversation. She asked her, "What are you in for?" and "What's your story?" Johnson said she was going to use an alibi, but Holloway suggested that she come up with something better because "if they find the body, they can always get some evidence, like hair or something, linking you to the crime." At that, Johnson laughed and said, "Don't worry about that. I put the body where the Lord himself couldn't find it."

QUESTION:

4. **At Johnson's trial for murder, the prosecutor plans to introduce Johnson's incriminating statements. Johnson argues that introduction of the statements will violate her Sixth Amendment right to counsel. The evidence is:**

    (a) Inadmissible because Johnson did not know she was speaking to an informant and was, therefore, unaware of her right to keep silent.

    (b) Inadmissible because Holloway was acting as an agent of the state and affirmatively induced Johnson to make incriminating statements.

    (c) Admissible because Holloway initiated contact with the police, was acting for her own benefit, and was not an agent of the state.

    (d) Admissible because Johnson did not know she was speaking to an informant and, therefore, was not under any pressure to make the statements.

    (e) Admissible because Holloway was told not to interrogate Johnson, and her failure to follow instructions means the state was not responsible for her behavior, and there was no state action.

Assume that the statements from the previous question are inadmissible and that Johnson's husband's body has not been found. At trial Johnson takes the stand and, during her direct examination, testifies that she is innocent and therefore does not know where her husband's body is located. During the State's rebuttal, the prosecutor called Holloway to the stand and asked Holloway to divulge what Johnson had revealed about the whereabouts of the body.

QUESTION:

5. **Assume that Johnson's counsel objects to the question asked of Holloway. What is the judge's likely ruling on the admissibility of the evidence?**

    (a) The testimony is admissible because it is being used to impeach Johnson's credibility.

    (b) The testimony is admissible because the police acted in good faith when they told Holloway not to ask about the crimes and the fact that she did not listen is not the kind of mistake that furthers the purpose of the exclusionary rule.

    (c) The testimony is inadmissible because it is the fruit of the poisonous tree.

    (d) The testimony is inadmissible because the statements did not lead to the body and therefore, the inevitable discovery doctrine does not apply.

(e) The testimony is inadmissible because the Sixth Amendment violation here, unlike Fourth Amendment violations, occurs when the evidence is admitted at trial.

* * *

Wisconsin police had probable cause to search a car parked on a public street. They did not have a warrant, although there was no exigency preventing them from getting one. A search of the car netted cocaine and illegal guns, and the owner of the vehicle, Miss Muggle, was charged with drug and gun possession. The Supreme Court of Wisconsin ruled that the search was illegal because there was no warrant. In reaching this conclusion, the Wisconsin high court relied on its interpretation of the Fourth Amendment of the U.S. Constitution and on an analogous provision of the state constitution. The state prosecutor appealed to the United States Supreme Court, arguing that Wisconsin was not free to disregard Supreme Court precedents establishing the "automobile exception" to the warrant requirement, that is, that police, with probable cause may search a car without a warrant.

QUESTION:

6. **Assuming the Wisconsin prosecutor is correct about the "automobile exception," which of the following statements is the most accurate and appropriate?**

   (a) Wisconsin is free to apply its own interpretation of Fourth Amendment requirements so long as it provides greater protections for the criminally accused, not fewer.

   (b) Wisconsin is free to apply its own interpretation of Fourth Amendment requirements unless the Supreme Court chooses to exercise its supervisory power to assure uniformity among the various state court judgments.

   (c) Wisconsin is free to interpret its own state constitution in any way it sees fit so long as the case involves only a local or state prosecution.

   (d) Wisconsin is free to interpret its own state constitution to give greater protections to the criminally accused than those provided by the federal constitution, but Wisconsin must provide a clear statement that that is what it is doing.

   (e) Wisconsin is not free to provide greater or lesser protections than those of the Fourth Amendment. If the Fourth Amendment is applicable to the facts, the State's constitutional provision is preempted.

* * *

In November seven members of the Del Ray Police Narcotics Squad arrested Steven Matt in his grocery store, Matt's Market. The officers had a valid arrest warrant, but, although they had probable cause to search and were in the process of securing a search warrant, they did not yet have a warrant to search the premises. Because they received credible information that Matt might be armed, the officers entered the store with weapons drawn. The few customers in the store were escorted out, and Matt, who was behind the counter, was seized, handcuffed, and informed of his Miranda rights. With matters in hand, the officers holstered their weapons. The officers then told Matt they would like to search his store and asked for his consent. At first Matt said nothing, and one of the officers said, "Look, you do what you want. We have sufficient information to get a search warrant and will secure one by this afternoon or tomorrow." Matt then said, "I want to talk to my lawyer." He went to a telephone and tried twice, unsuccessfully, to reach his lawyer. After hanging up, Matt said to the officers, "Look I know what you are here for," and led the officers to a stash of marijuana behind the counter. The officers seized the drugs and said, "well, that's nice, but we still want to search the whole store." Matt then agreed to let them search, and they uncovered cocaine in some boxes at the back of the store. Later, while in custody at the police station, Matt was approached for the first time by two officers from the Vice Squad who wanted to question him about a gambling operation they believed he was running out of his store. They administered Miranda warnings, and Matt agreed to talk and made incriminating statements.

[handwritten margin notes: "not an ambiguous invocation of Miranda rights ↓ has to be 'unambiguous'"]

QUESTIONS:

7. **Matt was charged with gambling offenses and, prior to trial, moved to exclude his statements at the station house. He contends that, because the police initiated questioning after he had invoked his right to counsel, none of his statements may be used in the case against him. The district court should:**

    (a) Deny the motion because Matt's reference to a lawyer while in the grocery store was an anticipatory invocation of counsel which does not trigger Miranda's right to counsel rules.

    (b) Deny the motion because the officers who questioned Matt about the gambling offenses did not know he had invoked his right to counsel in the grocery store.

    (c) Deny the motion because the officers who questioned Matt about the gambling offenses reread him his Miranda rights and secured a proper waiver.

    (d) Grant the motion because Matt had invoked his right to counsel, and, as a result, the police were not permitted to reinitiate questioning unless counsel was present.

    (e) Grant the motion because police had an affirmative duty to clarify whether Matt was seeking a lawyer in connection with the search of his store or whether he was seeking a lawyer for all of his dealings with the police.

8. **Matt also faces drug charges in connection with the cocaine found in his store. He has moved to exclude the admission of the drugs, arguing that he never voluntarily gave consent for a search. The district court should:**

   (a) Grant the motion because the officer's statements about getting a warrant rendered any consent invalid.

   (b) Grant the motion because, once Matt said he wanted a lawyer, consent could not be valid until a lawyer was present, or at least until Matt had an actual opportunity to consult with a lawyer.

   (c) Grant the motion because, once a person is in custody, he is rendered unable to give voluntary consent.

   (d) Deny the motion because the officers did not threaten or deceive Matt; they had probable cause to obtain a search warrant, and were, in fact, in the process of obtaining the warrant.

   (e) Deny the motion because Matt had been Mirandized and, therefore, knew that he did not have to say anything to the police, give consent, or say anything at all.

   * * *

   In the early morning hours of a December day, officer Kay Vincent spotted Alex Reuben speeding down Highway 22. After pulling him over, the officer approached the car. She smelled alcohol on his breath and observed that his eyes were glazed and bloodshot and that his face was flushed. Officer Vincent asked Reuben where he was coming from, and he answered, "The Flamingo Bar, up the road there." Officer Vincent then asked Reuben to exit the vehicle and to perform several standard sobriety tests, such as lifting one leg and walking heel to toe in a straight line while counting each of the paces. Reuben performed these tests poorly and told the officer it was because he had been drinking. Officer Vincent then handcuffed Reuben and transported him to a county Detention Center where all proceedings were routinely videotaped. Reuben had not been given any Miranda warnings.

   At the Detention Center, Officer Vincent asked Reuben for his name, address, height, weight, eye color, date of birth, and social security number. Reuben provided the information but stumbled over several answers. Officer Vincent then asked Reuben to perform sobriety tests similar to those he performed at the initial roadside stop and also asked him to count from one to thirty. Reuben performed poorly and, while doing so, commented about his state of inebriation. It was then that Officer Vincent advised Reuben of his Miranda rights. Reuben signed a statement waiving his rights, but then declined to answer any questions.

   At Reuben's trial for driving under the influence of alcohol, the government sought to admit into evidence the videotape of the proceedings at the Detention Center together with the arresting officer's testimony that Reuben failed the roadside sobriety tests and all of Reuben's incriminating statements.

QUESTION:

9. **Reuben sought to exclude all of the statements he made prior to receiving Miranda warnings and all videotaping of the proceedings at the Detention Center. The district court should:**

   (a) Exclude all of the statements and the video because Reuben was not free to leave once his automobile was pulled over, and therefore, all of his responses were obtained in violation of Miranda.

   (b) Admit all of the statements but exclude the video because Reuben was not advised that his actions and statements were being recorded.

   (c) Admit all of the statements and the video.

   (d) Exclude only Reuben's response to the request to count from one to thirty because, at that point, Reuben was in custody, had not yet been Mirandized, and the question called for a testimonial response.

   (e) Exclude only Reuben's response to the roadside question, "Where are you coming from," because, unlike the other questions and information, this interrogatory was neither a booking question nor a non-testimonial display of physical characteristics.

* * *

Robin Tiefer suffered bouts of mental illness. At particularly acute periods, she experienced hallucinations, heard voices, and became delusional. During these periods, she might appear quite normal, oriented to time and space, although sometimes she might also appear subdued or agitated. During one of her periods of illness, she became convinced that she was compelled by a vengeful god to follow divine instructions. Following these instructions, she walked into the third precinct station house and told the desk sergeant that five years ago she murdered her newborn baby, incinerated the remains, and sprinkled the ashes in her garden. The sergeant was astounded. He asked Ms. Tiefer to sit down, and he proceeded to ask her questions about the crime. Ms. Tiefer appeared coherent and rational. She provided details of the event, and at the conclusion of her account, the sergeant said, "Well, I'm going to have to arrest you, Ma'am." The sergeant placed her in a cell and, 15 minutes later, Detective Johnston arrived and told Ms. Tiefer that he wanted to ask her some questions. He read her the Miranda warnings, and asked her if she was willing to waive her rights. She said, "Yes, I am here to do god's will." She then answered questions, again confessing to the murder of her child.

At a hearing to determine the admissibility of her incriminating statements to the sergeant and the detective, uncontradicted expert testimony established that, at the time she spoke to both officers, she was in a psychotic state and suffering from serious mental illness. The medical experts explained that Ms. Tiefer suffered from "command hallucinations" which interfered with her volitional abilities and disabled her from making free and rational choices. They also testified that she was so detached from reality that she could not understand the rights she had when she was advised that she could remain silent, her words could be used against her, or that she was entitled to have the presence of a lawyer.

QUESTION:

10. **The defendant has moved to exclude all of her statements. The district court should:**

    (a) Grant the motion in its entirety because Ms. Tiefer was acting involuntarily and the use of any of her statements would violate Due Process of law.

    (b) Deny the motion in its entirety because none of the problems Ms. Tiefer was experiencing were caused by the police and, there was, therefore, no state action.

    (c) Grant the motion but only with respect to the statements made to the sergeant because Ms. Tiefer was questioned by the sergeant before she was advised of her Miranda rights.

    (d) Grant the motion but only with respect to the statements made to the detective because Ms. Tiefer did not validly waive her Miranda rights.

    (e) Grant the motion but only with respect to the statements made to the detective because Ms. Tiefer was never advised that the statements she made to the sergeant were inadmissible, and she may have agreed to answer the detective's questions because the "cat was already out of the bag."

* * *

Police Officers responded to a radio broadcast about a forcible theft of a wallet from Rye Allen, the victim, who provided a description of the suspect. They stopped a car driven by Leland Jordan who matched the description of the robber. In the car, the police found the stolen wallet, a knife, and a gun. In the preceding weeks and in the same general vicinity, there had been a series of robberies at gas stations, cash machines, and restaurants. Jordan was formally charged with one count of robbery in connection with the forcible theft of Rye Allen's wallet, arraigned on that charge, and released on bail. Shortly after his release, the prosecutor in the case sought a court order directing Jordan to appear in a line-up. His attorney was also notified, and she appeared with her client on the appointed day. Jordan was placed in a line-up with five other men who resembled him in appearance but were all somewhat shorter. Jordan's attorney objected vigorously and insisted that the police find other participants who were of the same height. The police officers told her "to pipe down," and called in, one at a time, Rye Allen and the nine other persons who had been robbed in other incidents. The witnesses were told to take their time and simply indicate that they had made an identification or they had not. After all nine had separately viewed the lineup, the line-up participants, including Jordan, were excused, and the witnesses were asked to remain so that the police could talk to them at greater length. Jordan's attorney insisted that she be allowed to remain to observe the conversations with the witnesses. The police refused, and she was ordered out of the room. Most of the witnesses, including Rye Allen, made a positive identification of Jordan.

Jordan was subsequently charged with six counts of robbery, one involving the wallet and five involving some of the earlier incidents. At his trial, his attorney objected to the introduction of the pretrial identifications, claiming a violation of Jordan's Sixth Amendment right to counsel. The trial court denied the request to suppress the pre-trial identification evidence and also denied defense counsel's request to introduce expert testimony from a professor of psychology regarding the reliability of eyewitness identifications. Jordan was convicted of all counts and has appealed.

QUESTIONS:

11. **Regarding Sixth Amendment challenge to the admission of post-charge line-up identification evidence generally:**

   (a) If the police do not permit the defendant's attorney to attend the line-up procedure, the admission of the line-up identification and any in-court identification are *per se* impermissible.

   (b) If the police do not permit the defendant's attorney to attend the line-up procedure, the admission of the line-up identification and any in-court identification will nevertheless be admissible if the government proves them to be reliable.

   (c) If the police do not permit the defendant's attorney to attend the line-up procedure, the admission of the line-up identification is *per se* impermissible, but an in-court identification may be allowed if the government proves by clear and convincing evidence that there was a reliable basis, apart from the line-up, to make the in-court identification.

Wade-Gilbert Rule

   (d) If the police do not permit the defendant's attorney to attend the line-up procedure, the admission of the line-up identification and the in-court identification will nevertheless be allowed unless the defendant proves that both are substantially likely to lead to mistaken eyewitness identification.

no, burden on government —

   (e) If the police do not permit the defendant's attorney to attend the line-up procedure, the line-up identification will be automatically excluded, and an in-court identification will be permissible only if a new line-up is conducted in front of the jury under the trial court's supervision.

12. **Regarding Jordan's motion to exclude the line-up identification evidence as a violation of his Sixth Amendment right to counsel:**

   (a) The motion should have been granted because Jordan's attorney was not permitted to remain for the discussion between the police and the witnesses.

(b) The motion should have been granted because Jordan's attorney identified flaws in the line-up procedures (the relative height of the defendant compared to the other participants), but her objections were ignored. ⤷ counsel: not an active participant, but passive observer.

(c) The motion should have been denied because Jordan's attorney was present to observe the confrontation of the defendant with the witnesses, and the right to counsel does not apply to witnesses' interviews after the line-up.

(d) The motion should have been denied because no right to counsel had attached to any of the charges Jordan faced.

(e) Even if Jordan's right to counsel had been violated in part, the motion should have been denied because, at trial, a full opportunity to conduct cross-examination would disclose any improprieties that occurred.

court of appeal / court's review standard

13. Regarding the trial court's exclusion of defendant's expert who would have testified about the reliability and unreliability of eyewitness identifications:

(a) On appeal, the trial judge's ruling will not be overturned unless it was an abuse of the court's discretion.

(b) On appeal, the trial judge's ruling is not subject to reversal because only the trial court could evaluate the witness's demeanor and determine whether her testimony would confuse the issues and mislead the jury. too extreme

(c) On appeal, the trial judge's ruling must be reversed because due process recognizes the right of a defendant to introduce such expert testimony in any case where identification is a critical part of the case against him.

(d) On appeal, the trial judge's ruling may be reversed if the appellate court concludes, on a *de novo* review, that the expert's testimony would have assisted the jury in deciding the identification question.

(e) On appeal, the trial judge's ruling on the admissibility of expert identification testimony is always considered harmless.

* * *

After months of thorough investigation, the Pontiac Police Department developed probable cause to believe that Dr. Mathis, the President of an "educational" non-profit, was funneling tens of thousands of dollars in drug proceeds through his non-profit. Although the paper trail was difficult to establish, the police obtained evidence that Dr. Mathis was involved with a violent gang widely known to control cocaine distribution channels and that he had the financial acumen to make the money appear legitimate. The police, while investigating, also noticed an unusual amount of foot traffic in and out of Dr. Mathis's house at odd hours throughout the day. After determining that enough reliable evidence was presented to her, the Magistrate issued a search warrant of Dr. Mathis's home, specifically noting that Dr. Mathis was to be arrested should he be present at the time of the search. The warrant targeted twenty separate categories of documents and things, focusing the search of the residence on evidence of money laundering, tax evasion, and documentation of the cocaine sales.

At 10:00 am on July 19, 2010, officers went to execute the warrant. They knocked, announced their presence, but nobody responded. Within minutes, the law enforcement officials knocked down the door with a battering ram, scaring Dr. Mathis's wife Janet and his daughter Melissa. Officer Langley, pointing his gun, ordered Janet and Melissa to "get down" immediately and placed them both in handcuffs. The officers proceeded to conduct a quick sweep of the home, after which Officer Langley displayed the warrant. Janet and Melissa remained in handcuffs for nearly three hours while the authorities scoured the premises. They were, however, permitted to use the restroom when needed. At the conclusion of the search, the officers seized two computers and six boxes of documents, leaving Janet with a copy of the warrant and a written inventory of the items seized. Janet was ultimately implicated and charged with violating a multiplicity of drug and tax laws.

QUESTION:

14. **Prior to Janet's trial, she moves to exclude the items seized during the search of her home. What is the most accurate and appropriate ruling on Janet's motion?**

    (a) The motion to suppress will be denied because the police used reasonable force in entering the house.

    (b) The motion to suppress will be granted because the police did not allow enough time to pass before knocking down the door with a battering ram.

    (c) The motion to suppress will be denied because the warrant was sufficiently particular in the items sought.

    (d) The motion to suppress will be granted because the officers were only looking for documents.

    (e) The motion to suppress will be denied because the manner of entry and the detention of Janet and Melissa were reasonable.

* * *

Michael Chase was the founder and executive director of The Chase Foundation, a major national charitable organization which collected money for veterans, homeless families, and sick children One day FBI Agent Roemer received an anonymous telephone call from a man identifying himself as "someone within the executive ranks of the Chase Foundation." The caller said that Chase was skimming money from the Foundation and using it for his own purposes, and then hung up. Two weeks later Agent Roemer received another call from the same anonymous person. The caller, sounding indignant, said, "Why haven't you done anything about that thief Chase? He's taking money from really needy folks and you're letting him get away with it." Struck by something in the caller's voice, Agent Roemer decided to do some investigating. She went to the Chase Foundation and talked to various officers, but she was unable to uncover anything. She then went to Chase's house and observed that it was quite grand, with manicured lawns and two luxury automobiles in the driveway. Agent Roemer decided that further investigation was required and, so, prepared an application for a warrant to search Chase's business office and his home for any documents "related to fraud by wire and mail fraud." The application referred to and included two documents, Attachment A and Attachment B. Attachment A described in detail the address, description, and location of Chase's office and his home. Attachment B described the categories of information to be seized as "Records, documents, computer disks, financial records, receipts, and banking and any other financial instruments related to fraud by wire and mail fraud," and it referred to an affidavit by Agent Roemer. The affidavit described the two anonymous calls, the agent's visit to Chase's house, and stated in relevant part, "Affiant does believe that evidence of fraud in the administration and finances of the Chase Foundation will be found at the office of Mr. Chase and at his residence and that such evidence will disclose violations of the federal wire and mail fraud statutes." Without hearing oral testimony, the Magistrate issued a search warrant to search the locations described in Attachment A and to seize the items identified in Attachment B. Through inadvertence, the affidavit was not physically attached to the warrant.

QUESTION:

15. **Several agents executed the warrant and thoroughly searched Chase's office and home and recovered 17 boxes of written materials which did disclose fraudulent activities and resulted in Chase's indictment on multiple counts of fraud. Before the trial court, Chase unsuccessfully moved to exclude the information seized in the search. He then entered a conditional plea of guilty, reserving his right to appeal the adverse ruling on his motion to suppress. On appeal, the appellate court should:**

    (a) Uphold the trial court's ruling because whatever deficiencies existed in the warrant were excusable under the "good faith exception."

    (b) Uphold the trial court's ruling because the Magistrate's decision to grant the warrant was not without some foundation and, therefore, substantial deference must be given to her judgment.

    (c) Reverse the trial court's ruling because the affidavit was not actually made a part of the warrant and, without it, the basis for the search did not rise to the level of probable cause.

    (d) Reverse the trial court's ruling because the trial court lacked a substantial basis for concluding that probable cause existed and the warrant was hopelessly overbroad.

(e)   Reverse the trial court's ruling because the Magistrate took no oral testimony on the application for the warrant and was simply a "rubber stamp."

* * *

Officer Knight noticed a van with a broken tail light and legitimately signaled it to stop. After checking the driver's license and registration, Officer Knight gave the driver a warning, told him he was free to leave, and began to walk away. Almost immediately, however, the officer turned back toward the driver and politely asked if he was carrying any guns or drugs. The driver said no, and Officer Knight then asked, "Well, do you mind if I search the car?" The driver turned to the other passengers in the vehicle and whispered something the officer could not hear. The driver then exited the vehicle. Officer Knight noticed a large bulge in the driver's pocket, which he appeared to want to conceal. Officer Knight then frisked the driver and noted that the bulge felt like a weapon. The officer instructed the driver to empty his pocket. At first the driver emptied the other pocket, but when Officer Knight repeated his order, he finally displayed the object—a pipe containing marijuana residue.

QUESTION:

16. **Prior to trial on a possession of marijuana charge, the driver moved to suppress the evidence of the pipe and the drug contained within it. The trial judge should:**

(a)   Deny the motion because the officer lawfully stopped the driver and developed a reasonable suspicion that he was armed and dangerous.

(b)   Deny the motion because once a vehicle is lawfully stopped, a police officer may, in the interest of safety, conduct a protective frisk of any occupant who exits the vehicle.

(c)   Grant the motion because, once Officer Knight told the driver he was free to leave, the original encounter was over; the subsequent questioning about guns or drugs amounted to an unjustified temporary detention, and the evidence derived from this unlawful stop was inadmissible.

(d)   Grant the motion because there was no evidence that the driver was involved in criminal conduct, and a frisk is improper unless an officer has reasonable suspicion that a person is armed and dangerous and is involved in criminal conduct.

(e)   Grant the motion because an officer may not frisk a person when there is no duty, as under these facts, for the officer to be in that person's presence.

* * *

Yasmin and Betty were driving down Route 66 in Yasmin's red pick-up truck. They were headed to the beach and had thrown their bags in the open flatbed back of the truck. Each had a large canvas duffel bag with her name flamboyantly embroidered on each side. Officer Brig stopped the truck after seeing it sway across the center line of the highway. Upon approaching the vehicle, Officer Brig smelled the odor of marijuana coming from the cab of the truck. He asked Yasmin and Betty to step out of the vehicle, took down their names, and directed them to stand apart, each one positioned at one of the truck's front headlights. Officer Brig then visually inspected the interior of the cab and opened and examined containers, such as a toolbox and a can of tennis balls. He found nothing to account for the marijuana smell. He then approached Yasmin and asked for her driver's license and registration. Yasmin appeared nervous and said, "Well I suppose you have your suspicions. Let me just admit that, yes, I had been smoking a marijuana joint, but I tossed it out the window just before you pulled us over. I don't want any trouble and Betty here is a good kid—she's never even tried a joint." Hearing this, Officer Brig looked again inside the cab and then went to the back of the truck. He began feeling the outside of the canvas bags, pressing and manipulating the contents. With Betty's bag, he pressed and pushed the outside of the bag so thoroughly that he was sure he felt a brick of marijuana. He then opened Betty's bag, retrieved a brick of marijuana, and arrested both women for possession of marijuana.

QUESTION:

17. **Prior to her trial on possession of marijuana Betty moves to suppress the brick of marijuana. The trial court should:**

    (a) Grant the motion because Officer Brig's manipulation of the bags amounted to a search, and although he had probable cause to search the cab and the containers within, he lacked probable cause to believe he would find evidence of a crime in the bags in the open flatbed back of the truck.

    (b) Grant the motion because, although Officer Brig may have had probable cause to search Yasmin's belongings, either in the cab or the flatbed back, he had no probable cause to search Betty's possessions which were plainly marked with her name.

    (c) Deny the motion because Officer Brig had reasonable suspicion to believe there were drugs in the vehicle, and his manipulation of the canvas bags was in reasonable proportion to the level of suspicion and the minor intrusion it involved.

    (d) Deny the motion because the smell of marijuana and Yasmin's admission gave the officer probable cause to believe there was marijuana in the truck, and he was entitled to search all containers that could contain it.

    (e) Deny the motion because, once Yasmin and Betty put their bags in the open flatbed area of the truck, anyone could have handled them and, so, neither of them had any expectation of privacy related to Officer Brig's touching or feeling of the outside.

* * *

A man placed a 911 call to police headquarters and reported that a 19-year-old African American male named "Lucky" had raped and murdered a female. The caller said that the victim's body could be found in the basement at 1704 N. 37th Street, a residence the caller described as "a drug house." The caller identified himself as "Anthony Carter" and stated that he lived "in the neighborhood." Two police officers immediately traveled to 1704 N. 37th Street. The building was a duplex with upper and lower units. The lower unit was 1704. Standing in front of the building was a young African-American male calmly holding a dog on a chain. The street was quiet. The man identified himself as Clarence Richardson and said he lived in unit 1704. The police officers explained to Richardson that they had received a 911 call reporting a murder. Richardson told the officers that nothing was going on and that "it's just another crank call from my nutty neighbors." Richardson then turned to take his dog inside the residence. The police officers instructed him to secure the dog on the porch because they needed to search the residence. As one officer put it, "Well, Mr. Richardson, we have to go on what we know. All we know is that we got a report of a murder and a body at this address, and we have to check it out to see if someone is dead or needs assistance. Sometimes victims are still alive so we have to check." The police entered the front door, looked in the bedroom and other areas of the 1st floor and then proceeded to the basement. Eventually they searched the entire house. They did not have a warrant. Throughout the house, the police saw illegal drugs and weapons. They did not find a female murder victim.

QUESTION:

18. **Based on the discoveries in the house, Richardson was charged with various narcotics and firearms offenses. Prior to trial, Richardson filed a motion to suppress all evidence gathered during the warrantless search of his home. The trial court should:**

    (a) Grant the motion because the report described the person as already dead, and there was no emergency need to enter the home without a warrant.

    (b) Grant the motion because the officers had an alternative to a warrantless entry, namely, they could have ordered Richardson and anyone in the house to come out and then secured the premises until a warrant was obtained.

    (c) Deny the motion because, in the circumstances, it was reasonable to believe that a person was dead or near death and to search for the victim on the premises.

    (d) Deny the motion because, although anonymous calls may not furnish a reasonable basis to justify an emergency warrantless entry, once an individual gives his name, police and other emergency personnel are duty-bound to act immediately.

    (e) Deny the motion because the police officer's comment to Mr. Richardson showed that they viewed the situation as an emergency requiring an immediate response.

* * *

Argonne Chemical Inc. manufactures and packages veterinary drugs. Food and Drug Administration Agents inspected Argonne several times over the last eighteen months to insure compliance with federal food and drug statutes. The FDA agents cited Argonne for several deficiencies. A month after the last inspection, FDA agents secured an administrative order for the seizure of various drugs alleged to violate the food and drug statutes. Relying on this order, the agents went to Argonne and seized over $100,000 worth of veterinary drugs from Argonne's premises.

The federal food and drug laws prohibit the adulteration or misbranding of any drug, whether for humans or animals. Virtually every phase of the drug industry is heavily regulated, from packaging, labeling, and certification of expiration dates, to prior approval before new drugs can be marketed. Strength, quality, and purity of drugs are extensively monitored. Manufacturing practices for the preparation of human and animal drugs are set forth in detail, and drug manufacturers must comply with detailed reporting and filing requirements. The federal food and drug laws identify various substantial interests to support close monitoring of the drug industry, and the laws provide for unannounced inspections of manufacturing plants and processes and for the swift seizure, pursuant to administrative orders, of misbranded drugs and their removal from the stream of commerce. Regulations governing seizure require that FDA officers file a verified complaint, under oath, describing with particularity the property that is to be seized and to file the complaint with the clerk of a federal district court, and serve a copy on the manufacturer at the time of seizure.

QUESTION:

19. **The FDA has now brought a condemnation action against the seized drugs, and Argonne has appeared to contest the constitutionality of the seizure. In deciding whether the seizure violated the Fourth Amendment, a court should conclude that,**

    (a) There was no violation of the Fourth Amendment because the Fourth Amendment does not apply to routine inspections of commercial premises; such inspections "touch at most upon the periphery of the important interests safeguarded * * * against official intrusions."

    (b) There was no violation of the Fourth Amendment because inspections of commercial premises, if routine and performed by government actors other than the police, do not require a warrant.

    (c) There was no violation of the Fourth Amendment because drug manufacturing is a highly regulated industry and the government's substantial interest in assuring properly manufactured and labeled drugs is furthered by the inspection program which provided an adequate substitute for a warrant.

    (d) There was a violation of the Fourth Amendment because even if, under the circumstances, a routine regulatory inspection need not proceed with a warrant, any *seizure* of items, as in this case, did require a warrant.

(e)   There was a violation of the Fourth Amendment because the FDA agents had previously inspected and noted the items they wanted to seize; their return over a month later demonstrates that there was no emergency and no reason why a warrant could not have been obtained.

* * *

Police have painstakingly put together enough information to arrest Dart Vander for murder. The police first developed basic information about the crime and, with the help of eyewitnesses, put together a description of the suspect. One witness said he knew the person as "Dodie or Dart Vander." Armed with this information, the police then went to the department of motor vehicles and learned that a person named Dart Vander and meeting the suspect's precise description lived at 2099 Mission Avenue. The police took all of their information to a magistrate and secured an arrest warrant for Mr. Vander. Warrant in hand, they immediately traveled to 2099 Mission Avenue. Once at the address, the police saw windows boarded up and high weeds growing on the front lawn. Although it was early evening, the house appeared dark. The police went to a neighbor's house to ask whether 2099 Mission was the address of one Dart Vander. The neighbor said, "Yes, that's his house. No one has seen him since about two months ago when he piled some stuff in his car and drove off. Are you officers here about the weeds, it's a terrible eyesore— we called a couple of times to complain." The officers said no and walked back to the house at 2099 Mission. They tried the door, but it was locked. They knocked loudly several times and called out, "Police, open up!" After a few minutes, they used a crowbar to break down the door. They entered the house, searched for Mr. Vander but found nothing but drug paraphernalia and a small amount of cocaine on the kitchen table.

QUESTION:

20.   **Later Mr. Vander was arrested and charged with drug offenses related to the items found at 2099 Mission. He moves to suppress all of it. The trial court should:**

(a)   Exclude the evidence because the police used too much force in gaining entry into the house.

(b)   Exclude the evidence because the police lacked a reasonable suspicion to believe that Mr. Vander was in the house.

(c)   Exclude the evidence because the police violated Mr. Vander's reasonable expectation of privacy in gaining access to his driver's license information without a warrant.

(d)   Admit the evidence because the police knocked, announced their presence, and waited for the suspect to appear before forcing open the door.

(e) Admit the evidence because the police were acting in good faith under the authority of a warrant issued by a magistrate.

* * *

Two uniformed police officers encounter Marcella as she alights from a train. The officers walk alongside of her as she travels down the concourse. One of the officers says, "hi," identifies himself, and then asks her some questions including whether she is carrying any guns or illegal drugs. When she answers "no," they then ask whether they can search her luggage.

QUESTION:

21. **Which of the following additional facts will best strengthen the conclusion that consent to search, if given, was voluntary?**

    (a) Marcella was informed of her right to refuse consent.

    (b) Marcella was a college graduate.

    (c) The encounter took place in a well-lighted, public area with other persons present.

    (d) Only one officer was present when the request to search was made.

    (e) The police and Marcella were all of the same race and ethnic background.

* * *

Police officers have set up a surveillance of Cruella's house. She is wanted for dog napping and other crimes. Cruella's partners in crime have turned themselves in and provided physical evidence and their own statements implicating her as the leader. At one point Cruella returns home and appears to be inside for the evening. She is completely unaware that the police are nearby. Officer Dithers decides he does not want to go through the headache of getting a warrant and, together with several other officers, enters the house and arrests Cruella. While in the house, Officer Dithers reads Cruella her Miranda rights and asks several questions about the dognapping scheme. Cruella makes several incriminating statements. Once outside of the house and while in a waiting cruiser, Cruella is again given Miranda warnings and again, in response to police questions, incriminates herself.

QUESTION:

22. **Which of the following statements is the most accurate and appropriate?**

    (a) The statements inside the house are inadmissible as a fruit of the illegal arrest; the statements made in the cruiser are admissible.

    (b) Both the statements inside the house and the statements made in the cruiser are inadmissible; both are products of the illegal arrest and the effect of that illegality was not cured by a fresh set of Miranda warnings.

(c)   Both the statements inside the house and the statements in the cruiser are inadmissible because Officer Dithers did not act in good faith; he knew of the need for a warrant and purposefully elected not to get one.

(d)   The statements inside the house are inadmissible as a fruit of the illegal arrest; the statements made in the cruiser may or may not be admissible depending on whether a court determines that the effect of the illegal arrest carried over to what took place in the cruiser.

(e)   Both the statements inside the house and the statements made in the cruiser were voluntary and, therefore, both are admissible.

* * *

Because of several anonymous calls to police headquarters, the police suspected that Johnny, 21 years old and living at home with his parents, was responsible for the murder of a 13 year old boy named Emory. Two officers went to Johnny's house and, being admitted by Johnny's father, told the father that they had come to talk to Johnny about the murder of Emory. They falsely told the father that they had conclusive evidence, including fingerprints, linking Johnny to the crime. The father then hollered to his son to come down from his room. No sooner had Johnny entered the living room than his father began beating him. As the police looked on, the father punched him and slapped him screaming, "You Killer! You no good bum!" The son then screamed—"No, no, no! Dad, wait, it was an accident. I can explain!" At that point, the officers pulled Johnny away from his father and placed him under arrest.

Once at the police station, the officers placed Johnny in an interrogation room and read Johnny his Miranda rights. Eventually, the police obtained a full written confession from Johnny.

QUESTIONS:

23. **Assume Johnny's lawyers file a motion to exclude Johnny's statements at home. The strongest argument in support of such a motion is . . .**

(a)   The statements are inadmissible because Johnny was never given an opportunity to invoke his Miranda rights.

(b)   The statements are inadmissible because the police obtained consent to enter the home on false pretenses.

(c)   The statements are inadmissible because the police had no probable cause to pursue Johnny at his home, and all of the statements were a product of that illegality.

(d)   The statements are inadmissible because the police lied about the evidence they had against Johnny.

(e) The statements are inadmissible because they were coerced by the father whom the police effectively used as their agent.

24. **Assume the statements in the house were excluded, which of the following statements is the most accurate and appropriate?**

(a) The giving of Miranda warnings at the police station was not sufficient in itself to break the chain between the in-house statements and the police station statements.

(b) The giving of Miranda warnings at the police station was sufficient to break the chain between the in-house statements and the police station statements. ↳No fruit in violation of Due Process of law is not admissible.

(c) The giving of Miranda warnings at the police station could cut off the connection between the in-house statements and the police station statements but only if the police warned Johnny that his in-house statements could not be used against him.

(d) The giving of Miranda warnings was unnecessary both at the house and at the police station because volunteered statements are always admissible.

(e) The giving of Miranda warnings was sufficient to break the chain between the in-house statements and the police station statements because the in-house statements were subject to interpretation and the "cat was not really out of the bag."

* * *

Jackie is arrested on a valid arrest warrant, brought to the police station, placed in an interrogation room, and advised of her Miranda rights. She responded, "Well, okay, I guess I'm in trouble. I understand my rights; I just hope my Dad gets me a good lawyer." The police then told Jackie, falsely, that they had her fingerprints on the murder weapon and an eyewitness who would identify her as the killer. Jackie sat for almost an hour responding only to three questions and even then, only with a nod or a one word response. The officers, growing impatient, went over their "evidence" again and told Jackie that her only hope of leniency, if any, was to make a full confession then and there. This sequence was repeated two more times until Jackie asked for a pen and paper and began scribbling a full confession.

QUESTION:

25. **Before trial, Jackie moves to suppress her confession. How should the trial court decide?**

(a) The confession is inadmissible because the police continued to question Jackie after she invoked her right to an attorney.

(b) The confession is admissible because none of Jackie's constitutional rights were violated.

(c)   The confession is inadmissible because Jackie, through her actions, evinced a desire to remain silent and the police did not scrupulously honor Jackie's desire to remain silent.

(d)   The confession is admissible because there was no police interrogation; the police merely advised Jackie of the situation she faced.

(e)   The confession is inadmissible because, given the totality of the circumstances, the police signaled to Jackie that they were going to continue their questioning until she responded.

* * *

Bugsy has learned that she is the target of a grand jury investigation into a securities fraud scheme. She promptly retains counsel. Thereafter, Bugsy calls the government lawyer and the detectives working on the investigation and tells them: "I know what is going on, and here's a flash for you: I have a lawyer, and I don't want nobody asking me questions without my lawyer, see?" Several weeks later, the detectives arrange for Ella, a friend of Bugsy's who has now turned government informant, to elicit incriminating statements from Bugsy concerning the securities fraud scheme. Ella is wired for sound and, during the course of several conversations with Bugsy, tapes incriminating statements about the securities fraud scheme. This additional evidence was then made available to the grand jury. The government now wishes to use those statements against Bugsy in a criminal prosecution for securities fraud.

QUESTION:

26. **Which of the following statements is the most accurate and appropriate?**

(a)   The statements are admissible because neither Fifth nor Sixth Amendment rights were violated.

(b)   The statements are admissible because neither the Fifth nor Sixth Amendment protect a person from a "false friend."

(c)   The statements are inadmissible because the government surreptitiously secured the incriminating statements about securities fraud knowing that Bugsy had retained an attorney on the securities fraud matter.

(d)   The statements are inadmissible because Bugsy's Fifth Amendment privilege not to incriminate herself before the grand jury was circumvented by Ella's acting as a transmitter of her words.

(e)   The statements are admissible because Ella was only an "ear"; she simply had a conversation with Bugsy and did not deliberately elicit the incriminating information.

* * *

Police developed probable cause to arrest Simone for theft. They also had probable cause to search her home for the stolen item, namely a valuable pendant inscribed, "To Fifi, with love." Police secured a search warrant but elected not to get an arrest warrant. Police went to Simone's house, and upon knocking and announcing themselves, let themselves in after no one answered the door after several minutes. Inside, the police saw an individual seated on the living room sofa listening to music through headphones. Police approached, explained their presence, and immediately arrested Simone when she identified herself. One officer then searched her and found the pendant inside her pants pocket. Another officer searched the area around the living room sofa and recovered an unregistered gun in a closed drawer of the coffee table.

QUESTIONS:

27. **Simone is charged with theft of the pendant and illegal possession of a gun. Prior to her trial, she moves to exclude both items as evidence. Which of the following statements is the most accurate and appropriate?**

    (a) The motion should be denied because a search warrant permits a search of every place, including persons and closed drawers, where evidence identified in the warrant might be found.

    (b) The motion should be denied because the pendant and the gun were seized pursuant to a valid search incident to arrest.

    (c) The motion should be granted because the police should have had an arrest warrant to arrest Simone in her own home, and all of the seized evidence was derivative of that illegality.

    (d) The pendant was properly seized pursuant to the search warrant but, once the police found it on Simone, they were not permitted to search any further.

    (e) The motion should be granted because police behaved unreasonably by entering the home without consent or before waiting a longer period for someone to answer the door.

                                    * * *

Assume that, in the question above, when the police entered Simone's house, Simone was seated next to her friend, Raul. Raul was a very good friend and planned to stay the night. After police found the unregistered gun in the coffee table drawer, they also arrested Raul. The police then searched the adjacent rooms. They found Raul's shaving kit in an upstairs dresser bureau and, inside the shaving kit, was a plastic bag containing marijuana.

28. Raul is charged with possession of an unregistered gun and marijuana. Prior to trial, he moves to exclude the gun and the marijuana. Which of the following statements is the most accurate and appropriate?

    (a) Both the gun and the marijuana will be excluded because the police had no probable cause to connect Raul to the gun and no basis to conduct a search of the adjacent rooms.

    (b) Both the marijuana and the gun will be excluded because the warrantless arrest of Simone in her own home was unlawful and all other actions were derivative of that illegality.

    (c) The gun will be admissible as a lawful search incident to the arrest of Simone, and its close proximity to Raul and Simone gave probable cause to arrest both; the marijuana will be excluded because the police had no basis to conduct a search of the adjacent rooms.

    (d) Neither the gun nor the marijuana will be excluded because, although Raul may have planned to stay the night, he had not yet done so and, thus, had no standing to complain of any search inside Simone's house.

    (e) The gun will be excluded because Raul had no connection to it, but the marijuana will be admissible because, pursuant to the search warrant, the police could search every room in the house and open any closed containers where the stolen pendant could have been located.

                                    * * *

29. Assume Raul, a citizen of France and present in the United States under a student visa, was on parole for a prior drug conviction. Assume further that, in addition to prosecuting Raul for illegal gun and marijuana possession, government officials have begun separate proceedings to revoke Raul's parole and to deport him to France. Assume that the trial judge in the criminal prosecution has ruled that both the gun and the marijuana were illegally seized in Simone's house. Which of the following statements is the most accurate and appropriate?

    (a) Until overturned on appeal, the judge's ruling excluding the gun and the marijuana in the criminal case must also be applied to use of the gun or the marijuana in the parole revocation hearing and the deportation hearing.

    (b) The exclusionary rule does not apply to parole revocation hearings or deportation hearings.

    (c) The exclusionary rule applies to parole revocation hearings because such proceedings are essentially criminal in nature, but does not apply to deportation hearings which are essentially civil in nature.

(d) The exclusionary rule applies in deportation hearings because it would have a significant deterrent effect on INS agents who might otherwise purposefully seize evidence in an unlawful way; the rule would not apply to parole revocation cases because police would not ordinarily jeopardize a criminal prosecution by illegally seizing evidence just to revoke someone's parole.

(e) The exclusionary rule does not apply to the proceedings against Raul because, as a citizen of France, he may not claim constitutional guarantees in collateral proceedings.

* * *

Spider was an informant for the Orange County police. He was paid small sums of money for his tips, which had always proved to be reliable. On April 13, Spider told Officer Fallon that Donnie was selling drugs from the bedroom of his home. Spider said that the day before, he was with Donnie when he made a drug sale, and he described the circumstances in full detail. Spider also said that Donnie planned to sell more drugs the next day. Spider gave Officer Fallon the names and descriptions of the two drug addicts who would be making the purchases. Officer Fallon went to Donnie's house the next day and did, in fact, observe the described persons enter Donnie's house and leave shortly thereafter carrying small packages. On December 2, Officer Fallon prepared an affidavit reciting the tip and his observations, although he did not identify the informant by name or mention his past record of reliability. A magistrate issued a warrant to search Donnie's house. With warrant in hand, Officer Fallon went immediately to Donnie's address. Officer Fallon knocked and announced his presence, and Donnie admitted him. Fallon did not immediately arrest Donnie but told him he was "not free to leave until the search was completed." Officer Fallon then thoroughly searched the premises and found several bags of cocaine in a guitar case in Donnie's bedroom closet. Officer Fallon then arrested Donnie.

QUESTION:

30. **Donnie is later prosecuted for possession of cocaine. Prior to trial, he moved to exclude the cocaine found in his bedroom. Which of the following is Donnie's best argument to support this motion?**

(a) Officer Fallon's failure to recite the informant's past reliability rendered the warrant invalid for lack of probable cause.

(b) Since the tip and Officer Fallon's own observations gave rise to probable cause to arrest Donnie, Officer Fallon should have obtained an arrest warrant before entering Donnie's house.

(c) Officer Fallon went beyond the scope of a proper search since the warrant did not particularly identify the guitar case as an item to be searched.

(d) The magistrate did not have probable cause to issue the warrant because there was no basis to believe that Donnie was then selling drugs from his house.

(e) Even though the police may refuse to inform the defendant of an informer's identity, Officer Fallon's lack of disclosure to the magistrate was misleading and fatally tainted the warrant.

* * *

Amy is arrested and jailed on manslaughter charges. At the jail, Detective Henderson gives the Miranda warnings to Amy, whereupon she says that she doesn't want to talk without a lawyer. All questioning stops. The next day, Amy's family hires a lawyer who comes to meet with her. Two hours after the meeting, Detective Henderson returns to the jail and tells Amy that he wants to talk to her. Amy says that she is just not sure whether she wants to talk or not without a lawyer and asks the detective what he thinks she should do. Detective Henderson says "Well, this is entirely your choice, you know. You have to make your own decision on this." He then advises her of her rights once more. Amy says that she understands, and then she asks to sign a waiver form. She confesses.

QUESTION:

31. **Amy now moves before trial to suppress the confession. Her best argument in support of her motion is that:**

   (a) The evidence should be suppressed because Detective Henderson's initiation of a conversation with Amy about the case in the absence of her lawyer violated her Sixth Amendment rights.

   (b) The evidence should be suppressed because Detective Henderson did not scrupulously honor Amy's request to be left alone.

   (c) The evidence should be suppressed because Detective Henderson's initiation of a conversation with Amy in the absence of her lawyer violated her Miranda rights.

   (d) The evidence should be suppressed because Amy did not knowingly and voluntarily waive her right not to talk without an attorney present.

   (e) The evidence should be suppressed because Amy's invocation of counsel was clear and unequivocal.

* * *

Marlene, the next door neighbor, came over to Nick's apartment to use the telephone. Marlene called Janice, and the two of them had a whispered conversation about Nick and his friend Tony. During the conversation, the two incriminated themselves and Nick and Tony in a conspiracy to illegally import endangered birds from Brazil. As it happens, however, the police placed a tap on the telephone. The police had extensive evidence, far more than probable cause, to establish that the four were involved in an illegal importation scheme, but, at that point, they were delayed by other pressing business and had not yet completed the paperwork to obtain a warrant for the tap.

QUESTION:

32. **Assume all four are tried, separately, for conspiracy to violate federal import statutes. Which of the following statements is the most accurate and appropriate?**

    (a) All four have standing to object to the illegal tap.

    (b) Only Nick, as the owner of the phone, has standing to object to the illegal tap.

    (c) Only Marlene and Janice, as the participants in the conversation, have standing to object to the illegal tap.

    (d) Only Tony lacks standing to object to the illegal tap.

    (e) None of the four can object to the tap because the police had probable cause, and they would have inevitably secured the warrant.

* * *

Officer Jones is part of a new community outreach program of the police department. He is going from door to door to introduce himself to the neighborhood and develop a cordial relationship with the residents. He gets to Elmer's house, walks up the steps, and knocks on the front screen door. Through the open wooden door, he sees a marijuana plant growing in a pot on a table in the open. The house is silent, and no one answers his knock.

QUESTION:

33. **Which of the following statements is the most accurate and appropriate?**

    (a) Jones may seize the marijuana because it is in plain view.

    (b) Jones may seize the marijuana because the owners have exhibited no reasonable expectation of privacy in it.

    (c) Jones may seize the marijuana immediately because of the exigent circumstance that it may promptly be destroyed.

    (d) Jones has violated the Constitution by entering upon the property and the curtilage of the defendant's house without justification and without a warrant.

    (e) Jones may apply for a search warrant using the evidence he obtained by looking through the open door because he violated no constitutional right in getting that information.

* * *

Kramer went across the hall to Jerry's apartment looking for Elaine. Jerry, his close friend, was not home, but the door was unlocked. Kramer let himself in as he usually did. He watched television and fixed himself lunch. No one turned up, so he took a nap on the couch. About two hours later, the police burst into the apartment, and the commotion awakened Kramer. He yelled: "What are you doing here, do you have a warrant?!" The officers answered: "It's none of your business, Bub," and proceeded to search the entire apartment including Kramer's backpack. In fact, the police had no warrant and no probable cause. In their search, the police found an unregistered gun in Kramer's backpack, and he was charged with illegal possession of a weapon.

QUESTION:

34. **Which of the following statements is the most accurate and appropriate?**

    (a) In order to exclude the gun as evidence, Kramer must prove by a preponderance of the evidence that he has standing to object to the officers' search.

    (b) Since Kramer was a regular guest of Jerry's and was, in fact, napping on his couch, he had standing to object to the search of the apartment.

    (c) Kramer has no standing to object to the search, and the gun will be admissible against him.

    (d) Kramer will have standing to object to the admission of the gun unless the police prove he was a "casual" or "fleeting" visitor.

    (e) Kramer has standing to object to the admission of the gun because, as a close friend of Jerry's and a frequent visitor to his apartment, Kramer was "legitimately on the premises" with Jerry's consent.

* * *

The police stopped a car containing four occupants almost immediately after receiving a report from a parking lot attendant that he had been robbed at gunpoint by two men. The car matched the description, and the description of the robbers matched two of the four occupants. Following the stopping of the automobile, the occupants were handcuffed and placed in a patrol car. The officers then searched the passenger compartment of the car and found a bag under the driver's seat. The officers felt the outside of the bag and noted that the items inside did not feel like a weapon but proceeded to open it anyway. Upon opening the bag, the officers found the proceeds of the robbery. The officers, wanting to locate the guns, then unlocked the trunk and found two handguns.

QUESTION:

35. **Which of the following statements is the most accurate and appropriate?**

    (a) The search is invalid because, although it was incident to the arrest, the items seized were beyond the control of the suspects.

    (b) The search of the passenger compartment was valid but the search of the locked trunk exceeded the scope of the officers' lawful authority.

    (c) The search of the passenger compartment of the car is invalid because the police were not permitted to open the bag once they determined that there were no weapons inside and the subsequent search of the trunk was fatally tainted by the search of the passenger compartment.

    (d) The search is valid because there was probable cause and the "automobile exception" applied.

    (e) The search of the passenger compartment is valid because it was reasonable to believe that evidence of the robbery would be found therein but the search of the trunk is invalid because the police can never search the trunk during a search incident to arrest.

* * *

Police were called to a local convenience store where they made an on-the-scene arrest of Tommy Henderson for robbery and assault with a deadly weapon. The police had no warrant but witnesses' accounts gave them probable cause to believe that Henderson brandished a gun and forcibly took money from two of the store's customers. Henderson was booked and charged with two counts of robbery and unlawful possession of a firearm. Under applicable state procedure, Henderson was brought before a magistrate within twenty four hours. At this initial appearance, there was no determination of probable cause, but Henderson was informed of the charges against him, advised that he was entitled to a preliminary hearing within thirty days, and bail was set at $5,000. Although Henderson was not asked to enter a plea, or indeed not invited to say anything, he interrupted the judge to say, "I shouldn't be here without a lawyer. My cousin is a lawyer. I'd like to call him. Otherwise, I need a public defender because I don't have any money." The judge simply said: "There will be time enough for that later, Mr. Henderson; we have other business at this point." Henderson, unable to make bail, was remanded to the custody of the local police. Three days later, Henderson was given Miranda warnings and interrogated about the incident at the convenience store. He waived his rights and, after talking with the police officers for about thirty minutes, made incriminating statements.

QUESTIONS:

36. **If Henderson brought a declaratory judgment action claiming he was entitled to a judicial hearing on the issue of whether there was probable cause to arrest and hold him, which of the following is the government's strongest argument to defeat his claim?**

    (a) Immediately after Henderson's arrest, the prosecutor filed an information reciting the basic facts on which the charges were based.

    (b) The day after Henderson's appearance before the Magistrate, the court released Henderson from custody on the condition that he wear a monitoring bracelet and remain at home.

    (c) There was no further need to establish probable because the police had made a public place arrest and their factual basis was obtained from information furnished by reliable eyewitnesses.

    (d) Under the applicable state procedures, Henderson was advised of his right to have a preliminary hearing within thirty days, but having failed to request such a hearing, he waived any further preliminary proceedings.

    (e) Immediately after Henderson's arrest, the grand jury handed up an indictment charging Henderson with two counts of robbery and one count of unlawful possession of a firearm arising out of the convenience store incident.

37. **Prior to trial, Henderson moves to suppress the incriminating statements he gave to the police. Which of the following statements is the most accurate and appropriate?**

    (a) Henderson's statements are admissible. None of his constitutional rights were violated.

    (b) Henderson's statements are admissible. Although Henderson could have insisted that his lawyer be present at any interrogation, his statements to the Magistrate were not a clear and unequivocal invocation of his right to counsel.

    (c) Henderson's statements are inadmissible. Once the right to counsel is invoked any subsequent waiver is necessarily the result of police coercion.

    (d) Henderson's statements are inadmissible. The Magistrate's failure to determine whether there was probable cause to hold him rendered his continuing custody a Fourth Amendment violation, and any statements secured while he was in illegal custody are inadmissible.

    (e) Henderson's statements are inadmissible. His comments to the Magistrate were a valid invocation of counsel, and thereafter, any attempt to interrogate him required that his lawyer be present.

* * *

Jules and Beezer were indicted for fraud in connection with selling stock in non-existent businesses. They were released on bail pending their trial. The two talked frequently about how they could best defend themselves. One day, Jules called Beezer to say that he learned that Miss Marple, an elderly widow and one of their best customers, was going to be the principal witness against them. Indeed it appeared that, if Miss Marple were unavailable to testify, the case against the pair would essentially evaporate. Jules told Beezer that he wanted his help in hiding some of the incriminating documents the police had not yet found and in "really scaring" Miss Marple so that she either "has a heart attack" or realizes that testifying against them "will definitely not be in her best interests." Beezer, worried that he was already in "too deep" and feeling concerned for the charming Miss Marple, tried to dissuade Jules from pursuing this course of action. When that failed, Beezer decided to go to the police. He told the police that he wanted to make a deal. In return for a promise of lenient treatment, Beezer told the police of Jules' plans. He also told them that the two of them talked regularly on the phone and would meet on Tuesday to discuss "all options" for their defense. The police then enlisted Beezer's help in order to prevent destruction of evidence and to protect Miss Marple. Beezer agreed to have a tap placed on his telephone and to wear a tape recorder when he met with Jules on Tuesday. The Tuesday meeting produced several statements by Jules which incriminated him in the fraud case and also implicated him in obstruction of justice and conspiracy to murder Miss Marple.

QUESTION:

38. **At his trial on the fraud charges, Jules objects to the government's use of the incriminating statements obtained from the Tuesday meeting. Which of the following statements is the most accurate and appropriate?**

    (a) The prosecution may use the statements because the government did not set up the Tuesday meeting between Beezer and Jules; it was merely the passive beneficiary of a contact already planned.

    (b) The prosecution may use the statements if the government proves, by a preponderance of the evidence, that its purpose in seeking the statements was only to gather evidence related to the future crimes of obstruction of justice and harm to Miss Marple.

    (c) The prosecution may use the statements because the government was investigating Jules' attempt to subvert the trial process in the fraud case against him.

    (d) The prosecution may not use the statements because they were obtained in violation of Jules' Sixth Amendment rights.

    (e) The prosecution may not use the statements because the real motive of the police was to gather evidence against Jules in his fraud trial and not really to uncover evidence of obstruction of justice or harm to Miss Marple.

* * *

Officers Kojo and Blaine were part of a drug detection unit assigned to the bus depot in Daytona Beach, Florida. They worked as a pair, and sometimes they would call upon another officer to bring a drug sniffing dog to sniff the outside luggage compartment of the bus and any luggage that might be resting on the walkway leading to the bus. As buses stopped to pick up new passengers and give on-board passengers a chance to stretch their legs, Kojo and Blaine would enter the bus, identify themselves as drug interdiction officers, and politely ask passengers if they would be willing to allow their bags to be searched. Hearing this routine, Deek Opperman, a passenger sitting in the back of bus #239 en route to North Carolina, stood up and in a loud voice yelled, "They have no right to do this! This is a free country! Just say no to these fascists!" Opperman clutched one of his two black bags and started jumping up and down, screaming, "Just say no, just say no!" Officer Blaine went to the back of the bus and, taking Opperman by the arm, said "Let's you and I just step off the bus and talk this over." Blaine then led Opperman off the bus. Meanwhile, Officer Kojo continued with their usual routine of asking passengers to identify which bags belonged to them and asking whether they would permit a search or not. After a few minutes, it became clear that there was one black duffel bag which no one claimed as his own. Officer Blaine held it up and said, "For the last time, does this bag belong to anyone?" When no one claimed it, Officer Blaine treated it as abandoned property and opened it. Inside he found cocaine and some papers with the name "D. Opperman." Based on this discovery, police charged Opperman with possession of cocaine.

QUESTION:

39. **At his trial for possession of cocaine, Opperman moves to suppress the cocaine found in the black duffel bag. Which of the following statements is the most accurate and appropriate?**

    (a) The evidence will be suppressed because the search of the bag was illegal, and the police would not have otherwise inevitably discovered the cocaine inside.

    (b) The evidence will be suppressed because the police had effectively arrested Opperman, the arrest was illegal, and all subsequent activity was derivative of that illegality.

    (c) The evidence is admissible because Opperman effectively abandoned the black duffel bag, and, as abandoned property, the police could search it without consent or probable cause.

    (d) The evidence is admissible because, even if the search of the bag was illegal, the police would have inevitably discovered it because they had drug sniffing dogs available.

    (e) The evidence is admissible because Opperman, having become rowdy on the bus, was properly taken into custody; the evidence in the duffel bag would have inevitably been discovered as a search incident to arrest.

* * *

Mitch Anderson was arrested in connection with the brutal murder of a small child. The community was shocked by the crime, and the police were intent on putting together a solid case against Anderson. In their zeal, however, the police mistakenly forgot to give Anderson his Miranda warnings before beginning to question him. Actually each detective simply assumed that the other had taken care of this small detail. Nevertheless, Anderson willingly agreed to talk. After a few minutes of his denials, the situation got heated as one of the detectives began yelling, "We want the truth and we want it now. Our patience is running real thin, real thin, Mr. Anderson." Anderson continued to claim innocence until one of the detectives said, "Look we can do this the hard way or the easy way. If you don't admit your guilt right here and right now, we will put you in the general prison population and let the word leak out that you are a child molester. And God help you then because your life won't be worth two cents." Anderson then said, "Well, can we make some kind of a deal? I'll confess, but you have to protect me and no death penalty." The police agreed and Anderson confessed, giving the police full details of the crime and providing ample and unmistakable corroboration of his guilt. Prior to his trial for murder, the trial judge suppressed the confession given to the police and the evidence derived therefrom. At trial, Anderson took the stand in his own defense and proceeded to tell a story completely at odds with his confession. He repeatedly perjured himself.

QUESTION:

40. **The prosecutor now seeks to use Anderson's confession to impeach his trial testimony, and Anderson objects. Which of the following statements is the most accurate and appropriate?**

    (a) The statements may be used for impeachment because the ultimate purpose of a criminal trial is ascertaining factual guilt, and Anderson's confession was, in fact, reliable.

    (b) The statements may be used for impeachment if the prosecutor can show the court that Anderson's direct testimony was perjurious.

    (c) The statements may not be used for impeachment because Miranda holds that statements obtained in violation of its requirements "may not be used for any purpose."

    (d) The statements may not be used for impeachment because they were not voluntarily given.

    (e) The statements may not be used for impeachment because they were unreliable.

* * *

Taking as its guide the federal bail statute, Massachusetts enacted a bail reform act that provides that trial judges may, in deciding whether to release a defendant prior to trial, impose a variety of conditions on a defendant, including the posting of money bail. The judge may impose these conditions, or decide to detain the defendant, if necessary to assure the defendant's appearance at trial or to protect any person or the community from danger posed by the defendant. If the government is seeking pretrial detention, a hearing must be held to determine if the defendant poses a flight risk or is a danger. However, persons charged with aggravated sexual battery against a minor or charged under the state's "Sexual Predator" statute are automatically assumed to pose a danger to others.

Benny is charged with aggravated sexual battery on a minor, and Andy is charged with obstruction of justice in connection with trying to cover up Benny's activities. At their arraignment, Benny's counsel asks that he be granted bail, but the judge denies the request saying that he is subject to pretrial detention under the statute. Andy's counsel also asks that her client be granted bail. The judge notes that Andy is unemployed, has no known address, and few ties to the community. She sets bail at $10,000, but Andy is indigent and unable to post the required amount. He, too, is remanded to jail until trial or until he can meet the bail amount.

QUESTION:

41. **Both defendants have raised constitutional claims challenging the court's bail decision. Which of the following is the *strongest* argument either could make to challenge the court's bail ruling?**

   (a) Bail set at an amount too great for an indigent defendant to meet violates the Eighth Amendment's guarantee that excessive bail shall not be required.

   (b) Bail set at an amount too great for an indigent defendant to meet violates the presumption of innocence of Due Process of law since a jailed defendant is effectively punished before being convicted of any crime.

   (c) The automatic detention of persons charged with aggravated sexual battery on a minor violates procedural Due Process.

   (d) Preventive detention violates the basic Eighth Amendment principle that assuring the defendant's appearance at trial is the only legitimate objective of the bail system.

   (e) Bail set at an amount too great for an indigent defendant to meet violates the Equal Protection Clause because being set at liberty prior to trial, like having a lawyer for one's defense or having access to a transcript on appeal, should not depend on how rich or poor a person may be.

* * *

Ashton, an American citizen, landed in Atlanta after a long flight from the Philippines. Ashton was so exhausted from traveling and was so eager to get through customs that he filled out his declaration form with the utmost care, hurried to the baggage carousel to pick up his checked baggage, and headed over to the customs inspection point. Upon reaching the customs agent, he was told he was selected at random for secondary questioning. The second agent asked Ashton questions about his whereabouts, the length of his trip, and its purpose. While inspecting the contents of his luggage, the agent asked him to turn on his computer in order to make sure it was operating properly. When the computer booted up, there were several icons and the agent opened a file entitled "Kodak Pictures." In the file were several nude pictures of women. Homeland Security agents from the immigration department were called in and they took Ashton to a separate room, detained him for several hours, and proceeded to search his computer and external hard drive. They found what they believed to be child pornography, released Ashton but seized the equipment. A week later, they obtained a warrant to search the equipment, and Ashton is now charged with several crimes arising from the incident.

QUESTION:

42. **Prior to trial, Ashton moves to suppress the images found on his computer arguing that the search was invalid under the Fourth Amendment. Which of the following statements is the most accurate and appropriate?**

    (a) The suppression motion should be granted because Ashton's effects were searched without any particularized suspicion.

    (b) The suppression motion should be granted because people have a heightened expectation of privacy in their computers due to the massive amount of personal and business information capable of being stored on them.

    (c) The suppression motion should be granted because Ashton's computer was seized without a warrant.

    (d) The suppression motion should be denied because individualized suspicion was not necessary to search the computer.

    (e) The suppression motion should be denied because, by failing to password protect the files on the computer, Ashton did not take affirmative measures to protect his expectation of privacy.

END OF EXAM I QUESTIONS

EXAM II
CRIMINAL PROCEDURE MULTIPLE CHOICE OBJECTIVE QUESTIONS

Swaggart was a suspect in his live-in girlfriend's murder. The police found the woman dead in the basement of his townhouse, apparently the result of blows to the head from a blunt instrument. Swaggart initially told police he knew nothing of what happened, that his girlfriend must have been killed by an intruder while he slept upstairs, and that he did not want to cooperate further. A few days after the murder, Swaggart called Detective Dano, the detective in charge of the investigation, to get an "update on what was happening." The detective invited him to come to the police station "to talk things over." Swaggart went to the police station where he met with Detective Dano and another officer in a small room with only a table and some chairs. The detective told Swaggart that he was not under arrest and gave him Miranda warnings. Swaggart then signed a Miranda waiver form and agreed to take a polygraph test and answer questions. After the polygraph was administered, Detective Dano asked a couple of preliminary questions and then matter of factly informed Swaggart that the polygraph test indicated that he was lying. This was an exaggeration since the test revealed only that it was unclear whether Swaggart was telling the truth. At that point, Swaggart said that he would like to obtain counsel. Detective Dano said, "you may or may not need a lawyer, I don't know-you should just tell me the truth." Swaggart then admitted that he sometimes quarreled violently with his girlfriend but that he did not kill her. Swaggart then stood up and left the station.

Over the next two weeks, the police developed further evidence linking Swaggart to his girlfriend's murder and arrested him. Detective Dano again advised Swaggart of his Miranda rights. Swaggart signed a waiver card and answered questions for about fifteen minutes. The detective then asked Swaggart if he would provide the police with "body samples." The following exchange then occurred:

Officer: Would you be willing to uh, give us hair samples, blood sample [sic]. Anything that we might need for our investigation?

Swaggart: Yeah, just as soon as I talk to a lawyer.

Officer: Okay, you have a right to do that.

Swaggart: I don't, you'll have to get me one 'cause I ain't got one.

Officer: Okay. That's right, now are you wanting the lawyer just, just for the decision on that . . . before you talk to me?

Swaggart: No. you can leave this [tape recorder] on.

Officer: That's what I'm saying, are you wanting to stop it now since you know you told me you wanted a lawyer?

Swaggart: Well, when can you get me a lawyer?

Officer: That'll be up to the courts, they'll get you one, ya know, that's no problem. I just need to know, you know if you're through talking to us or if you want to continue to talk?

Swaggart: No, I'll talk to you.

Swaggart then made incriminating statements.

QUESTIONS:

1. **Assume that Swaggart moved to exclude the initial incriminating statement that he sometimes quarreled violently with his girlfriend. Which of the following statements is the most accurate and appropriate?**

    (a) The statement will be admissible because Swaggart was not in custody at the time the statement was made.

    (b) The statement will be admissible because Swaggart was not responding to a question, and thus was not being interrogated at the time he made the statement.

    (c) The statement will be admissible because the Detective scrupulously honored Swaggart's decision to terminate the meeting.

    (d) The statement will be inadmissible because the Detective continued the interrogation after Swaggart said he wanted to obtain counsel.

    (e) The statement will be inadmissible because the Detective misled Swaggart about the polygraph results.

2. **Assume Swaggart moved to exclude the incriminating statements he made during his second encounter with Detective Dano. Which of the following statements is the most accurate and appropriate?**

    (a) The statements will be admissible because there was a decent interval between the first questioning session and the second.

    (b) The statements will be admissible because Swaggart might have wanted an attorney only in connection with giving body samples, and he did not clearly and unequivocally ask for a lawyer before answering any questions.

    (c) The statements will be admissible because any problem with the first interview was cured by the giving of a fresh set of Miranda warnings and the signing of the waiver card at the second questioning session.

    (d) The statements are inadmissible because Swaggart raised the issue of having a lawyer, and it was the Detective's job to clarify what he meant.

(e)   The statements are inadmissible because, even though Swaggart's reference to a lawyer at the second questioning session was unclear, he had already requested counsel at the first interview and that constituted invocation of his right to counsel.

* * *

In the early morning hours of November 12th, Officers Dole and Langen saw Eddie Turner driving erratically. They pulled him over and asked for his driver's license. Turner gave officer Dole a piece of paper on which was written a false name and other information. Dole asked Turner if he had been drinking or using drugs. Turner denied he had been drinking, but did not reply to the question about drugs. Dole asked Turner to exit the car and walk to the rear. Turner complied but seemed a bit unsteady on his feet.

Officer Lalla then arrived at the scene to administer sobriety tests to Turner. Based on the tests, Lalla believed that Turner was impaired by a substance other than alcohol. Lalla arrested Turner, advised him of his Miranda rights, and placed him in a patrol car. Meanwhile, a fourth officer on the scene, Officer Kron, searched the car to see if she could find the substance Turner may have ingested, as well as to see if there were any weapons in the vehicle. During the search, Officer Kron saw an unfastened canvas bag on the floor of the passenger side. Inside the bag, Kron found an unloaded semi-automatic weapon, a loaded clip for the weapon, and a container of crack cocaine. As Lalla was pulling away with Turner in the back, Turner stated: "All right, I'll tell you my real name" and gave Lalla his real name, date of birth, social security number, and other personal information. When Turner arrived at the jail, another officer conducted a urine drug test which showed that Turner had consumed phencyclidine (PCP). During the testing, Turner was cooperative and answered questions appropriately.

After the testing, Detective Henderson interviewed Turner. Henderson again advised Turner of his Miranda rights. Turner signed a waiver form, initialing each admonition. Turner then admitted that he had stolen the crack cocaine and the gun in Kansas City and was going to sell them in order to get money to buy Christmas presents for his daughter. During the interview, Turner was cooperative.

Following the interview, while in jail, Turner exhibited "bizarre" behavior. About one week later, on November 20th, Dr. Remi Cadoret, a psychiatrist, examined Turner and diagnosed a psychotic disorder and substance abuse. Several months later, in March, and again in July, another psychiatrist examined Turner and diagnosed a PCP-induced psychotic disorder. In August, pursuant to a court-ordered sanity and competency evaluation, a forensic psychologist examined Turner. The doctor reported to the court that Turner's I. Q. was in the low-average to borderline range, his "verbal comprehension was stronger than his verbal expressive abilities," and his profile was consistent with that of a malingerer. The doctor testified that, at the time of his arrest, Turner's functioning was affected by the influence of PCP, but he noted that Turner was able to follow directions, respond appropriately to questions, and was "goal-oriented" in that he stated his intention to sell the gun and the cocaine for money. The doctor opined that, at the time of his arrest, Turner "had the ability to appreciate the nature of his actions" and was competent to stand trial.

Before trial, Turner moved to suppress the gun and the cocaine as invalid under the Fourth Amendment. He also claimed that use of his admission of his name and related information would violate Miranda, and that his confession had to be excluded because he did not have the mental capacity to voluntarily and knowingly waive his rights. At a suppression hearing, Turner presented several witnesses including a psychiatrist who testified that, because of a low I.Q. and PCP use, Turner "was incapable of forming an intelligent and knowing waiver of his Miranda rights." Although the doctor diagnosed Turner as suffering from a PCP-induced psychosis, the doctor admitted that, at the time of Turner's arrest, he might have only been intoxicated by PCP. On cross-examination, the doctor admitted that a person intoxicated by PCP might understand verbal and written communication.

QUESTIONS:

3. **Assume the district court rejected Turner's claim that he lacked the mental capacity to waive his Miranda rights and refused to suppress his confession. Which of the following statements is the most accurate and appropriate?**

    (a) In reviewing the district court's suppression ruling, the Court of Appeals may set it aside only if it was clearly erroneous.

    (b) In reviewing the district court's suppression ruling, the Court of Appeals may decide the question de novo.

    (c) In reviewing the district court's ruling, the Court of Appeals must evaluate all facts in a light most favorable to the defendant.

    (d) In reviewing the district court's ruling, the Court of Appeals reviews the district court's finding of facts for clear error, and reviews de novo the ultimate determination whether the accused voluntarily and knowingly waived his rights.

    (e) In reviewing the district court's ruling, the Court of Appeals must show "due deference" to the trial court's findings of fact and conclusions of law.

4. **Assume that the district court has yet to decide the issue of whether Turner validly waived his Miranda rights. Which of the following statements is the most accurate and appropriate?**

    (a) The waiver was valid because, even if Turner was suffering from a drug-induced psychosis, the police questioning was neither improper nor coercive; in other words, the police were not the cause of the defendant's mental infirmities, and there was no state action.

    (b) The waiver was valid because, even though Turner was under the influence of PCP and later exhibited signs of mental illness, he was sufficiently intelligent and competent to understand his rights at the time of his confession.

(c) The waiver was valid because Turner specifically initialed each Miranda admonition after it was read to him.

(d) The waiver was invalid because PCP intoxication is a *per se* basis on which to conclude that the defendant lacked the mental capacity to waive his rights.

(e) The waiver was invalid because the police officers sought a waiver from Turner at a time when they knew he was under the influence of some substance.

5. **Assume the district court is asked to decide whether Turner's statements of his name, age, social security number and other personal information are admissible and assume that the information is somehow incriminating. Which of the following statements is the most accurate and appropriate?**

(a) These statements are admissible because they were part of routine booking questions

(b) These statements are admissible because they were spontaneous and volunteered.

(c) These statements are admissible because asking for information such as a name, age, or a social security number is not an attempt to compel "testimony" but only a way to learn basic information which each individual constantly exposes to the public.

(d) These statements are inadmissible because Turner was being held by the police, had been asked for his driver's license prior to receiving Miranda warnings, and would not have provided the information had he not been placed under arrest.

(e) These statements are inadmissible because persons need not cooperate with the police, and Turner signaled that he did not want to reveal personal data when he gave the police a false name.

6. **Assume the district court is asked to decide whether the weapon, ammunition, and cocaine found in the car are admissible. Which of the following statements is the most accurate and appropriate?**

(a) The items are admissible because they were properly obtained as part of a protective sweep of the car for the officers' safety.

(b) The items are admissible because they were properly discovered as part of a search incident to an arrest.

(c) The items are admissible as a frisk of the car incident to the officers' reasonable suspicion to stop Turner for erratic driving.

(d) The items are inadmissible because there was no reason to believe evidence of erratic driving would be found in the car.

(e) The items are inadmissible because the police lacked reasonable suspicion to think Turner was armed and dangerous and had no probable cause to search the bag.

* * *

Mia was indicted on six counts of mail fraud in connection with a scheme to swindle senior citizens out of their life savings. Police decided not to arrest Mia at the time of the indictment because they believed she was involved in an ongoing drug distribution ring. Over the next two weeks, pursuant to a lawful warrant, they tapped her phone and obtained incriminating statements from her conversations with police informers about the drug operation and the mail fraud scheme.

QUESTION:

7. **Which of the following statements is the most accurate and appropriate?**

   (a) All of Mia's incriminating statements are inadmissible because a wiretap requires at least one party's consent to the tap.

   (b) All of Mia's incriminating statements are admissible because a warrant for the tap, valid on its face, was obtained.

   (c) Mia's incriminating statements as to the mail fraud involvement are inadmissible.

   (d) Mia's incriminating statements as to the drug operation are inadmissible.

   (e) All of Mia's incriminating statements are inadmissible because the police violated Mia's Due Process rights by failing to arrest her promptly after her indictment.

* * *

Dennis Mobley lived alone in a one bedroom apartment, leased in his name. Armed with an arrest warrant, three FBI agents arrived at Dennis Mobley's apartment one morning at 8:30. The warrant was based on information from wiretaps and police informants and recited that there was probable cause to believe Mobley was engaged in a conspiracy to distribute crack cocaine. The agents knocked at the door, and when Mobley, who was naked, opened the door, the agents stepped across the threshold and secured Mobley against the wall. As two of the agents were effecting the arrest of Mobley, the third, Agent Lin, did a security sweep of the premises. While in the bedroom, Agent Lin noticed a nightstand drawer standing slightly open with some papers protruding out. He walked to the table and, pulling the drawer slightly open, was able to see betting slips and other betting paraphernalia inside. He removed the items and returned to the living room where the other agents and Mobley were now standing. Once all of the agents determined that there was no one else in the apartment, they seemed to relax. The lead Agent, Borah Martin, officially informed Mobley that he was under arrest, and she told him that several other agents were about to arrive with a search warrant to look for narcotics on the premises. Mobley was allowed, under surveillance, to go to his bedroom and dress. He returned to the living room where Agent Martin informed him of his Miranda rights. Mobley said he wanted a lawyer. As Mobley and all three agents were leaving the apartment, Agent Martin turned to Mobley and said, "Since the other agents will be coming to conduct a search, is there anything in the apartment that would pose a threat to them, like a weapon?" Mobley replied that there was a gun in the bedroom closet, and he then led the agents to it. The gun was located amidst Mobley's sweaters in a clothes closet in his bedroom. Ultimately Mobley was indicted for illegal possession of gambling paraphernalia and illegal possession of a firearm.

QUESTIONS:

8. **Prior to trial, Mobley filed a motion to suppress his statements concerning the gun, arguing that the FBI agents obtained them by improperly questioning him after he invoked his right to have a lawyer. The district court should:**

    (a) Grant the motion because, even if the agent's question was actually prompted by concern for the safety of the other agents, once Mobley invoked his right to counsel, no public safety exception could apply.

    (b) Grant the motion because the question violated Miranda rules, and the public safety exception did not apply because Mobley was being led out, the agents knew that there was no one else in the apartment, and they knew that Mobley was unarmed.

    (c) Deny the motion because the public safety exception permits a question about the whereabouts of weapons if an officer has an actual safety concern and, here, the agent sincerely had the welfare of the other agents in mind.

    (d) Deny the motion because the agent's question was spontaneous and was not designed to elicit an incriminating response.

    (e) Deny the motion because Miranda rules were never designed to foreclose questions about firearms, and officers may always ask suspects about the whereabouts of guns.

9. **Prior to trial, Mobley filed a motion to suppress the betting slips and other evidence found in the nightstand, arguing that the search of the nightstand was unreasonable under the Fourth Amendment. The district court should:**

    (a) Grant the motion because the agents lacked probable cause to believe that anyone else was lurking in the house and, therefore, no protective sweep, and hence no discovery of evidence in the nightstand, was justified.

    (b) Grant the motion because the agent went beyond the scope of a cursory visual inspection of those places where a person might be hiding.

    (c) Deny the motion because the agent was properly conducting a protective sweep and, since Mobley left the nightstand drawer open, he assumed the risk that someone in the bedroom would look in the drawer.

    (d) Deny the motion because, in conducting the protective sweep, the agent was in a spot he was lawfully entitled to be, and he could see papers sticking out of the drawer in plain view.

    (e) Deny the motion because the agents were arresting Mobley on a charge of conspiracy to distribute crack cocaine and, therefore, there was reasonable suspicion that weapons would be found in a protective sweep of obvious hiding places, like the nightstand.

10. **Assume for the purpose of this question that Mobley's statements about the gun could not be used at trial; in deciding whether the gun itself would be admissible, the district court should rule that:**

    (a) The gun is admissible because derivative evidence rules do not apply to non-testimonial physical fruits recovered as a result of statements obtained after the suspect has invoked his Miranda rights.

    (b) The gun is admissible because it would have inevitably been discovered during the search of the apartment for narcotics.

    (c) The gun is admissible because, even if Mobley should not have been asked about weapons, he voluntarily led the agents to the place where the gun was stashed.

    (d) The gun is inadmissible because it is a fruit of the poisonous tree and allowing officers to obtain derivative evidence from Miranda violations will invite purposeful disregard of the Miranda rules.

    (e) The gun is inadmissible because, once Mobley invoked his right to counsel, the agents were not permitted, absent initiation of conversation by Mobley himself, to obtain any evidence from him unless counsel was present.

11. **Assume for purpose of this question that the district court admitted Mobley's statements about the gun and the gun itself and that Mobley was convicted of the gun offense; if on appeal, the Court of Appeals rules that the gun was properly admitted but the statements were not, the Court of Appeals should:**

    (a) Reverse the conviction unless the error was harmless beyond a reasonable doubt.

    (b) Reverse the conviction automatically because the error was of constitutional dimension, and no constitutional violation will be regarded as harmless.

(c) Reverse the conviction because the admission of statements obtained after a suspect has asked for counsel is an error so intrinsically harmful that reversal is mandated without regard to the effect of the error on the outcome of the trial.

(d) Sustain the conviction unless the defendant proves, by a preponderance of the evidence, that the error actually affected the jury's verdict.

(e) Sustain the conviction unless the defendant shows that reversal will operate as a deterrent to future police misbehavior.

* * *

One morning Officers Gunny and Gander responded to a 911 call of a home being burglarized. Upon reaching the victim's home, they encountered the homeowner running toward them yelling, "They took my TV and everything!!" The homeowner said that the perpetrators were teenagers who had just fled toward a house at the end of the block. The officers ran to the house (411 Mayberry Street) and, beneath an open rear window, found a box containing a TV and other household items. The officers entered the Mayberry Street house to see if the burglars, or other victims, might be inside. They found no one inside but did see a gun on the kitchen table. The officers then radioed headquarters to direct another officer to pick up the gun later, and they returned to the burglary victim to obtain more information. That afternoon, Officer Hunter entered the house, retrieved the gun, and determined that it was unregistered.

QUESTION:

12. **Assuming someone has standing to raise the issue, which of the following statements most accurately and appropriately describes the admissibility of the unregistered gun?**

(a) The gun is admissible because the police had probable cause to think that the burglars or other victims might be inside the Mayberry Street house, were in hot pursuit of the perpetrators, and saw the gun in plain view.

(b) The gun is admissible because the police entered the Mayberry Street house under exigent circumstances, and once they saw the gun, the owner no longer had any expectation of privacy with respect to it.

(c) The gun is inadmissible because the police had no probable cause to enter the Mayberry Street house since they had no description of the burglars and did not see them enter the premises.

(d) The gun is inadmissible because Officer Hunter did not obtain a warrant to seize the gun.

(e) The gun is inadmissible because initially the police should have secured the Mayberry Street house from the outside and waited for a warrant to enter.

* * *

Late one afternoon, Bobbie was leaving her sister's house and walking to her car. In an instant, she was tackled by a mugger who emerged from behind a tree. The attacker threw her to the ground, grabbed her pocketbook, and fled. Bobbie managed to catch a glimpse of the perpetrator as he took the pocketbook and ran. Using a cellular phone which was attached to her belt, Bobbie called the police and described the mugger as a twenty-something white male wearing khaki pants, a green t-shirt, and a St. Louis Cardinals baseball cap. Almost immediately after this description was broadcast to officers in the area, Officers Pizzaro and DeSoto apprehended Kenny approximately two blocks from the incident. Kenny is a twenty-three year old white male who, at the time of his arrest, was wearing khaki pants, a green t-shirt, and a St. Louis Cardinals baseball cap. The officers took Kenny to the station house and, en route, read him his Miranda rights. In reply, Kenny said, "I'm not saying anything until I have a lawyer, period." At the station Kenny was fingerprinted, photographed, and placed in a holding cell. Officers Tolstoy and Grisham, not knowing that Kenny had asked for a lawyer, visited with Kenny, gave him a fresh set of Miranda warnings, and asked him questions about Bobbie's mugging and other assaults in the neighborhood. Kenny knew and liked Officers Tolstoy and Grisham based on prior dealings. He agreed to answer the questions and implicated himself in the mugging and the other assaults. Meanwhile, Officers DeSoto and Pizzaro arranged for Bobbie to look at Kenny's booking photo as part of an array of eight other photos of persons similar in appearance to Kenny. Bobbie immediately identified Kenny as the man who mugged her.

QUESTIONS:

13. **Kenny is prosecuted for robbing Bobbie, and the prosecutor seeks to use as evidence Bobbie's pretrial photo identification. If Kenny's lawyer moves to exclude the evidence claiming a violation of his constitutional rights, the trial court should:**

    (a) Grant the motion because the entire pre-arrest procedure was tainted when Officers Tolstoy and Grisham questioned Kenny after he had invoked his right to counsel.

    (b) Grant the motion because, looking at the totality of the circumstances, the identification was unreliable and likely to lead to mistaken identification.

    (c) Grant the motion because Kenny did not have counsel present when Bobbie viewed the photo array.

    (d) Deny the motion because there is no constitutional basis to exclude evidence of the pretrial identification.

    (e) Deny the motion because Kenny did not object to having his photo taken.

14. **Kenny is subsequently prosecuted for the other assaults in the neighborhood. The prosecutor plans to introduce his incriminating statements given to Officers Tolstoy and Grisham. Kenny's lawyer again files a motion to exclude, claiming that use of the evidence would violate Kenny's constitutional rights. The trial court should:**

   (a) Grant the motion because Kenny was interrogated after he had invoked his Miranda right to counsel.

   (b) Grant the motion because, although Kenny voluntarily agreed to answer questions from Officers Tolstoy and Grisham, he did not know that they would ask him about matters unrelated to Bobbie's mugging.

   (c) Deny the motion because Kenny knew and liked Officers Tolstoy and Grisham, and his conversation with them was not only voluntary but volunteered.

   (d) Deny the motion because Officers Tolstoy and Grisham approached Kenny in good faith and were completely unaware of Kenny's comments to Officers Pizzaro and DeSoto.

   (e) Deny the motion because, although Kenny's statements regarding the mugging of Bobbie are inadmissible against him, the statements made about the other assaults are admissible because Kenny was not then in custody on those charges.

* * *

Bugsy was arrested for grand larceny. At her arraignment, she asked for counsel, and a lawyer was appointed by the court to represent her. The court imposed bail in an amount Bugsy was unable to post, and she was detained in the City jail awaiting trial. Police also believed that Bugsy was a participant in a recent kidnapping; and they "planted" an undercover agent, posing as a prisoner, in her cell. The agent struck up a conversation with Bugsy and eventually asked whether she had committed any other criminal acts. Bugsy talked about the kidnapping and answered the agent's questions about many of the details. Prosecutors want to use these statements against Bugsy in her trial for kidnapping.

QUESTION:

15. **Which of the following statements is the most accurate and appropriate?**

   (a) The statements are inadmissible because they violate Bugsy's Fifth and Sixth Amendment Rights.

   (b) The statements are inadmissible because they violate Bugsy's Fifth Amendment Rights.

   (c) The statements are inadmissible because they violate Bugsy's Sixth Amendment Rights.

(d)   The statements are admissible because they were not compelled.

(e)   The statements are admissible because they do not violate either Bugsy's Fifth or Sixth Amendment rights.

* * *

Police arrested Hunter for burning down a warehouse the previous day. He was taken to headquarters and placed in an interrogation room outfitted with one-way glass that allowed outsiders to look in but the suspect could not see out. Detectives Maddie and Addison brought a witness, Mr. Jackson, to view Hunter while he sat in the interrogation room. The witness hesitated at first but then said, "Yes, I think that is the man I saw run from the burning building." The detectives then entered the interrogation room, read Hunter his Miranda rights, and began to question him. Hunter said he wanted a lawyer. The detectives persisted in their questioning and commented, "What do you have to hide. . . . don't involve lawyers, just answer our questions." Hunter refused to answer any questions. Later that day Hunter was put in a line-up, and all participants, who closely resembled each other, were asked to say, "Burn, burn, nothing like a big roaring fire!" Hunter said he wanted a lawyer with him at the line-up to insure that he was treated fairly and that the line-up was conducted properly. The detectives said that they could not get him a lawyer at that time, and Hunter was put in the line-up and told to speak the words when his turn came. Another witness, Mrs. Jefferson, identified Hunter as the person she saw on the premises of the warehouse and running from the warehouse after the fire started. As Hunter left the line-up area to return to his cell, Detective Maddie said, "You didn't do too good, looks like we have you now." Hunter, startled, blurted out, "No way, no one could see me."

QUESTIONS:

16. **At his trial for arson, Hunter objects to the introduction of Mrs. Jefferson's line-up eyewitness identification. Which of the following statements is the most accurate and appropriate?**

(a)   The motion will be denied because the line-up was constitutional.

(b)   The motion will be denied because Hunter ultimately participated in the procedure and effectively waived his right to have counsel present.

(c)   The motion will be granted because Hunter requested counsel and proceeding in the absence of counsel violated his Sixth Amendment rights.

(d)   The motion will be granted because the police persisted in questioning Hunter after he requested counsel, and the line-up identification was derivative of the violation of Hunter's Fifth Amendment rights.

(e)   The motion will be granted because Hunter had invoked his right to counsel and requiring him to speak the words, "Burn, burn, nothing like a big roaring fire!" violated Hunter's rights against self-incrimination.

17. **Hunter also objects to the introduction of evidence of Mr. Jackson's identification of him at police headquarters. Which of the following statements is the most accurate and appropriate?**

    (a) The identification is admissible because, although Hunter had requested counsel earlier, he was not "confronted" with a witness against him since he could not see the witness observing him through the glass.

    (b) The identification is admissible because Hunter asked for a lawyer only in connection with the interrogation; he did not, at that point, request counsel for any identification procedures.

    (c) The identification is admissible because no right to counsel had yet attached, and no Due Process violation occurred because the identification, although suggestive, was necessary; it came soon after the crime and police needed to know if they were on the right track.

    (d) The identification is inadmissible because Hunter had requested counsel during the interrogation, and he had no opportunity to invoke his right again at the identification because the police allowed the identification to be done surreptitiously.

    (e) The identification is inadmissible because it was unnecessarily suggestive and, unless the witness had a reasonable basis to make the identification based on his view at the time of the fire, it is unreliable.

18. **Hunter also moves to exclude his statement to Detective Addison following the line-up, "No way, no one could see me." Which of the following statements is the most accurate and appropriate?**

    (a) The statement is admissible because it is not necessarily incriminatory; Hunter can argue that he meant "no one could see" him because he wasn't at the scene of the fire.

    (b) The statement is admissible because there was no right to have a lawyer at the line-up, and the detective simply told Hunter that the line-up results were very bad for him.

    (c) The statement is inadmissible because it was the product of custody plus interrogation, and Hunter's lawyer was not present.

    (d) The statement is inadmissible because it was deliberately elicited and violated Hunter's Sixth Amendment right to counsel.

    (e) The statement is inadmissible because it was immediately derivative of the unconstitutional line-up.

* * *

Assume that Hunter was arraigned on arson charges the day after the line-up. At the arraignment, Hunter asked for counsel to be appointed to represent him, but there were no lawyers immediately available to defend him and no assignment was made. Hunter, however, was released on bail pending his trial for arson. Three days after being released on bail, Hunter was walking down the avenue and encountered Officer Riley who knew him and who knew of his "troubles" with the law, even the recent arson charge. Officer Riley said, "You know, my boy, maybe we ought to have a talk about some of the trouble you have gotten yourself into." At that point, Officer Riley started questioning Hunter about the arson and probing about other crimes. Hunter confessed to several "mistakes," including the arson and the robbery of an elderly man six months ago.

QUESTIONS:

19. **Prior to his trial for arson Hunter moves to exclude his admission to Officer Riley that he burned down the warehouse. Which of the following statements is the most accurate and appropriate?**

    (a) The motion should be denied because Officer Riley's discussions with Hunter took place a decent interval after his station house interrogation.

    (b) The motion should be denied because Hunter was represented by counsel.

    (c) The motion should be denied because even if Hunter secured counsel in the days following the arraignment, Hunter implicitly waived his right to counsel by making the statement.

    (d) The motion should be granted because Hunter had invoked his right to counsel when he was first interrogated, and the police ignored him; Officer Riley's later questioning in the absence of counsel was derivative of that initial violation.

    (e) The motion should be granted because Hunter had a Sixth Amendment right to counsel, had asked that counsel be appointed, and Officer Riley deliberately elicited incriminating statements in the absence of counsel.

20. **Hunter now faces a charge of robbery in connection with his admission that he robbed an elderly man six months ago. Prior to trial on that charge, Hunter moves to exclude his admission to Officer Riley that he committed the robbery. Which of the following statements is the most accurate and appropriate?**

    (a) The motion should be denied because, at the time Hunter made the statement, he was not in custody and his right to counsel had not attached.

    (b) The motion should be denied because Hunter's meeting with Officer Riley was completely happenstance and, therefore, there was no deliberate attempt to elicit incriminating statements from him.

    (c) The motion should be denied because, by voluntarily speaking to Officer Riley, Hunter waived his Fifth and Sixth Amendment rights.

    (d) The motion should be granted because Hunter had asked for an attorney at his earlier interrogation and again at his arraignment, and thereafter, any police initiated questioning in the absence of counsel violated his constitutional rights.

    (e) The motion should be granted because Hunter did not receive a fresh set of Miranda warnings, and there could be no waiver of Fifth or Sixth Amendment rights under those circumstances.

While on routine patrol along Highway 80, police noticed Barney speeding and driving in a reckless manner. They pulled him over, and despite the fact that he appeared to be a frail and elderly gentleman and despite the fact that it was bitterly cold, the police ordered him out of the car. As Barney exited the car, several pieces of paper fell from his pocket and onto the ground. As Barney was standing near his vehicle and straightening himself up, Magnum, one of the officers, looked down at the papers and, seeing that they were stock certificates, wrote down the stock numbers and other identifying information. Officer Magnum also walked around the vehicle and peered through the windows. She saw more papers on the front seat and wrote down the numbers she saw displayed on these papers as well. The other officer, Kojak, approached Barney and told him he was under arrest for reckless driving. Because Barney seemed shaky on his feet, Officer Kojak asked him whether he had any alcoholic beverages to drink. Barney replied, "Well yes, I've just come from a party, and let me tell you, the liquor was flowing pretty good over there." Officer Kojak then said, "Well consider yourself under arrest for drunk driving too." As Barney sat handcuffed in the patrol car, both officers searched the interior of the car and recovered a gun in the glove compartment. They also searched the trunk and opened several tightly rolled up paper bags and found marijuana.

QUESTIONS:

21. **Barney has been charged with a weapons violation and, prior to trial, moved to suppress the gun discovered in the glove compartment. The motion should be:**

    (a) Granted because Barney was handcuffed and seated in the police cruiser and the police did not reasonably believe that evidence of the crime of arrest was in the vehicle.

    (b) Granted because the glove compartment is not within the scope of a search incident to arrest.

    (c) Denied because police were entitled to make a protective frisk which would include the glove compartment or any space where a gun could be found.

    (d) Denied because the gun was found as part of a proper search incident to arrest.

    (e) Denied because, once Barney admitted he had been drinking, the officers had probable cause to search anywhere in the car where evidence of alcohol could be found.

22. **Barney is charged with illegal possession of drugs and, prior to trial, moves to exclude the marijuana recovered from the trunk. Which of the following statements is the most accurate and appropriate?**

   (a) The motion should be granted because the search of the trunk went beyond the scope of a search incident to arrest.

   (b) The motion should be granted because, although the police were permitted to search the trunk in order to protect themselves, they were not permitted to open containers.

   (c) The motion should be denied because police had probable cause to believe that the car itself contained evidence of weapons or alcohol.

   (d) The motion should be denied because, once Barney was placed under arrest, police could search anywhere in the immediate area, whether or not Barney had a realistic possibility of lunging for a weapon.

   (e) The motion should be denied because the police may always conduct an inventory search of a car, either on the spot or at headquarters.

23. **The securities that had fallen out of Barney's pocket turned out to be stolen, and Barney faces prosecution for possession of stolen securities. Barney now moves to exclude Officer Magnum's testimony concerning the stolen securities. Which of the following statements is the most accurate and appropriate?**

   (a) The evidence should be excluded because the police acted unreasonably in ordering Barney, an elderly and frail individual, out of the car and into the bitter cold; the securities would not have fallen to the ground if Barney remained in the car.

   (b) The evidence should be excluded because the police did not give Barney an opportunity to pick up the securities before Officer Magnum quickly copied down the identifying information.

   (c) The evidence should be admitted because Barney did not immediately retrieve the securities, and police could reasonably assume he had abandoned them.

   (d) The evidence should be admitted because there is no reasonable expectation of privacy concerning the details of public documents such as securities.

   (e) The evidence should be admitted because the officer made the observations from a lawful vantage point.

24. **Barney is prosecuted for drunk driving. Prior to trial he moves to exclude his statement that he had been drinking at a party. Which of the following statements is the most accurate and appropriate?**

   (a) The motion should be denied because Officer Kojak's comment was just a remark and not an attempt to elicit an incriminating response.

   (b) The motion should be granted because Barney was in custody and no Miranda warnings were given before he made his statement.

(c) The motion should be denied because Barney's statement came prior to his arrest for drunk driving.

(d) The motion should be granted because Barney was not validly subject to arrest, and any statements were a product of that illegality.

(e) The motion should be denied because the question was only an attempt to clarify the situation and did not rise to the level of interrogation.

25. **The slips that Officer Magnum observed on the front seat of Barney's car were betting slips. Barney is now charged with illegal gambling. Prior to his trial he moves to exclude Officer Magnum's testimony concerning the betting slips. Which of the following statements is the most accurate and appropriate?**

(a) The motion should be granted because the car stop was illegal, and the papers were a direct product of that illegality.

(b) The motion should be denied because Magnum never actually searched anything; the exclusionary rule applies to physical objects, like persons, houses, and effects.

(c) The motion should be granted because Magnum did not have any reasonable suspicion to think that there was criminality associated with the papers.

(d) The motion should be denied because Magnum observed and recorded the information about the betting slips without violating any of Barney's Fourth Amendment rights.

(e) The motion should be granted because Magnum's actions amounted to a search, and she had no probable cause to view and record the numbers on the betting slips.

* * *

A Vermont statute requires all farms engaged in the production of maple syrup to register with the State Maple Syrup Board (MSB). Registered farms are, by statute, subject to periodic inspection to determine whether syrup production practices meet the high requirements set by the MSB. Boffo owned and operated a Vermont farm that produced maple syrup. But Boffo was engaged in more than maple syrup production. He was also growing marijuana on his property and had never actually registered with the MSB. Police had heard rumors about Boffo's drug activities but had nothing reliable to go on. Officer Friendly called MSB officials and suggested that they inspect his farm. She also arranged to accompany the MSB on their inspection of Boffo's farm. While on the inspection, Officer Friendly looked into various sheds and buildings hoping to find evidence of a marijuana growing operation. She found and seized 50 plants growing in a small garage 100 yards from Boffo's house.

QUESTION:

26. **In his prosecution for possession of marijuana, Boffo has moved to exclude the marijuana plants. Which of the following statements is the most accurate and appropriate?**

    (a) The evidence will not be excluded because the garage was not part of the curtilage.

    (b) The evidence will not be excluded because it was discovered in the course of a lawful inspection of Boffo's farm.

    (c) The evidence will not be excluded because Officer Friendly gained her vantage point from a spot where she was legally entitled to be.

    (d) The evidence will be excluded because the search was pretextual, and Officer Friendly lacked probable cause and a warrant.

    (e) The evidence will be excluded because Boffo was not registered under the statute and was, therefore, not subject to syrup production inspections.

* * *

The police received an anonymous tip that a white man, approximately 20 years old and wearing a green t-shirt and black jeans, was standing on the corner of Main and Crescent streets, at the head of Warner municipal park, and that he had a bag of cocaine in his pants pocket. Two uniformed officers drove their squad car to the corner of Main and Crescent, a high crime area and a spot frequented by drug dealers. They saw several men on the corner, just talking. One of the men, known as Schroeder, was a twenty something white male wearing a green t-shirt and black jeans. As soon as the officers pulled up alongside the curb where the men were standing, the man standing next to Schroeder, Linus, looked at the officers and immediately turned on his heel and took off running. Officer Lightfoot ran after him and chased him for several blocks. At one point during the chase, Linus discarded a small package, which Officer Lightfoot picked up and then continued the pursuit. Eventually Officer Lightfoot cornered Linus and arrested him. Meanwhile Officer Lopez approached Schroeder and the third man, Charlie. Officer Lopez ordered both of them to "Stop, don't move, just stand where you are." Charlie simply ignored the officer and sat on a nearby park bench with his back to the officer. Officer Lopez went over to Charlie and asked him some questions, but Charlie refused to say anything and even refused to give his name. Officer Lopez then frisked him, found a knife, and placed him under arrest. Officer Lopez then returned to Schroeder, patted him down, and felt an object in his pants pocket. After feeling and turning the object several times from the outside, Officer Lopez believed that it was a package of cocaine. He then reached in to Schroeder's pocket and removed a package of cocaine.

QUESTIONS:

27. **The package that Linus discarded contained heroin, and Linus now faces a drug charge. If Linus asks the court to exclude the heroin as evidence, the court should:**

    (a) Allow the evidence to come in because Linus was not seized by the officer and, when he threw away the heroin, he could no longer claim any reasonable expectation of privacy in it.

    (b) Allow the evidence to come in because, although a chase under these circumstances was effectively a seizure, Linus was properly chased since he ran from a police officer while in a high crime area.

    (c) Allow the evidence to come in because Linus was in close proximity to a person matching the description given by the anonymous tipster.

    (d) Exclude the evidence because the officer lacked reasonable suspicion to chase Linus.

    (e) Exclude the evidence because Linus was not the person the officers were originally sent to investigate.

28. **Charlie is prosecuted for possession of a dangerous weapon, namely, the knife. Prior to trial he moves to exclude the knife as evidence. Which of the following statements is the most accurate and appropriate?**

    (a) Grant the motion because, although police had sufficient justification to detain Charlie, they lacked an independent justification to pat him down.

    (b) Grant the motion because police had no probable cause or reasonable suspicion to seize Charlie, and his refusal to co-operate, without more, did not provide a basis to search or seize him.

    (c) Grant the motion because the police had no reason to attribute any reliability to an anonymous tip, and the entire encounter, from beginning to end, started with the unreliable tip.

    (d) Deny the motion because Charlie has to take his friends as he finds them, and his association with persons suspected of drug possession or who flee headlong when the police arrive furnishes sufficient justification to detain him and, under the circumstances, pat him down.

    (e) Deny the motion because the tip, the high crime area, and the refusal to cooperate gave the police sufficient justification to stop and frisk Charlie.

29. In his prosecution for possession of illegal drugs, Schroeder moves to exclude the packet of cocaine found in his pants pocket. Which of the following statements is the most accurate and appropriate?

(a) Deny the motion because the police independently corroborated essential parts of the informant's tip and, therefore, they had reasonable suspicion to pat down Schroeder and, hence, recover the cocaine from his person.

(b) Deny the motion because a tip alleging the possession of drugs, especially in an area where children congregate such as a park, presents a public safety exception and police had a special need, beyond ordinary law enforcement, to recover the drugs.

(c) Deny the motion since, as it turned out, the tip was reliable; Schroeder did indeed have cocaine in his pants pocket.

(d) Grant the motion because police had no reasonable suspicion to stop Schroeder, and, in any event, the officer's actions in touching his outer pocket several times went beyond the reasonable scope of a frisk.

(e) Grant the motion because the tip described only clothing and appearance which were too common to permit the police to conclude that the anonymous tipster had made a reliable identification.

* * *

Louise was sick and tired of being beaten by her boyfriend, Kenny. One night she and her friend, Thelma, caught Kenny as he was getting out of his car and proceeded to beat the daylights out of him. He begged them to stop before they killed him, but they said that the only way they would stop was if he turned himself in to the police for assaulting Louise. They then drove him to the police station. When he hesitated about going in, they started beating him again. Officer Jones was sitting at his desk looking outside the window of the police station and saw the commotion. He then saw Thelma and Louise drag Kenny into the station, kicking and hitting him. Officer Jones told them to, "Stop it right now" and asked, "What the heck is going on here?" Louise, holding Kenny by the hair, said that Kenny had come to confess to something. Kenny looked at Jones and said that he had been forced to come to the station. He then went on and confessed as the two women stood there, grinning. Jones arrested him, and charged him with assaulting Louise.

QUESTION:

30. Before his trial, Kenny moves to suppress his statements to Jones. This motion will most likely be:

(a) Granted, because the statements were the product of coercion and thus invalid under the Due Process clause.

(b) Denied, because the police did not violate any of Kenny's constitutional rights.

(c) Granted, because a reasonable person in Kenny's shoes would not have believed he was free to leave, and Jones did not read Kenny his Miranda rights before he confessed.

(d) Denied, because Kenny's Sixth Amendment right to counsel had not yet attached.

(e) Denied, because Officer Jones' question about what was going on was a spontaneous question.

* * *

Police received an anonymous tip that Nina had a large marijuana growing operation in the basement of her home. Since large amounts of heat are associated with significant, in-house marijuana growing operations, police acquired a thermal imaging device that would measure the amount of heat coming from Nina's house. The trouble was that Nina lived in a rural part of town, and her house was surrounded by acres of thick woods. In addition she had eight-foot high fences, marked "No Trespassing," surrounding the entire property. The police decided to climb over the fence at the rear of the property. After they climbed over the fence, the officers walked through woods for about five minutes. Eventually they emerged from the thicket and were able to walk onto the deck attached to the back of the house. They began to use the imaging device and were getting remarkably high readings. Just then they realized that, from that vantage point, they could see directly into the kitchen at the back of the house. They saw Nina and a friend having coffee and, immediately next to them, were several pots with marijuana growing in them. The police decided to confront Nina and went to the door and rang the bell. Nina hollered, "Who is it" and, at that, the officers raced in and seized the marijuana plants in the pots.

QUESTION:

31. **In a subsequent prosecution for possession of marijuana, Nina moves to exclude the marijuana found in the pots seized from the kitchen. Which of the following statements is the most accurate and appropriate?**

    (a) The marijuana will be admissible because the heat readings gave the police probable cause to believe a major marijuana operation was underway in Nina's house.

    (b) The marijuana will be admissible because the police made plain view observations of the marijuana from outside of the house, and they were justified in seizing it immediately because Nina and her friend would destroy the evidence before a warrant could be secured.

    (c) The marijuana will be excluded because police went beyond the open fields of the house, and Nina's reasonable expectation of privacy was intruded upon.

(d)   The marijuana will be excluded because the police entered the house without consent.

(e)   The marijuana will be excluded because the police unreasonably interpreted Nina's remark of "Who's there" to be consent to enter.

* * *

Detective Dano arrested Hilde for murder. Detective Dano was quite familiar with Hilde since he had arrested her three times before. Two of these charges had been dropped, but the third, theft, was still awaiting grand jury action.

Hilde's mother heard neighborhood rumors that Hilde had been arrested again, perhaps for something very serious this time. Frantic, she called the police station but was given no information. Hilde's mother then called Peralee Manson, the public defender who already represented Hilde on the theft charge. Ms. Manson promptly called the police station and asked about Hilde. Detective Dano took the call and acknowledged that Hilde was in custody. Ms. Manson said she wanted to see her client, and insisted she not be questioned until they conferred, whereupon Detective Dano said, "Relax, we're through with her for tonight. Come around tomorrow." Nevertheless, one half hour later, Detective Dano took Hilde to an interrogation room and administered Miranda warnings, including the warning that she had a right to have a lawyer present during interrogation. Hilde said, "Oh, detective, we've been through this so many times before. I don't really mind talking to you." She then signed the Miranda card, began answering questions, and within minutes, confessed to the murder.

QUESTION:

32. **Prior to her trial for murder, Hilde moves to exclude her confession. Which of the following statements is the most accurate and appropriate?**

    (a)   Grant the motion because Detective Dano's misrepresentation to Ms. Manson violated Due Process of law.

    (b)   Grant the motion because Detective Dano's deception undercut the validity of Hilde's waiver.

    (c)   Grant the motion because Detective Dano's deception violated Hilde's Sixth Amendment right to counsel.

    (d)   Deny the motion because Hilde's waiver was valid, and Detective Dano did not have to tell Hilde of any events occurring outside of the interrogation room.

    (e)   Deny the motion because Hilde was not subjected to any coercion, threats, or false promises.

* * *

Florida drug enforcement agents observed passengers board a Trailways bus traveling from Miami to New York City. Among the passengers was Fred who clutched a single carry-on bag. Fred was the last to board and took a seat by himself in the back of the bus. After the bus left Miami, one of the agents called other drug agents, Wilma and Betty, who were watching the bus station in Jacksonville, Florida. The Miami agents described Fred and told Wilma and Betty "you might want to keep an eye on that guy; we have nothing on him, but he gave us both a weird feeling." Some hours later the bus made a ten minute intermediate stop in Jacksonville. Fred remained on the bus. Wilma and Betty boarded the bus and moved to the back of the bus where they saw Fred. Standing over Fred, Betty said, "Hi there. We're drug enforcement agents, and we were wondering whether you'd like to answer some questions. You don't have to, of course." Fred said, "What's up. . . . what do you want to know?" Betty then asked some questions and determined that Fred was on his way to New York City, that his bag had a name that did not match his identification, and that he was quite vague about whom he was visiting and how long he would stay in New York. As passengers were beginning to reboard the bus, Betty said, "well maybe we should talk privately, so please accompany us to our office in the bus station." Fred went with the agents to a small room where Betty and Wilma closed the door and asked Fred some further questions. They noticed he was sweating. They asked him whether they could search his bag. Fred said nothing but simply handed the bag to the agents. Inside Betty found a brick of marijuana.

QUESTION:

33. **If Fred is charged with possession with intent to distribute marijuana, what is his strongest argument to exclude the drugs discovered in his bag?**

    (a) The marijuana should be excluded because the agents had hours to anticipate Fred's arrival in Jacksonville, and it was unreasonable for them to engage in any investigative actions without having arranged to have a drug sniffing dog available.

    (b) The marijuana should be excluded because Fred never actually consented to the search; he simply handed over his bag.

    (c) The marijuana should be excluded because the agents lacked reasonable suspicion to approach Fred and stand over him as he sat on the bus.

    (d) The marijuana should be excluded because, although the agents had reasonable suspicion to approach Fred on the bus, the encounter was beyond the scope of a stop because, under the circumstances, Fred was not free to leave.

    (e) The marijuana should be excluded because consent to search was a product of an arrest without probable cause.

* * *

Jake asked Maggie if he could leave his green and red Travelpro suitcase in her house for temporary safe keeping. The suitcase was closed but unlocked. The police, meanwhile, were watching Maggie's residence after receiving a reliable eyewitness tip that Maggie was storing drugs in a green and red Travelpro suitcase in her house. The police obtained Maggie's consent to enter her house, and upon seeing Jake's suitcase under a table in the hallway, asked Maggie, "What is in there." Maggie said she did not know because it was her friend Jake's who left it with her for temporary safekeeping. "You can do whatever you want with it," she said. The police then seized the suitcase, took it outside, and searched it while they sat in their patrol car. Inside they found an unregistered gun, and Jake was later prosecuted for illegal gun possession.

QUESTION:

34. **Which of the following statements is the most accurate and appropriate?**

    (a) Jake can successfully suppress the gun because the police did not obtain a warrant to search the suitcase.

    (b) Jake can successfully suppress the gun because the police did not have probable cause to believe there were any drugs in Maggie's house.

    (c) Jake can successfully suppress the gun because the police seizure of the suitcase was unlawful.

    (d) Jake cannot suppress the gun because Maggie had common authority over the suitcase which would allow her to consent to its search.

    (e) Jake cannot suppress the gun because the police had probable cause to search the suitcase, and Maggie's consent to enter the house excused the need for a warrant.

* * *

In December IRS Agent Anita Hernandez met with Juan Sandoval and his wife Maria. Maria Sandoval had been convicted of embezzling money from her employer, and the IRS sought to revise the Sandoval's joint tax return to reflect an increased tax obligation based on the embezzled income. During the meeting, Maria Sandoval remarked that her former employer and some of his employees were not reporting all of their income. Agent Hernandez expressed interest. She told the Sandovals that the IRS had a reward program for reports of such information, but she did not explain the program.

A few months later, Juan Sandoval called Agent Hernandez and told her: "How can I say this? I would like to make a deal with you." Agent Hernandez later testified that she felt "something wasn't right" with this offer and decided that she would refuse any offer of information and insist on an illegal bribe instead. Several days later, Sandoval explained his telephone reference to a deal by stating, haltingly, "We know a public official who is taking bribes, but what would be in it for me to get you all of this stuff?" Agent Hernandez commented several times, "What's in it for me?" "This isn't the way the system works." "Information, that's not enough."

In subsequent conversations, despite the Agent's repeated efforts to direct Sandoval to a bribe, Sandoval continued to offer only information. Then, finally, after a lengthy discussion, Sandoval finally understood that Agent Hernandez was speaking of a bribe and not merely information. After a long pause, Sandoval slowly said, "I don't know. Let me think about this a little bit."

In the face of Sandoval's reluctance, Agent Hernandez reminded him of the large tax liability he and his wife faced. Several days later, Sandoval agreed to pay Hernandez $3,000 in cash in exchange for favorable tax treatment. The next month, Sandoval delivered the payment, remarking that he had "never done anything like this before." Shortly thereafter Sandoval was arrested and prosecuted for bribing a public official.

QUESTIONS:

35. **Sandoval is now relying on the defense of entrapment. Which of the following statements is the most accurate and appropriate?**

   (a) The entrapment defense will not succeed. The government will be able to establish Sandoval's predisposition because Sandoval clearly intended to strike some sort of deal, legal or illegal, with the IRS.

   (b) The entrapment defense will not succeed. Even though Agent Hernandez's efforts to persuade Sandoval were significant and persistent, Sandoval's prompt acceptance of the opportunity to commit the crime will be enough to prove predisposition.

   (c) The entrapment defense will succeed. The government employed significant and persistent encouragement to induce Sandoval to make the bribe, and the facts are insufficient for the government to prove Sandoval's predisposition to commit the crime.

   (d) The entrapment defense will succeed if Sandoval can establish that he was solicited to give the bribe and did not know that it was a crime to comply.

   (e) The entrapment defense will succeed because Sandoval's statement that he "had never done anything like this before" will negate the government's attempt to prove predisposition.

* * *

Assume that it had been established that the government had induced Sandoval to offer a bribe and that, after the close of the case against Sandoval, the trial court read the following entrapment instruction to the jury:

"If you should find beyond a reasonable doubt from the evidence in the case that, before anything at all occurred respecting the alleged offense involved in this case, the defendant was ready and willing to commit a crime such as charged in the indictment, whenever opportunity was afforded, and that government officers did no more than offer the opportunity, then you should find that the defendant is not a victim of entrapment. On the other hand, if the evidence in the case should leave you with a reasonable doubt whether the defendant had the previous intent or purpose to commit an offense of the character charged, apart from the inducement or persuasion of some government officer, then it is your duty to find the defendant not guilty. The burden is on the government to prove beyond a reasonable doubt that the defendant was not entrapped."

36. Which of the following statements is the most accurate and appropriate?

  (a) The instruction is improper. Entrapment is an affirmative defense, and the defendant bears the burden of proving that he was entrapped.

  (b) The instruction is improper. The jury should not have been instructed on predisposition because predisposition is a question of law, not fact.

  (c) The instruction is improper. Even if the jury finds entrapment, the defendant should not necessarily be found not guilty; all other facts and circumstances must still be taken into account.

  (d) The instruction is proper. The government bears the burden of proving predisposition, and it is proper for it to use evidence such as the defendant's prior convictions, if any, to show the defendant was ready to commit the offense when the opportunity arose.

  (e) The instruction is proper but incomplete. Propensity may be established either by evidence of the defendant's behavior before the government contacted the defendant, or it may arise during the course of the government's attempted inducement.

* * *

Based on underground rumors, the police have a hunch that Patty is responsible for making fourteen bombs that have been mailed to various victims over the last six months. Many of the victims have been maimed or killed. Recently the police discovered a hideaway in the woods where they believe most of the bombs were assembled. None of the evidence in the hideaway can be tied to Patty. However, based on the condition of the hideaway, police believe that one of the bombs exploded prematurely spraying debris throughout the one room structure. Police think it is possible that the bomb-maker may have sustained injuries and may even have physical evidence lodged in his or her body. Patty recently went to the hospital for an infectious wound in her leg. She was treated with antibiotics, but she refused permission for surgeons to remove what appeared to be a 1/4 inch sliver of metal. Removal of the sliver would require a surgical operation under anesthesia, some probing to recover the sliver near bone and tendons in the knee, and some chance of nerve damage. Leaving the sliver in would cause no immediate danger, but potentially serious medical consequences could occur if the infection flared up again or if the sliver migrated to nerves or veins.

As it happens, the materials used to make the bombs are quite unusual, particularly the metal. Indeed the police regard the unusual metal components as the "signature" of the bomber. If the police were to find a sliver of the unusual metal in Patty's leg, they would have a direct way to tie Patty to the bombings. The police would like to get a search warrant directing the removal of the sliver from Patty's leg, but they lack probable cause or even reasonable suspicion to link Patty to the bombings. The police ask the prosecutor if she would be willing to take the matter before a grand jury and obtain a subpoena duces tecum ordering Patty to have the sliver removed and provided to the grand jury. The prosecutor agrees and the subpoena is obtained.

QUESTIONS:

37. **Sally files a motion to quash the subpoena claiming that its enforcement will violate her constitutional rights. The supervising judge holds a hearing on the matter. Which of the following statements is the most accurate and appropriate?**

    (a) The subpoena is enforceable because the grand jury has broad powers to seek evidence, and so long as the prosecutor can show that the evidence is relevant to its investigation, there are no further Fourth Amendment limitations.

    (b) The subpoena is enforceable because it relates to physical evidence and a physical condition which Patty already exposed to third parties, namely, her doctors, when they treated her and viewed the x-rays.

    (c) The subpoena is enforceable because the bombings present a serious public safety danger, the perpetrator is still at large, and the evidence may be the only way to tie Patty to the crime.

    (d) The subpoena should be quashed because it would shock the conscience, and hence violate Due Process of law, to force any person to undergo an unwanted medical procedure.

    (e) The subpoena should be quashed because, under the circumstances, the degree of intrusion is unreasonable.

* * *

While the police await the actions of the grand jury, they remain anxious that Patty, if she really is the bomber, might make more devices and harm more people. They decide to monitor her actions as closely as possible. Officers are assigned to follow her every movement. They watch her house twenty four hours a day, with officers parked out front and on the street behind her house. If she travels by vehicle, they trail behind her. If she walks her dog, they walk nearby. If she goes to the grocery store or to the bank or enters other buildings, they follow. They have even monitored her phone calls by arranging with the phone company to obtain a record of numbers dialed from her home phone. This police behavior persists for over three months. And, during all of that time, the police did not have and still do not have probable cause or even reasonable suspicion to link Patty to the bombings.

38. What is Patty's *strongest* argument that this police activity is unlawful?

(a) Constant surveillance for the three month period was an illegitimately long period of time and produced fright and embarrassment, and the police needed either reasonable suspicion or probable cause to justify such an intense pursuit.

(b) The telephone company lacked the authority to give third party consent to permit access to Patty's list of dialed telephone numbers.

(c) Under the federal wiretapping statute, it was unlawful to obtain the list of telephone numbers without a judicial warrant.

(d) The police were free to follow Patty when she was out and about, but they needed either reasonable suspicion or probable cause to follow her into buildings, such as the bank.

(e) Since Patty was already a target of the grand jury, police efforts to obtain incriminating evidence against her violated Due Process of law.

* * *

State trooper Delino Hill was driving in the left lane of Route 99 when he noticed that a blue Nissan Maxima, positioned slightly ahead of him in the right lane, displayed license plates from Baja California, Mexico. Officer Hill was aware that California law required foreign vehicles traveling on state roadways to be properly registered in their home jurisdictions. Officer Hill looked for a valid registration sticker on the back of the vehicle because, as he later testified, he had been instructed at the Police Academy that Baja California requires motorists to place registration stickers on the back window so they could be viewed from the rear. The police academy training was in error. In fact, the applicable Baja California law requires that a vehicle registration sticker be displayed on the front windshield. Seeing no sticker from the rear, the officer, in good faith, stopped the vehicle on suspicion that it was not properly registered. As he put on his flashing lights, the vehicle turned into a parking lot of a housing complex where, as it happened, the driver of the vehicle lived. Upon parking, the driver, Rachael Gold and her passenger and owner of the car, Dorrito Vaughn, exited the vehicle and locked it. Officer Hill called to both of them to stay with the vehicle. The pair continued walking and were a considerable distance from the vehicle when officer Hill approached at a run, yelling at them to stop. Officer Hill told the two to stand apart from one another. He first turned his attention to Vaughn having noticed that Vaughn had his hand in his belt and looked to be holding some sort of hard object. Officer Hill, fearing it was a gun, ordered Vaughn to put his hands over his head, and he patted him down. He found a gun in his pocket and placed him under arrest. These events caused a small crowd to gather, including Vaughn's brother who also lived in the housing complex. As he was being led away, Vaughn called out to Rachael Gold, "Don't give them the keys to the car." A back-up officer, Trooper Kennedy, then told Gold that the police were going to impound the car and that she should surrender the keys. When she refused, Trooper Kennedy arrested her for obstruction of justice and reached into her pocket and took the keys. Within ten minutes of Gold's arrest, police officers unlocked the blue Nissan and began to search its contents. Finding nothing of interest in the passenger area, they then opened the trunk where they uncovered a substantial quantity of heroin in a black plastic bag.

QUESTIONS:

39. Vaughn is charged with illegal possession of a handgun and possession with intent to distribute heroin. He moves to suppress the handgun arguing that the initial stop was unlawful and, therefore, that any evidence derived therefrom was unconstitutionally seized. Which of the following statements is the most accurate and appropriate?

(a) The stop was illegal because, even though it may have been made in good faith, it was based on a mistaken view of the law and was not objectively reasonable.

(b) The stop was illegal because, even if the vehicle was not properly registered, the driver and passenger were no longer in the vehicle, had lawfully parked the car on private property, and were walking away from it when the officer finally accosted them.

(c) The stop was legal because, even though Trooper Hill was wrong about Baja California's registration requirements, his mistake was reasonably based on the training he received at the police academy.

(d) Vaughn has no standing to complain about the stop because he was not the driver of the vehicle.

(e) The stop was legal because, at the time Vaughn was detained, Trooper Hill was no longer relying on his suspicions related to the vehicle's registration, but, rather, he was relying on his reasonable suspicion that Vaughn was armed.

* * *

Assume that the trial court ruled that the stop was legal. Vaughn now moves to exclude the heroin found in the trunk. The government defends the seizure of the car as a valid decision to impound, and it defends the search as a valid decision to inventory an impounded vehicle. Although the police department has no written policies regarding impounding vehicles, officers at the defendant's suppression hearing testified that it was the custom and practice of the police to act in "furtherance of public safety" and exercise a "community care-taking function" by impounding vehicles once the owner or person in control of the vehicle has been arrested. According to the police witnesses, cars would be impounded under such circumstances for the protection of the owner of the vehicle and to protect the police department against liability should vandals or others injure the vehicle.

40. Which of the following statements is the most accurate and appropriate?

   (a)   The car was illegally impounded because impoundment based solely on an arrestee's status as a driver or owner is unreasonable and inconsistent with caretaking functions, particularly since Rachael Gold and Vaughn's brother were immediately available to take control of the legally parked car.

   (b)   The car was illegally impounded because the police did not have written policies establishing the standards for impoundment.

   (c)   The car was illegally impounded because Vaughn was not the driver of the vehicle at the time the car was stopped.

   (d)   The car was illegally impounded because police only acted to take control of the car once Vaughn told Gold not to surrender the keys; since Vaughn's comments caused the police to believe that evidence of a crime would be found in the car and since their real motive was to find evidence of a crime, the police needed probable cause to search the vehicle.

   (e)   The car was legally impounded because both Vaughn and Gold were arrested, and there was no way for the police to know whether there was any other person available to provide for the speedy and efficient removal or custody of the car.

* * *

Pursuant to a district-wide regulation, the City of New Amsterdam regularly conducted random searches of students' personal belongings. In so doing, the public schools would randomly select a classroom, order the students to empty their pockets and leave all personal items in the room, which they were required to leave while the search was conducted. If contraband was discovered during the search, it was routinely turned over to law enforcement authorities. All students in the New Amsterdam Public Schools received a student handbook describing the search policy, thus effectively putting them on notice. The student handbook even went on to explain that the search policy was in response to an uptick in drug use and school violence across the country.

In September of 2010, Martha Graham's classroom was randomly selected for a search. Upon completion, Martha and one other student were separately escorted to the principal's office for possessing contraband. The authorities found a container with marijuana residue and seeds in Martha's purse and three prescription strength Tylenol pills in Jack McArthur's backpack. Martha was ultimately charged with a possession offense.

QUESTION:

41. **Prior to trial, Martha moved to suppress the evidence of the school search, alleging that the search violated the Fourth Amendment. How should the District Court decide?**

(a) The search was constitutional because the concerns about student welfare and safety provided the requisite justification for the search.

(b) The search was constitutional because the search for contraband was sufficiently analogous to the permissible practices of subjecting students to metal detectors and canine sniffs.

(c) The search was constitutional because students do not have a reasonable expectation of privacy in the items they carry with them to school.

(d) The search was unconstitutional because the concerns described in the student handbook failed to provide the individualized suspicion necessary for the search at issue.

(e) The search was unconstitutional because the search could have been conducted in a less intrusive manner.

* * *

Assume the facts from the previous question still apply and that the legality of the initial search is not in issue. When Martha, a 14-year-old high school freshman, and her escort reached the principal's office, a police officer had already been summoned. Altogether, four people were in the office: Martha, Officer Laminick, the school official who searched Martha's belongings, and the principal himself. The door was closed and the window had been covered with blinds. The principal asked Martha if she knew why she was in the office, to which Martha responded "no." Officer Laminick jumped right in, realizing that she might be able to make headway in an unrelated drug investigation where Martha was one of several suspects. Officer Laminick implored Martha to tell the truth, telling Martha "that the truth will set you free."

For the next 30 minutes or so, the officials peppered Martha with questions about drugs, suppliers, etc. Officer Laminick eventually became annoyed and declared, "I'm not going to play these games. If you want to confess, confess. We have enough evidence to put you away." Martha kept thinking about how the "truth will set you free."

Martha began to choke up, but was able to hold back the tears. At that point, the principal saw that Martha wasn't going to speak so he placed the container on the table and asked if she had anything to say. Officer Laminick told Martha that there was a lot more evidence and that she should just come clean. Only then, 50 minutes after arriving at the office, Martha told them everything they wanted to hear. At no point were Miranda warnings given.

QUESTION:

42. **At her trial, Martha moves to exclude her incriminating statements. Which of the following is the most accurate and appropriate?**

    (a) The statement will be excluded because the authorities used deception and trickery to secure the confession.

    (b) The statement will be admitted because school investigations involve special needs and therefore, strict adherence to constitutional requirements is unnecessary.

    (c) The statement will be excluded because the surrounding circumstances suggest that Martha would have felt compelled to speak.

    (d) The statement will be admitted because Martha was never told she was under arrest, no weapons were displayed, and the questioning lasted under an hour.

    (e) The statement will be excluded because confronting a suspect with evidence against her is interrogation.

END OF EXAM II QUESTIONS

EXAM III
CRIMINAL PROCEDURE MULTIPLE CHOICE OBJECTIVE QUESTIONS

At 6:17am, police arrived at the home of Arlene and Seymour Tankleff in response to a 911 call from Tankleff's son, Martin. They found seventeen-year-old Martin outside of the house shouting that someone had murdered his parents. Mrs. Tankleff was dead in the master bedroom, and Mr. Tankleff was unconscious but gravely wounded in the study. Martin told police he found the bodies when he got up for school and that he thought that his father's business partner committed the crime. One officer instructed Martin and his brother-in-law, who was also present, to leave the house and go sit in separate police cars so they wouldn't "contaminate each other's stories." At 6:37am, Martin went outside and sat in the front seat of a police car with the door swung open. At around 7:40am, homicide detectives interviewed Martin as he then stood near a police car. No Miranda warnings were given. Among themselves, the detectives noted inconsistencies in Martin's statements, and they decided it would be advisable to take him to headquarters for further questioning. They did not believe Martin was telling the whole truth and truly considered him a suspect. At 8:40am Martin agreed to go with Detective McCready to the police station because he wanted to "help the police find the person who killed my parents." At 9:40am, Detectives McCready and Rein took Martin to a ten-foot by ten-foot, windowless room where he was interviewed for the next two hours.

Martin was questioned in detail about inconsistencies in his story, and the detectives openly expressed disbelief with his version of events. They asked Martin to demonstrate how he performed CPR on his father. Detective McCready then leaned forward and said that Martin's account was "ridiculous and unbelievably absurd." The detectives at times raised and lowered their voices, they accused Martin of showing insufficient grief, and said they "could not accept" his explanations. They never yelled at or threatened Martin.

At about 11:40, Detective McCready pretended to get a phone call and left the room. He spoke in a loud voice so he would be overheard by Martin. When he returned to the room, he said that he was told that Mr. Tankleff had just been pumped with large doses of adrenaline, had come out of his coma, and had named Martin as his attacker. This was untrue. Mr. Tankleff never regained consciousness and died two weeks later. Martin continued to deny having committed the crime and said his father might have accused him because Martin was the last person he saw before falling unconscious. Detective Rein asked if Mr. Tankleff was conscious when Martin "beat and stabbed him." Martin then asked to take a lie detector test which the police refused to administer. Rein asked, "Marty, what should we do to a person that did this to your parents?" Martin said, "Whoever did this needs psychiatric help." Martin then said, "Could I have blacked out and done it?" and asked whether he could have been "possessed." One of the detectives encouraged Martin to say more, and Martin uttered, "it's coming to me."

At that point, however, concerned that the interview had taken a different turn, Detective McCready stopped the questioning and administered Miranda warnings. He added, "Martin, nothing you've said so far can be used against you, but from here on in, anything you say can and will be used against you— do you understand? Do you still want to talk to us?" Martin nodded, waived his rights, and the interrogation continued. Martin stated that he needed psychiatric help. He then described the reasons for his actions and the manner in which he attacked his parents. He was placed under formal arrest later that afternoon.

QUESTIONS:

1. **Martin has moved to exclude all of the stationhouse statements he made to the police prior to receiving Miranda warnings. Which of the following statements is the most accurate and appropriate?**

   (a) Martin was in custody at least by the time of the phone call ruse because a reasonable person would have felt he was under arrest; statements given after that point and until Miranda warnings were given are inadmissible.

   (b) Martin was not in custody because he was never formally placed under arrest until the afternoon nor was he ever told he was not free to leave; all of his pre-Miranda statements are admissible.

   (c) Martin was not in custody because he consented to accompany the police to headquarters, and he voluntarily agreed to answer questions; all of his pre-Miranda statements are admissible.

   (d) Martin was in custody once the police decided he was a suspect; all of his answers to questioning after that point and until Miranda warnings were given are inadmissible.

   (e) Martin was in custody once he was in the police car and transported to headquarters; all of his answers to police questioning after that point and until Miranda warnings were given are inadmissible.

2. **Martin also moved to exclude all of the statements he made immediately following the giving of Miranda warnings. Regarding this request, the district court should:**

   (a) Deny the motion because the failure to give Miranda warnings was a "mere Miranda violation," and any voluntary statements given after warnings were administered are admissible.

   (b) Deny the motion because, although this was a single interrogation session, the police introduced a sufficient curative measure to separate the pre-warning statements from the post-warning statements.

(c) Grant the motion because all of the stationhouse questions were part of a single interrogation and, until that session ended, all statements during that session were inadmissible.

(d) Grant the motion because the pre-warning statements were obtained by hostile questioning and were involuntary; the post Miranda statements were a direct product or "fruit" of that coercive questioning and are also inadmissible.

(e) Grant the motion because, despite later warnings, once the police violated Miranda and secured Martin's incriminatory statements, the psychological impact of having already "confessed" was a form of compulsion making later statements involuntary.

* * *

The police arrested Anibal Ortiz at his place of employment on charges of money laundering. The arresting officer, Agent Doo, read Ortiz his Miranda warnings. When asked if he wanted an attorney, Ortiz said, yes, he did. Agent Doo immediately ceased questioning Ortiz, handcuffed him, seated him on a couch, and left the room. Shortly thereafter, Agents O'Neil and Navarro approached Ortiz, and Navarro reread him his Miranda rights. Indeed he read them twice, once in English and once in Spanish. Agent Navarro asked Ortiz whether he wanted to cooperate. Ortiz said he did and asked the agents, "What are the charges against me?" Navarro told him the charge was money laundering and then carried on further conversation with Ortiz. Navarro then asked Ortiz if he wanted to waive his Miranda rights and, after Ortiz said yes, the officers secured his signature on two waiver forms. Ortiz then answered questions and gave incriminating replies.

QUESTION:

3. **Prior to trial, Ortiz moves to exclude the incriminating statements he gave to Agent Navarro. The District Court should:**

(a) Deny the motion because, once Ortiz initiated conversation with Navarro by asking him about the charges he faced, the officer was permitted to seek a waiver and, upon obtaining it, reinterrogate him.

(b) Deny the motion because Agents O'Neil and Navarro did not know that Ortiz told Agent Doo that he wished to have a lawyer, they gave him a fresh set of Miranda warnings, and Ortiz voluntarily agreed to waive his rights and answer questions.

(c) Deny the motion because, whether or not the agents knew of Ortiz' prior request to have a lawyer, suspects are always free to waive their rights if they have been warned and waive voluntarily.

(d) Grant the motion because, under the circumstances, once Ortiz invoked his right to a lawyer, Agents Navarro and O'Neil were not permitted to approach Ortiz and ask whether he wanted to cooperate, and statements obtained thereafter are inadmissible.

(e)   Grant the motion because, once a suspect invokes his right to counsel, there are no permissible circumstances where the police may attempt reinterrogation in the absence of counsel.

* * *

The police were investigating a robbery and murder at the Kum and Go convenience store in Wichita, Kansas. Hearing he might be wanted, Mr. Cody Glover voluntarily presented himself at the police station for questioning about the incident. Mr. Glover was arrested at the station on an outstanding warrant. The police read Mr. Glover his Miranda rights, which he acknowledged and voluntarily waived. Mr. Glover denied involvement in the crimes. The interrogation was underway for about forty minutes when Glover and one of the detectives, Detective O'Mara, began talking with raised voices. Soon the second detective, Detective Hennessy, joined in. Hennessy told Glover he was lying and that he was involved in the robbery. Glover then stated: "If you are going to continue talking about this, I want an attorney." The detectives said "that was his right," and the questioning immediately ceased. A third detective, Detective Rich, was then enlisted to transport Glover to a detention facility. Rich handcuffed Glover and placed him in the back of his vehicle. A few minutes into the drive, Glover peered out the window and commented, "Boy, those guys were jerks. All they did was yell." Rich responded by defending his colleagues, adding "all they wanted was the truth . . . and it's always best to tell the truth. I have my kids, you know, look me in the eye and just tell the truth. That's always best." Shortly thereafter, when they arrived at the detention facility, Detective Rich parked at the curb and told Glover that he did not know whether Glover was involved in the robbery, but, based on his twenty years of police experience, he thought he had something to do with it Glover responded, "I know something about it, I'll talk to you about it." Rich reported that Glover was willing to talk, and the police conducted another interrogation. But, this time, Glover gave incriminating statements and eventually a full confession.

QUESTION:

4.   **Prior to trial, Glover moves to exclude his incriminating statements and confession. The district court should:**

(a)   Deny the motion because, in context, Glover's invocation of counsel was ambiguous, and the police could have proceeded with additional questions immediately.

(b)   Deny the motion because Glover reinitiated conversation about the investigation when he commented about the other detectives being "jerks."

(c)   Deny the motion because Detective Rich's statements to Glover in the police car were just routine conversation and did not amount to interrogation.

(d)   Grant the motion because once Glover invoked his right to have counsel available, the police could not interrogate him further unless counsel was present, and Glover did not indicate a desire to open a discussion related to the investigation.

(e) Grant the motion because, once the first interrogation degenerated into a shouting match, anything Glover stated in the second interrogation was a product of that coercive environment and, therefore, inadmissible.

* * *

Bernard Montgomery was indicted for the possession and manufacture of methamphetamine, an illegal drug. The police had gathered substantial evidence against Montgomery but continued their investigation even after his indictment. Their investigation led them to Lance Blondin, an employee of a chemical company. Blondin identified Montgomery at trial as the purchaser of a large quantity of red phosphorous—a key ingredient in the manufacture of methamphetamine. The police had presented Blondin with a photograph of Montgomery and asked him "if he knew the guy in the photo." Blondin said, yes, it was a man using the name of "Jim Luna." Blondin said that he dealt with "Jim Luna" on several occasions, and he added that, on the last occasion, Luna had purchased a large amount of red phosphorous on a rush basis. "Jim Luna" was Montgomery. Months after this identification and several weeks prior to Montgomery's trial, Blondin asked the police to fax him a copy of the photo of Montgomery so he "could have it right in his mind to identify Montgomery." The police did fax the photo, and on receipt of the faxed photo, Blondin immediately called the police to say, "yes, it's the right photo, it's the guy I dealt with." Blondin pinned the photo to the wall of his office and looked at it several times prior to testifying.

The day before Blondin was scheduled to testify, he asked the police if there was any way he could see Montgomery so "I could have it straight in my mind that Montgomery was the fellow that had purchased chemicals from me." At Blondin's request, a police officer escorted Blondin into a courtroom where, unobserved by Montgomery, he could see Montgomery who was seated at the defense table. Blondin took a brief look, saw Montgomery mostly from behind, and then left the courtroom. At trial Montgomery moved to strike Blondin's in-court identification testimony after cross-examination uncovered these pre-trial identification events. The trial court denied the motion, and Montgomery was convicted.

QUESTIONS:

5. **Montgomery claimed that the use of the pre-trial photos rendered Blondin's in-court identification of Montgomery fundamentally unfair and a violation of Due Process of law. The trial court agreed. On this point, the trial court's ruling should be:**

(a) Upheld on appeal because, given Blondin's original opportunities to view Montgomery as a customer and his prompt and certain identifications of his photograph, the defendant could not prove that the pretrial identifications would lead to a very substantial likelihood of irreparable misidentification.

(b) Upheld on appeal because, even if the pre-trial identifications were unreliable, Montgomery had a full and fair opportunity to cross examine Blondin at trial and, thus, the in-court identification could not be fundamentally unfair.

(c) Upheld on appeal because Due Process limits only suggestive identification procedures, and the photos, as presented to Blondin initially and later by fax, were presented without any coaching or indication of what the police thought, and were not suggestive.

(d) Overturned on appeal because, under the circumstances, the government could not prove by clear and convincing evidence that the unnecessarily suggestive pre-trial photo identifications did not taint the in-court identifications.

(e) Overturned on appeal because the trial court was required to hold a separate hearing on whether the pre-trial identifications were unreliable, and its failure to do so requires reversal.

6. **Montgomery also claimed that when the police officer granted Blondin's request to take him to the courtroom to view Montgomery, this identification without notice to Montgomery's counsel, rendered the in-court identification a violation of his Sixth Amendment right to counsel. The trial court ruled it was not a Sixth Amendment violation. On this point, the trial court's ruling should be:**

(a) Upheld on appeal because, at the time, Montgomery had not invoked his Sixth Amendment right to counsel.

(b) Upheld on appeal because the initiative and the request came from Blondin, and the police officer's escort was insufficient to create state action.

(c) Upheld on appeal because the observation of Montgomery in the courtroom was not a critical stage, that is, an adversarial confrontation between a witness and the accused where the accused would face the intricacies of the law and the advocacy of the prosecutor.

(d) Overturned on appeal because the viewing of the defendant was akin to a line-up without notice to Montgomery's attorney, and the in-court identification was necessarily tainted by the close-up, sneak peek of the defendant in person.

(e) Overturned on appeal because the Sixth Amendment, which was not honored here, applies to any stage of the proceedings, in-court or out, where the presence of the defendant's attorney will assure a full and fair opportunity to cross examine witnesses and receive a fair trial.

* * *

Skip was a participant in a heroin ring. On various occasions, he would receive shipments of heroin and then be instructed to deliver portions of it to designated addresses. A police informant of proven reliability told police that she was with Skip that morning, observed the heroin in his house, and overheard Skip's plan to take the heroin that afternoon at 3 p.m. in a red, white, and blue duffel bag and deliver it to a house at 15 Damascus Road. Officer Chang was sent to Skip's house to investigate. At approximately 3 p.m., he observed Skip leaving the house and carrying the red, white, and blue duffel bag. He watched Skip place bag in the trunk of his car. He then followed Skip as he drove to 15 Damascus Road, and there he observed Skip remove the bag from the trunk and carry it onto the porch at that address. Officer Chang raced up the stairs and placed Skip under arrest. Officer Chang then transported Skip to the police station, and the next day Officer Chang picked up the duffel bag and returned to police headquarters. After filing out some initial paperwork, Officer Chang then opened the duffel bag and placed the heroin in an evidence container. He had no warrant.

QUESTION:

7. **Skip has moved to suppress the heroin in his trial on narcotic charges. Which of the following statements is the most accurate and appropriate?**

   (a) The heroin is admissible because the bag was opened as a valid search incident to an arrest.

   (b) The heroin is admissible because any search at police headquarters is a valid inventory search.

   (c) The heroin is admissible because it was in a container placed in a car, and the "automobile exception" excused the need for a warrant.

   (d) The heroin is inadmissible because Officer Chang never corroborated that the bag contained heroin and, therefore, the arrest and the search were invalid.

   (e) The heroin is inadmissible because Officer Chang searched the bag without a warrant.

QUESTION:

8. **Which of the following statements is the most accurate and appropriate? Consistent with the Fourth Amendment, when the police enter a house and arrest someone they have probable cause to believe has committed a violent crime, they may, in order to protect themselves . . .**

   (a) Conduct a protective sweep of the immediate area including closets as well as the other rooms in the house without any further suspicion.

   (b) Conduct a protective sweep of the immediate area including closets as well as the other rooms in the house only if they have reasonable suspicion that someone who could pose a harm to them could be in any of these areas.

(c) Conduct a protective sweep of the immediate area including closets without any further suspicion, but a protective sweep of the other rooms in the house only if they have reasonable suspicion that someone who could pose a harm to them could be in any of these areas.

(d) Conduct a protective sweep of the immediate area including closets without any further suspicion, but a protective sweep of the other rooms in the house only if they have probable cause to believe that someone who could pose a harm to them could be in any of these areas.

(e) Conduct a protective sweep of the immediate area including closets, only if they have reasonable suspicion that someone who could pose a harm to them could be in that area, and a protective sweep of other rooms in the house only if they have probable cause that someone who could pose a harm to them could be in those areas.

* * *

Police officer Arlene Jenkins stopped Bobby Potter for speeding. Seated next to Potter in the front passenger seat was Daisy Lambert. Jenkins checked Potter's license and registration and, finding everything in order, wrote out a ticket. She was about to hand the ticket to Potter when she noticed that Potter was sweating and fidgeting and appeared extremely nervous. Jenkins suspected that Potter had illegal drugs on him. She directed him to step out of the vehicle and began to search him. She found a small crack pipe in his jacket pocket, and said, "What's this?" Potter replied, "It's my crack pipe. I smoke crack. I'm an addict, if you must know." Hearing that, Jenkins ordered Potter's passenger out of the car and searched the entire interior of the car including Daisy Lambert's handbag which was on the floor on the front passenger's side of the car. Before the search, Ms. Lambert called out, "Wait just a minute, now. That's my bag and I insist you give it to me right now." Officer Jenkins ignored the comments, conducted the search, and found cocaine in the handbag.

QUESTION:

9. **If Ms. Lambert is tried for possession of cocaine, what is the most likely outcome of her motion to suppress the drugs found in her handbag?**

(a) The drugs will be excluded because Officer Jenkins' search incident to the arrest of Mr. Potter did not lawfully include Ms. Lambert's personal items which she specifically identified as belonging to her.

(b) The drugs will be excluded because Officer Jenkins did not have reasonable suspicion to search Mr. Potter, and all other evidence was derivative of that illegality.

(c) The drugs will be admissible because Officer Jenkins had probable cause to search Mr. Potter for drugs and to act for his own safety; once Officer Jenkins discovered the crack pipe and Potter made his admissions, Officer Jenkins had probable cause to search the car and all containers within it for drugs.

(d) The drugs will be admissible because Ms. Lambert, as a mere passenger, has no standing to complain of a search of Mr. Potter, Mr. Potter's vehicle, or any containers she voluntarily placed in the vehicle.

(e) The drugs will be admissible because Ms. Lambert has no standing to complain of the search of Mr. Potter and, after the search of Mr. Potter and his admissions, Officer Jenkins had probable cause to search the interior of the vehicle and all containers, including the handbag, where drugs could be found.

* * *

Police had probable cause to believe that Elmer was developing and selling obscene photographs from his house. They obtained a search warrant to search and seize all obscene photographs, equipment, accounts, and proceeds from the illicit photography business. The officers waited until Wednesday evening to execute the warrant because they knew Elmer would be out bowling. They knocked at the door and announced themselves. When no one answered, they broke open the front door and entered. Officers farmed out through all of the rooms, but the photography operation appeared to be run out of the basement. There the police found hundreds of photos, a dark room, accounts, records, phone messages, and piles of cash. Despite this discovery, officers continued looking elsewhere in the house. One officer opened mail addressed to Elmer found on the dresser in his bedroom. The bedroom was located three stories above the basement. The envelope from the dresser contained an incriminating letter from Max, one of Elmer's obscene photo customers. Among other relevant tidbits, the letter included a threat by Max to turn Elmer over to the police unless he improved the quality of his work.

QUESTION:

10. **Assume police found Max and asked Max to testify against Elmer in his obscenity trial. Max jumped at the chance, but Elmer is now seeking to suppress his testimony. Which of the following statements is the most accurate and appropriate?**

(a) The testimony should be permitted because Max is a willing witness and, even though police obtained his name illegally from the envelope, Max's independent desire to testify has broken the chain between the illegality and the evidence.

(b) The testimony should be permitted because the police obtained Max's name by looking in a place where they reasonably believed they would find evidence of Elmer's obscenity activities.

(c) The testimony should be suppressed because the police unreasonably forced their way into Elmer's house at a time when they knew he wasn't at home, and all ensuing actions were derivative of that initial illegality.

(d) The testimony should be suppressed because, once the police discovered the obscenity operation in the basement, they no longer had a basis to search elsewhere in the house, and the letter identifying Max was beyond the proper scope of a search at that point.

(e) The testimony should be suppressed because unopened first class letters are within the reasonable expectation of privacy of both the author and the addressee, and at least one of them had to consent to the letter being opened.

* * *

Police suspected that Winchell murdered his brother. They purposefully failed to get a warrant to arrest Winchell at home. Instead they made a non-consensual entry into his home and arrested him. While in the home, Winchell made incriminating statements in response to the officers' comments, between themselves, that "the victim was shot up so badly that he must have made somebody pretty mad." After Winchell was placed in a squad car, he was advised of his Miranda rights. Again he made incriminating statements. At police headquarters he again received Miranda warnings, and again, repeated the same incriminating remarks he made in the squad car and in his home.

QUESTION:

11. **Which of the following is the *strongest* basis to exclude the incriminating statements Winchell made in the squad car and at headquarters?**

(a) The officers' comments in the house were the equivalent of interrogation.

(b) The officers lacked probable cause to arrest Winchell.

(c) The officers did not have a warrant to arrest Winchell in his own home.

(d) The officers purposefully and in bad faith did not obtain an arrest warrant.

(e) While in the squad car and at headquarters, the officers failed to warn Winchell that his statements in the house were inadmissible.

* * *

A fight broke out among a small group of five to ten patrons in a tavern. During the melee, one person was stabbed to death. Police were called to the scene, and officers immediately told all of the approximately fifty patrons to "freeze." The police then went to each person and asked "What happened?

What did you see?" When they approached Buffy, she said, "I'm not saying anything. I want to see a lawyer before I make any comments." Police took her name, said that she should not try to leave town, and permitted her to depart. Later that night, police developed enough evidence to arrest Buffy for the murder of the tavern patron. They brought her to headquarters, gave her Miranda warnings, and proceeded to ask her questions about what happened in the tavern. Buffy said, "I'll tell you what happened, but I'm not signing anything and I won't put anything in writing." She then incriminated herself in the stabbing.

QUESTION:

12. **The prosecutor now wishes to use Buffy's statements against her in a prosecution for murder. Which of the following statements is the most accurate and appropriate?**

    (a) The statements are inadmissible because Buffy did not actually comprehend the rights she gave up when speaking to the police.

    (b) The statements are inadmissible because, once Buffy invoked her right to counsel, the police could not reinterrogate her unless her counsel was actually present.

    (c) The statements are inadmissible because the police effectively seized all of the patrons without probable cause, and but for that seizure, they would not have known Buffy's identity.

    (d) The statements are admissible because Buffy validly waived her rights against self-incrimination.

    (e) The statements are admissible because the errors the police made at the tavern were cured by giving Miranda warnings at the police station.

* * *

Police suspected that Marty murdered his brother. They developed probable cause and secured a warrant for Marty's arrest. Marty was taken into custody and questioned after he was advised of his Miranda rights. Marty neither invoked nor waived his Miranda rights but did acknowledge that he understood them. Marty's lawyer called the station to make the police aware that the wanted Marty left alone. The police gave their assurances that they would stop talking to Marty until the lawyer was able to speak with him. Nevertheless, the officers continued to question Marty as he sat silently. Two hours later, Marty had still not confessed and the police learned that a grand jury had just handed up an indictment against Marty charging him with the murder of his brother. The police advised Marty about the indictment, gave him a fresh set of Miranda warnings, and continued their questioning. After another two hours, the police gave up for the night, placing Marty in a holding cell until the next morning.

Early the next morning, Marty's attorney called the station again. The attorney indicated that he was aware of the indictment and instructed the police officers not to speak with his client. Knowing that Marty was to be taken to court for an arraignment in the late afternoon, the police realized this could be their last chance to secure a confession because of the possibility Marty would be transferred. The officers read Marty his Miranda rights again but did not inform him that he was going to be arraigned that afternoon. Marty gave a full confession.

QUESTION:

13. **Marty wants his confession suppressed. Which of the following would be Marty's strongest argument at a suppression hearing?**

   (a) The police should have informed Marty that he was indicted; by failing to do so, the police deprived Marty of his Sixth Amendment rights and the statement is accordingly inadmissible.

   (b) In the State procedural system, Marty would have been appointed an attorney at the arraignment. Because the police deliberately failed to tell Marty that he was going to be arraigned and would get an attorney at this arraignment, the police violated Marty's Sixth Amendment rights. This violation requires the confession to be suppressed.

   (c) Marty's four hour silence clearly indicated his desire to remain silent. Because the police did not respect this desire, the confession must be suppressed.

   (d) Marty's lawyer called the police station before Marty's indictment and told the police not to interrogate him. The police agreed but never told Marty that he was represented. Because this information was withheld, the waiver was legally insufficient.

   (e) Marty's lawyer called the police station immediately after Marty's indictment to advise Marty not to say a word. Marty was not informed of this and as such, Marty's waiver was not knowing and intelligent. *have to tell because 6th Amd. Right to counsel attached*

   Because upon indictment - Miranda warning is enough for both 5th & 6th Amd.
   right to counsel. ⟺ waiver has to be knowing + voluntary

* * *

Police detectives developed probable cause to arrest McGiver for fraud. McGiver was a small time con artist who, because of the people with whom he associated, sometimes had valuable information about drug deals and planned robberies. The detectives decided that they really didn't want to lock McGiver up; instead, they wanted to apply some pressure and perhaps acquire useful information. On May 5th, they entered McGiver's house yelling: "Police! Police!—You're under arrest!" They had no warrant. McGiver made some incriminating statements about his con schemes. The detectives were about to handcuff McGiver when his wife entered the house. As she started to complain about McGiver's drinking and slovenly ways, McGiver picked up a knife and threatened to kill her.

QUESTION:

14. **McGiver was never prosecuted for fraud but was tried for making the May 5th threats against his wife. Which of the following statements is the most accurate and appropriate?**

    (a) All of the May 5th statements made by McGiver in the house are inadmissible because the detectives lacked a warrant to enter the house.

    (b) All of the May 5th statements made by McGiver in the house are admissible because the detectives had probable cause to arrest and the entry into the house protected only McGiver's privacy interest in the house.

    (c) The May 5th threats are admissible because the threats were a new crime not considered a product of the unlawful entry.

    (d) If it is established that the detectives blatantly schemed to violate McGiver's Fourth Amendment rights, then, no matter how strong the other evidence against him is, admission of any of the in-house statements could never be deemed harmless.

    (e) All of McGiver's May 5th statements are inadmissible because McGiver had not received Miranda warnings.

*   *   *

Ferris is a target of a grand jury investigation into drug dealing. Ferris is not informed of his status as a target nor is he given Miranda warnings at any time during his testimony before the grand jury. Ferris does not specifically waive his Fifth Amendment rights but simply answers all questions because he thinks he has to. Ferris is later prosecuted for perjury for making certain false statements before the grand jury and for the drug dealing activities.

QUESTION:

15. **Which of the following statements is the most accurate and appropriate?**

    (a) Ferris' grand jury statements can be used against him because the grand jury, because of its unique nature and historic function, is entitled to all relevant evidence.

    (b) Ferris' grand jury statements cannot be used against him because he was not informed of his target status.

    (c) Ferris' grand jury statements cannot be used against him because he did not receive Miranda warnings.

    (d) Ferris' grand jury statements cannot be used against him because he did not specifically waive his protection against self-incrimination.

    (e) Ferris' grand jury statements can be used against him for the perjury counts.

* * *

The police arrested an assistant United States Attorney on charges of robbery and assault in connection with high level shakedowns of drug suppliers. When the police handcuffed the suspect and began reading him his rights, the suspect said, "Oh, cut the bull. I'm a prosecutor . . . I know my rights. Just take my statement." The police then took notes as the suspect confessed.

QUESTION:

16. **Which of the following statements is the most accurate and appropriate?**

    (a) The confession is admissible because the defendant waived the reading of his Miranda warnings.

    (b) The confession is inadmissible because Miranda rights were not given.

    (c) The confession is admissible because it was volunteered.

    (d) The confession is inadmissible because, at that point, the defendant had a right to counsel which was not specifically waived.

    (e) The confession is inadmissible because the defendant did not knowingly and intelligently waive his rights.

* * *

Officers arrest Flanders in Marge's home pursuant to a valid arrest warrant. Cocaine is seen on the table in Marge's bedroom, and Marge is arrested. Marge moves to suppress the drugs.

QUESTION:

17. **Which of the following statements is the most accurate and appropriate?**

    (a) The cocaine is inadmissible against Marge unless the officers had a search warrant.

    (b) The cocaine is admissible pursuant to the plain view exception to the warrant requirement of the Fourth Amendment.

    (c) The cocaine is admissible under the "wing span" search permitted as a search incident to an arrest.

    (d) The cocaine is inadmissible unless probable cause existed and the seizure wasn't inadvertent.

    (e) The cocaine is inadmissible unless the police had probable cause to believe Flanders would be found in Marge's home.

* * *

Eleanore, visibly upset, reports to the police that she was just robbed of her purse while getting into her car outside of a convenience store. She says the suspect ran away in the direction of town. Police drive her around the neighborhood, and when she spots Drummond, she says, "That's the man who robbed me." The police arrest Drummond, search his person, and find cocaine.

QUESTION:

18. **Which of the following statements is the most accurate and appropriate?**

    (a) The police should have detained Drummond under *Terry v. Ohio* while they sought an arrest and search warrant.

    (b) Eleanore's identification must be suppressed because Drummond was not provided with a lawyer at this pretrial identification procedure.

    (c) Eleanore's identification is inadmissible because the police did not stage a lineup.

    (d) Since Eleanore's account to the police mentioned only the details of the robbery and did not provide the police with a detailed description of Drummond, there was no probable cause for Drummond's arrest.

    (e) Even though Eleanore has had no previous dealings with the police and thus no track record of reliability, as an ordinary citizen in these circumstances, Eleanore is presumed reliable.

* * *

On August 1, Detective Holmes was conducting an investigation of Moriarity. Moriarity had previously made a cocaine sale to Detective Holmes' colleague, Detective Watson, in the parking lot of Moriarity's apartment complex. Moriarity had arranged for another parking lot transaction with Watson to take place at 1 pm on August 1. Holmes arranged to watch the transaction from an observation post across the street from the apartment complex. From that post, Holmes could see through a large glass window in Moriarity's building into the hallway outside Moriarity's apartment, but not into the apartment itself.

At around the scheduled time of the sale, Holmes saw Moriarity and a friend, later identified as Pinky, emerge from Moriarity's apartment. Holmes was not acquainted with Pinky and had no information concerning him. Moriarity and Pinky conversed briefly in front of the large window in the hallway outside of the apartment. Moriarity then entered the apartment alone while Pinky lingered momentarily at the window and then reentered Moriarity's apartment. Moriarity then left the apartment and met Watson in the parking lot and sold him a small amount of cocaine. Moriarity then returned to his apartment, and approximately twenty minutes later, Moriarity and Pinky left the apartment and started walking up the street. Holmes and Watson then ran up to them, spun them around, frisked them, and placed them under arrest.

QUESTION:

19. **Which of the following statements is the most accurate and appropriate?**

    (a) The arrest of Moriarity and Pinky was unlawful because there was no emergency and no flight, and the police had ample opportunity to obtain a warrant.

    (b) The stop and frisk of Moriarity and Pinky was lawful but, neither was, at that particular moment, subject to arrest.

    (c) The detectives' failure to obtain a warrant for Moriarity's arrest on the earlier drug sale tainted the stakeout and the subsequent surveillance of Moriarity and Pinky.

    (d) The arrest of Moriarity was lawful but the arrest of Pinky was not.

    (e) The stop and frisk of Moriarity and the arrest of both was lawful.

* * *

Police in Punta Gorda, Florida were investigating a series of robberies and had little to go on except a set of the assailant's fingerprints. The police interviewed approximately thirty to forty possible suspects and, although they developed no specific information amounting to probable cause, began to focus on eight of the interviewees. The police then obtained home addresses, visited each of the eight, and asked if they would provide fingerprints. All agreed except Woody who refused. The police then told Woody he had "no choice," and then hustled him to a waiting squad car and drove him to police headquarters, about two miles away. At headquarters they instructed him to submit to fingerprinting. He did not physically resist, but he never consented to the procedure. The entire episode, from the house to fingerprinting, lasted about one hour. Woody was then taken back home.

QUESTION:

20. **Which of the following statements is the most accurate and appropriate?**

    (a) The police action in taking Woody to police headquarters was justified by "reasonable suspicion," but the actual taking of his fingerprints violated his Fifth Amendment right because he was compelled to submit to the procedure.

    (b) The police action violated Woody's Fourth Amendment rights because they did not have probable cause to take him to police headquarters.

    (c) The police action in taking Woody to police headquarters was justified by reasonable suspicion, but the police, absent any emergency, needed probable cause and a warrant for obtaining the fingerprints.

(d) In the absence of consent, fingerprints can only be obtained by a grand jury pursuant to a subpoena duces tecum.

(e) The police action in taking Woody to the police headquarters and in obtaining his fingerprints was justified by reasonable suspicion.

* * *

A young woman informed the police that a husband and wife had kidnaped and sexually abused her in an apparent attempt to force her into prostitution. During her stay at the couples' apartment, the woman observed a diary in which the couple wrote details of their plans to obtain, condition, and coerce young women and even boys and girls to serve in their prostitution ring. On the basis of the woman's complaint, the police obtained a search warrant for the apartment. The warrant described the diary and other evidentiary items.

At the same time, a federal grand jury investigating violations of interstate prostitution laws issued a subpoena duces tecum to the husband and wife to produce the diary.

QUESTION:

21. **Which of the following statements is the most accurate and appropriate?**

(a) The only legal way to obtain the diary is for a grand jury to issue a subpoena duces tecum.

(b) If the police seize the diary pursuant to a warrant, any constitutional objection will give way to the "good faith exception."

(c) The diary can be obtained pursuant to the warrant or a grand jury subpoena duces tecum.

(d) The diary cannot be seized pursuant to the warrant or a grand jury subpoena duces tecum because such a seizure would violate the Fifth Amendment.

(e) Although the police pursuant to a warrant or the grand jury pursuant to a subpoena duces tecum can obtain the diary, either way, the husband and wife may have a Fourth Amendment "act of production" immunity.

* * *

Officer Segal clocked Lance Feather, who was riding a scooter, at 50 miles per hour in a 35 mile per hour zone. Officer Segal turned on his lights and pursued Feather who pulled over almost immediately, dismounted from his scooter and, pursuant to Officer Segal's instructions, walked a good distance from the scooter.

Feather was wearing only cut-off jean shorts and tennis shoes (in a State without a mandatory helmet law). Officer Segal noticed that Feather was acting erratically. Standing 20–25 feet away, Officer Segal observed that

Feather appeared uneasy on his feet and was screaming gibberish peppered with an occasional expletive. Officer Segal ordered Feather to stop his antics, but Feather continued to rant. Wanting to assert control over the situation, Officer Segal drew his taser and shot Feather from 20 feet away. Feather was immediately (and temporarily) paralyzed and dropped to the ground, breaking several teeth and his jaw. Feather was then arrested and charged with speeding and disturbing the peace.

QUESTION:

22. **Feather has challenged his arrest on the grounds that Officer Segal used excessive force in effectuating the arrest. Which of the following statements is the most accurate and appropriate?**

    (a) The use of force was reasonable because a taser is non-lethal force.

    (b) The use of force was unreasonable because the use of the taser was lethal force and such force was not justified.

    (c) The use of force violated Feather's due process rights.

    (d) The use of force was unreasonable under the Fourth Amendment balancing test.

    (e) The use of force was reasonable because Feather posed a threat to Officer Segal and the force was reasonably calculated to protect Officer Segal from Feather.

* * *

After a magistrate refused to issue a search warrant for want of probable cause, the police, following their instincts that criminal activity was underway, went to a house registered under the names of Mr. and Mrs. Smith at 302 Broadway. Mr. Smith answered the door but declined to give the officers consent to search and slammed the door in the officers' faces. The police left and returned the next day, at a time they know Mr. Smith will be out at work. During this second visit, only Mrs. Smith was home. The officers truthfully told Ms. Smith that they were investigating illegal drug activity, and then asked her for permission to search the house. Mrs. Smith said, "Well, you are the police and I guess you can search if you want to. Come in." The police searched the house ultimately finding cocaine in the bedroom. Later, the police learned that at the time of the search, Mr. and Mrs. Smith were going through a messy divorce and that Mrs. Smith was only there to remove her belongings.

QUESTION:

23. **In the trial of Mr. Smith for illegal possession of cocaine, which of the following statements is the most accurate and appropriate?**

    (a) The cocaine is inadmissible against Mr. Smith because he did not consent to the search.

    (b) The cocaine is admissible against Mr. Smith because he lacks standing to object to the search.

(c) The cocaine is inadmissible against Mr. Smith because the police lacked probable cause to search.

(d) The cocaine is admissible against Mr. Smith because the search was made with consent.

(e) The cocaine is inadmissible against Mr. Smith because the police returned to the house after Mr. Smith refused to give consent knowing that he would not be present to object to the search.

* * *

Without any warrant, the police forced their way into Tommy's house, confiscated stolen property found in the bedroom, and placed Tommy under arrest. Tommy, hoping to get favorable treatment, told the police that, yes, he and Rebecca did deal in stolen goods, and they kept most of the stolen items at Rebecca's house. Still without any warrant, the police then went to Rebecca's house, seized the stolen property found there, and placed Rebecca under arrest. After being arraigned, Rebecca was released on her own recognizance. The next day, Rebecca's mother learned of the arrest and told her daughter that she should probably "make some kind of a deal" or, at least, "come clean for the sake of it." Rebecca thought it over and returned to the police station and gave a confession.

QUESTION:

24. **Which of the following statements is the most accurate and appropriate?**

(a) Rebecca's confession is inadmissible because it was the derivative fruit of a warrantless and unlawful search and seizure and arrest.

(b) Rebecca's confession is inadmissible because, in the absence of specific warnings, it was not "knowingly and intelligently" given.

(c) Rebecca's confession is admissible because the original illegality was the arrest and search and seizure at Tommy's house, and Rebecca has no standing to object to those acts.

(d) Rebecca's confession is admissible because intervening events purged the taint of the unlawful search and seizure and arrest.

(e) Rebecca's confession is inadmissible because arraignment is a critical stage, and her right to counsel had attached.

* * *

Fire inspectors, having no warrant but having probable cause to believe that a specific house contains fire code violations, enter the house without consent and conduct an inspection. They find the violations as expected.

QUESTION:

25. **Which of the following statements is the most accurate and appropriate?**

    (a) The search is proper as an "administrative" or "regulatory" search because, as such, it is sufficient that the fire inspectors had probable cause to believe the house contained fire code violations.

    (b) The search is proper so long as the fire inspectors are acting pursuant to statutory authority and so long as they conduct the searches on a regularized, systematic, and non-arbitrary basis.

    (c) The search is proper if there was probable cause and if the code violations were criminal and not just administrative in nature.

    (d) The search was improper because there was no warrant.

    (e) The search was improper because administrative searches can only be conducted with consent—even though the withholding of consent can be made a crime.

* * *

One afternoon a police officer stopped a man in a narrow alley. A second man was standing nearby to the one stopped. The officer later testified that the reason he stopped the first man was because "the situation looked suspicious, and I had never seen that subject in the area before." After stopping him and asking him some questions, the police officer then patted down the first man and took a cigarette flip-top-box from his shirt pocket. Looking inside the officer found a packet of heroin.

QUESTION:

26. **Which of the following statements is the most accurate and appropriate?**

    (a) The heroin will be inadmissible because the officer lacked reasonable suspicion to stop the man, and the look into the cigarette pack was beyond the scope of a stop and frisk search.

    (b) The heroin will be inadmissible because the officer went beyond a proper frisk; there was reasonable suspicion to stop.

    (c) The heroin will be inadmissible because the officer lacked reasonable suspicion to stop; the search was a proper frisk.

    (d) The heroin will be admissible if the officer's encounter with the man was for a brief period only.

    (e) The heroin will be admissible if the officer's actions, under the particular facts of this case, were the least intrusive means reasonably available to dispel the officer's suspicions.

* * *

A police officer observed Smith driving recklessly down the road, pulled him over, and asked him to step out of his vehicle. When Smith exited the car, the officer noticed that Smith had bloodshot eyes and appeared to have trouble standing. The officer decided he was going to arrest Smith for drunken driving but said nothing to him. Instead, the officer asked Smith "Have you been drinking?" Smith replied that he had a "couple" of beers at an office party an hour earlier. At that point, the officer asked Smith to take a breathalyzer test, which Smith took and failed. Smith was placed under arrest for driving while intoxicated and charged with the same offense.

QUESTION:

27. **Which of the following statements is the most accurate and appropriate?**

   (a) Smith's statement is inadmissible because the officer did not give him Miranda warnings.

   (b) Smith's statement is inadmissible because it was the fruit of the breathalyzer test which, under the circumstances, constituted an unlawful search.

   (c) Smith's statement is inadmissible because it was given in response to a question at a time when Smith was not free to leave and was effectively under arrest.

   (d) Smith's statement will be admissible if the stop was made with probable cause.

   (e) Smith's statement is admissible because Miranda warnings were not required, and Smith was not coerced to speak.

* * *

Although they have no hard evidence yet, the police firmly believe that Harry and Bob are responsible for a recent burglary. They decide to confront them. One evening at around 11 pm, four officers go to Harry's house. They have no arrest warrant and no search warrant. The four go through an unlocked door and surround Harry in his bed, their guns drawn. One officer says "Come clean, Harry, we know you did it." Harry immediately confesses saying he was grateful to have the opportunity to come clean. He tells all of the details of the robbery and also implicates Bob. The police take a statement and, trusting Harry's promises to turn himself in in the morning, tell him he won't be arrested and can remain free until morning.

QUESTION:

28. **Which of the following statements is the most accurate and appropriate?**

   (a) There is no Miranda violation because there was no interrogation.

   (b) There is no Miranda violation because there was no arrest.

(c) There is no Miranda violation because Harry's statements were voluntarily given.

(d) Harry's statements are inadmissible against him.

(e) Harry's statements cannot be used as a basis to establish probable cause to arrest Bob.

* * *

Flood and Brubaker became friendly while living in California as they were both tangentially involved in the marijuana distribution business. Eventually, both moved back to the East Coast and became involved in marijuana distribution in Philadelphia. Large quantities of marijuana were periodically delivered to Flood's residence. From there, Brubaker and others would divide the marijuana and allocate it among several local suppliers. Brubaker was eventually arrested on a possession charge and agreed to work as a confidential informant and consented to wear a recording device during his meetings with Flood, whom the police had been investigating.

About a month after Brubaker's arrest, he and Flood discussed new shipments of marijuana from the west coast. One was supposed to arrive the first week of September and a second shipment the week after. Officer Manges learned about these shipments by listening to Brubaker's conversations with Flood and on both occasions Officer Manges applied for, and was issued, a search warrant. However, Brubaker later told Officer Manges that the first shipment was rerouted and the second was delayed for unknown reasons.

Brubaker learned that a third shipment was running according to schedule and was to be delivered on September 19. Brubaker reported this to Officer Manges who then secured a third search warrant for Flood's residence. The warrant contained information only relating to the place to be searched and the items to be seized.

When the third shipment arrived, Brubaker called Officer Manges to report the number of people at Flood's house and the amount of marijuana delivered. When the police arrived they did not knock to announce their presence but rather moved in, secured the residence and found over 500 pounds of marijuana and $25,000. Flood confessed to possession with the intent to distribute on the spot.

QUESTION:

29. **Flood files a motion to suppress the evidence arguing that his Fourth Amendment rights were violated. What will the court rule on this motion?**

(a) The motion will be granted because the drugs were not at the residence when the third warrant issued and the failure of the first two deliveries shows that Brubaker was not a reliable informant. Thus, the warrant was not supported by probable cause.

(b)   The motion will be granted because the police did not comply with the knock and announce rule which is part of the Fourth Amendment reasonableness analysis.

(c)   The motion will be denied because the warrant was supported by probable cause.

(d)   The motion will be denied because the police never need to knock and announce their presence when a drug transaction is involved.

(e)   The motion will be denied because Flood assumed the risk that Brubaker was an informant and therefore he waived his reasonable expectation of privacy in regard to the recorded conversations.

* * *

During the course of a murder investigation, police developed evidence, including an eyewitness account and fingerprints on the candlestick used as the murder weapon, to believe that Col. Mustard murdered Mr. Green in the conservatory of Mustard's home. Police decided to arrest Col. Mustard, but he had apparently gone into hiding. Police watched airports and train and bus depots and placed two officers to watch his home. One late evening, two weeks later, the officers watching Mustard's home observed Mustard enter a back door. Over the next hour, they saw him go to the kitchen, have a snack, and then go into an upstairs bedroom, put on pajamas, and shut off the light. The police then entered the house and arrested Col. Mustard without a warrant. They asked him no questions, took him to headquarters, read him his Miranda warnings, and booked him.

QUESTION:

30. **Which of the following statements is the most accurate and appropriate?**

(a)   The arrest was valid because a warrant is not necessary when police arrest a dangerous fugitive who was avoiding capture.

(b)   The arrest was invalid because the police lacked probable cause and a warrant.

(c)   The arrest was valid because, had the warrant been obtained at the beginning of the investigation, it would have been stale, and had the police waited at the house to get a warrant, Col. Mustard could have fled.

(d)   The arrest was valid because, under the murder crime scene exception, police are permitted to enter premises where the murder occurred.

(e)   Any statements made by Mustard in the house would have been inadmissible against him.

* * *

Mrs. Peacock and two confederates robbed and murdered Mrs. White. Several days later, Mrs. Peacock went to the police to say she had witnessed the crime, but she denied any involvement, claiming she had fled for fear of being implicated in the terrible deed. She gave a description of the perpetrators but denied knowing them. The police disbelieved her, based on her inconsistent account and on other evidence implicating her in the crime, and they arrested her on the spot. After her arraignment on robbery and murder charges, Mrs. Peacock was put in a cell with a Miss Scarlet. Unknown to Peacock, Scarlet had agreed to act as a police informant. The police hoped that Peacock would reveal the names of her confederates. According to her arrangement with the police, Scarlet did not ask Peacock any questions but simply kept her ears open for incriminating information. One day, while Peacock was looking out of the cell block window in the direction of where the crime took place, she murmured that she was sorry she ever planned the robbery and that the killing of Mrs. White was an accident.

QUESTION:

31. **Scarlet reported this statement to police, and, later, prosecutors sought to introduce it into evidence against Peacock. Which of the following statements is the most accurate and appropriate?**

    (a) The statement is admissible because although police had arranged for and hoped to be the beneficiaries of a voluntary statement by Peacock, their actions did not violate her Sixth Amendment right to counsel.

    (b) The statement is inadmissible because, in the circumstances, the use of a police informant was the equivalent of secret state interrogation which violated Peacock's Sixth Amendment right to counsel.

    (c) The statement is inadmissible because placing Peacock in a cell which faced the direction of the crime, and the use of the informant were devices deliberately designed to elicit incriminating statements, and thus, the police violated Peacock's Sixth Amendment right to counsel.

    (d) The statement is inadmissible because Peacock was in custody and not aware that Scarlet had become a police agent; therefore, all statements were obtained in violation of Peacock's Sixth Amendment right to counsel.

    (e) The statement is inadmissible because Peacock's right to counsel had attached, and only statements made by her in defendant-initiated conversations would be admissible.

                                    * * *

Police officers received an uncorroborated and anonymous tip that a farmer was growing marijuana on his secluded property at the edge of the county line. The police went out to the farm, and finding no one home, looked into the windows of the house, went around the back, and followed a path that led out to the adjacent fields where cattle and horses were grazing. At the farthermost point on the property, about one quarter of a mile from the house, there were about two dozen marijuana plants. The plants were obscured by a high hedge fence, but the officers walked through the hedges and found the plants.

QUESTION:

32. **Which of the following statements is the most accurate and appropriate?**

    (a) The farmer has no Fourth Amendment expectation of privacy in the plants because they were contraband.

    (b) The farmer has no Fourth Amendment expectation of privacy in the plants because they were located in open fields.

    (c) The farmer has no Fourth Amendment expectation of privacy in the plants because they could readily be observed by air craft or a helicopter flying at very low altitudes.

    (d) Whatever Fourth Amendment expectation the farmer has in the plants, the police had adequate reasonable suspicion to look around the property.

    (e) The farmer has a Fourth Amendment expectation of privacy in the plants because they fell within an area known as the curtilage.

* * *

Bart was evicted from his apartment and had no place to go. He packed his meager personal belongings into several cardboard boxes and asked his friend Milhous if he could store them in his garage until he found a new home. Milhous agreed, but later, when police said that they were investigating Bart for robbery, Milhous directed the police officers to the particular area of the garage where Bart's stuff was stored, saying, "Here's his stuff, in that corner next to my car. See, he stored it here until he finds some place to live." Milhous then consented to a search of the garage. The officers conducted the search and found gun parts in one of the cardboard boxes linking Bart to the robbery.

QUESTION:

33. **Which of the following statements is the most accurate and appropriate?**

    (a) The gun parts may not be used as evidence against Bart because he retained an expectation of privacy in the boxes.

    (b) The gun parts may be used as evidence against Bart because he was not an overnight guest in the house; indeed he was homeless at the time.

(c) The gun parts may be used as evidence against Bart because Milhous's full access to the garage negated any expectation of privacy Bart may have had in the boxes.

(d) The gun parts may be used as evidence against Bart because Milhouse had mutual and joint access to the garage and was free to give consent to the search.

(e) The gun parts may not be used as evidence against Bart because the police lacked probable cause to think that evidence of the burglary would be found in the boxes.

* * *

Scully was riding an interstate bus traveling from New Orleans to Atlanta. The bus made a scheduled stop in Mobile, Alabama where the driver told all passengers they would have to get off the bus temporarily. Before the passengers could leave, however, two drug interdiction officers, both in full uniform and armed, boarded the bus. One officer identified the pair as members of the Mobile Police Department's drug interdiction unit. The officer then stated: "With your cooperation, we want to check for on-board contraband drugs and weapons. I'd like to ask you to bring down your on-board luggage if you have any overhead and have it open so we can do a quick on-board inspection." The officers said nothing more, and after waiting for the passengers to ready their bags, one remained at the entrance while the other went down the aisle, from front to back, and checked each passenger's open luggage. Once the searching officer finished with a row, the passengers in that row were free to exit the bus. When the officer searched Scully's bag, she found a brick-like object wrapped in heavy paper. The officer asked Scully to exit the bus with her. Outside, the officer exposed the bag to a narcotics-detection dog. The dog alerted to the bag. Scully then admitted it contained cocaine, and she was placed under arrest.

QUESTION:

34. **Which of the following statements is the most accurate and appropriate?**

    (a) Unless the officers brandished guns or otherwise manifest the threat of physical force, the police tactics on the bus were a consensual encounter, and the nature of the object in the bag gave the police reasonable suspicion to subject it to a dog sniff.

    (b) The tactics on the bus were a consensual encounter, and the dog sniff of the luggage, without more, was valid even if there was no reasonable suspicion.

    (c) The tactics on the bus amounted to a detention because the officers conveyed a message that compliance with their requests was required; all ensuing events were the product of the unlawful detention and invalid.

(d) The tactics on the bus amounted to a detention, but because Scully voluntarily admitted that she was transporting cocaine, the narcotics will be admissible against her.

(e) The tactics on the bus amounted to a detention because police must advise passengers that they may refuse consent to search; all ensuing events were the product of the unlawful detention and invalid.

* * *

Brandi Cooper became the target of an IRS investigation when the government received information that she was involved in the laundering of illicit drug proceeds. The IRS set up a sting operation as part of its investigation. Special Agent Rock Irons was detailed to make contact with Cooper and pretend to be a drug dealer interested in moving large amounts of tainted money through legitimate businesses. Irons hung out in a bar Cooper was known to frequent and, seeing her there, struck up a conversation and bought her a drink. The two hit it off immediately and agreed to see each other again. At their next meeting, Irons told Cooper that he was trying to "recycle" a large amount of drug money and asked Cooper whether she could be of any help. Cooper expressed interest. At subsequent meetings, the two worked out a method whereby Cooper would use some of her legitimate business activities to launder funds. At the same time that these arrangements were being worked out and during the entire course of the IRS' year-long investigation, Cooper and Irons were romantically involved and were intimate on many occasions. The IRS never authorized the use of sex as a tool in the sting operation, (indeed the IRS had written policies prohibiting such behavior), would not have approved of it had it been known, and never learned of the behavior throughout the investigation.

QUESTIONS:

35. **After the IRS completed its investigation, federal prosecutors charged Cooper with thirty six counts of money laundering. Cooper's attorney has now filed a motion claiming that the IRS agent's sexual relationship with Cooper and his use of that relationship to gather evidence against her constituted outrageous governmental conduct and, thus, a Due Process violation requiring dismissal. Which of the following statements is the most accurate and appropriate?**

(a) The motion should be denied because the agent was acting on his own and without the approval of the IRS when he carried on a sexual relationship with Cooper.

(b) The motion should be denied because Cooper demonstrated a propensity to engage in the criminal conduct even before the sexual relationship began.

(c) The motion should be denied because the agent's behavior was not so extreme and outrageous as to offend the fundamental requirements of Due Process.

(d)   The motion should be granted because sexual relations between a government agent and a suspect and the use of that relationship to gather evidence against the suspect always constitutes outrageous governmental conduct and requires dismissal.

(e)   The motion should be granted because the agent's actions were a direct violation of written, internal IRS policies which each agent was sworn to uphold.

36. With respect to the defense of outrageous governmental conduct in general, which of the following statements is the most accurate and appropriate?

(a)   The defense is never applicable if the defendant's conduct involved violence.

(b)   If the defense is put in issue by facts shown by the defendant, the government must then prove, beyond a reasonable doubt, that its conduct complied with Due Process standards.

(c)   The question of outrageousness is a question of fact for the jury to determine.

(d)   The defense is not available if, under the applicable statute, Congress clearly expressed its intention to eliminate it.

(e)   If a court finds that the government's behavior was so outrageous that fundamental principles of Due Process were violated, the government would be absolutely barred from invoking judicial processes to obtain a conviction.

* * *

Eddy Tee, who had served eight years of a ten year sentence, was released on parole. Mr. Tee's parole officers heard rumors that Mr. Tee had lost his job and had returned to his criminal ways in order to pay rent at the house in which he was living. Despite efforts to investigate these rumors, the parole officers were unable to corroborate them. After several days of fruitless investigation, the parole officers decided to pay Mr. Tee a home visit, bringing police officers along for back up.

When Mr. Tee opened the door, the parole officers told him that they were conducting a search of his residence pursuant to the applicable Montana statute governing the supervision of parolees and Mr. Tee's agreement to abide by the conditions of his parole. The officers went through the home and seized guns and ammunition. As the officers were finishing the search, Mr. Tee said, "I'm a gun addict. It's a sickness." When the search was completed, Mr. Tee was arrested and ultimately charged with being a felon in possession of firearms.

QUESTION:

37. **Prior to trial, Mr. Tee moved to suppress the evidence seized during the warrantless home search conducted by the parole officers and the statement he made during this allegedly illegal search. Which of the following statements is the most accurate and appropriate?**

    (a) The evidence and the statement are admissible because the parole officers had reasonable suspicion to believe that evidence of a parole violation would be found in Mr. Tee's home, and no warrant was necessary.

    (b) The evidence is inadmissible because the officers entered Mr. Tee's home without a warrant and without consent; the statement is admissible because it was voluntary and not given in response to any police questioning.

    (c) The evidence is inadmissible because the officers entered Mr. Tee's home without reasonable suspicion; the statement is inadmissible because it was the product of the illegal entry.

    (d) The evidence is inadmissible because the parole officers relied on ordinary law enforcement personnel, namely the police, to assist them when they conducted the search; the statement is admissible because it was voluntary and not given in response to any police questioning.

    (e) The evidence and the statement are admissible because neither individualized suspicion of wrongdoing nor a warrant is required when conducting a search of a parolee.

* * *

On August 15, at approximately 4:25 p.m., Officers Mauet and Roeper, received a radio dispatch that an assault involving a weapon was in progress at nearby apartment complex located in a neighborhood known for drug and gang activity. This dispatch was based on a 911 call from an anonymous caller. The dispatcher described the assailant as a 6-foot-tall Latino male wearing gray sweatpants and a black leather jacket. Within minutes, the officers arrived at the apartment complex. Neither officer saw evidence of an assault but when they looked in the lobby, they saw Simmons, a Latino male standing 5 feet 10 inches tall who was clad in gray sweatpants and a black leather jacket. The two officers entered the building. As soon as Simmons spotted the officers, he began to walk away briskly. Officer Mauet told Simmons to stop, but Simmons kept walking. Officer Mauet again ordered Simmons to stop and instructed Simmons to remove his hands from his jacket pockets. Again, Simmons did not comply. Officer Roeper ran behind Simmons, grabbed him and felt an object in his pocket that felt like a gun. At this point, Officer Roeper told Simmons to put his arms above his head and placed handcuffs on Simmons. Two loaded guns were found, one in each of Simmons' jacket pockets. Simmons was then formally arrested. Officer Roeper asked Simmons if there were any more weapons he should know about. When Simmons said no, Officer Roeper read Simmons his Miranda rights.

QUESTION:

38. **Simmons has moved to exclude the weapons as the fruit of an illegal arrest. Which of the following statements is the most accurate and appropriate?**

    (a) The evidence should be admitted because the totality of the circumstances gave the officers the probable cause they needed to stop and question Simmons.

    (b) The evidence should be admitted because the 911 caller described an ongoing emergency and the police were entitled to act accordingly.

    (c) The evidence should be excluded because the officers did not have probable cause to arrest Simmons.

    (d) The evidence should be excluded because Simmons' failure to comply with the officers' requests cannot be credited in the probable cause determination.

    (e) The evidence should be excluded because the anonymous 911 caller's description of Simmons was too vague to act on and the officers never confirmed that an assault took place.

* * *

Police suspect that Nora Lewes robbed the clerk at the local convenience store. One evening, as Nora sat at home watching a Women's World Cup soccer match, four police officers asked to be admitted to her house and then confronted her with the evidence they had gathered against her. Although the officers did not expressly place her under arrest, and although they in good faith believed they did not convey the impression that she was under arrest, Nora reasonably and objectively believed that she was in custody. Without giving any Miranda warnings, the officers asked Nora if she would be willing to answer their questions about the incident. Nora readily agreed, saying she "welcomed the chance to clear things up." For about thirty minutes, she answered questions and shortly thereafter began to give incriminating statements. At her trial for robbery, the prosecution sought to introduce these statements and Nora objected, claiming a violation of her Miranda rights. The state trial judge ruled that because there was absolutely no compulsion exerted against Nora to speak, the court would not apply the severe medicine of the exclusionary rule. Excluding the evidence, the trial judge said, would punish the police for a mere technical violation of Miranda, and such a harsh result was not constitutionally required.

QUESTION:

39. **Which of the following statements is the most accurate and appropriate?**

    (a) The evidence was properly admitted because the police would have inevitably discovered the same evidence; that is, even if Miranda warnings were given, Nora displayed such unmistakable willingness to answer questions that she would have given the police the same information.

    (b) The evidence was properly admitted; even if the police actions technically violated Miranda, their actions were excused because they acted in good faith.

    (c) The evidence was properly admitted because states are free to fashion their own rules of procedure so long as they are equally as effective as Miranda in preventing truly compelled statements.

    (d) The evidence was wrongfully admitted because the prophylactic Miranda warnings are constitutionally based requirements, and state courts are bound to exclude Miranda violative statements.

    (e) The evidence was wrongfully admitted because Miranda warnings are constitutionally compelled requirements of the Fifth Amendment, and the remedy in all courts, state and federal, is exclusion of the improperly obtained statements.

* * *

Police developed probable cause to believe that Dan Couche was carrying drugs in his large green briefcase. With the briefcase in his possession, Couche flew from Miami to New York, and police watched him as he exited the airport. Couche waited in a line to get a taxi, and, eventually, the dispatcher directed him to go to the next available cab. The taxi driver opened the trunk and invited Couche to place his briefcase inside. At first Couche hesitated but then put the bag in the trunk and settled into the backseat. It was customary at the airport to double up riders going to the same part of town and, right before the taxi was about to pull away from the curb, an undercover police officer got into the backseat with Couche. As the taxi left the airport, other undercover officers followed in an unmarked vehicle. They maintained close visual surveillance of Couche at all times. Shortly into the trip, Couche began to think he was being followed, and he also became highly suspicious of the "passenger" sitting in the back seat with him. At a traffic light, he jumped out of the cab and ran away leaving the briefcase behind. The police, startled by this development, were slow to react, and Couche got away. Meanwhile the police signaled the cab to pull over. The police removed the green briefcase from the trunk, opened it, and found cocaine. They then searched the interior of the taxi and found obscene pictures under the taxi driver's front seat. They had no warrant.

QUESTION:

40. **The taxi driver is prosecuted for possession of obscene materials and moves to suppress the introduction of the pictures found under his seat in the cab. Which of the following statements is the most accurate and appropriate?**

    (a) The pictures are inadmissible because the police lacked probable cause to search under the taxi driver's front seat.

    (b) The pictures are inadmissible because the police lacked a warrant to search the taxi, and there was no emergency since the taxi driver was cooperative and the suspect had already fled.

    (c) The pictures are admissible because the taxi driver was not the target of the police investigation and had no standing to object to the seizure of the briefcase or the search of the cab.

    (d) The pictures are admissible because the police had probable cause to believe that Couche was transporting drugs, and the "automobile exception" excused the need to obtain a warrant.

    (e) The pictures are admissible because a taxi driver, by operating a taxi, implicitly consents to the inspection of the interior of his vehicle.

*   *   *

John was driving with his girlfriend Marybeth from Boston to Las Vegas. Somewhere west of Omaha, Nebraska, John was pulled over by Officer Parson, who clocked John's speed at 75 miles per hour in a construction zone with a 55 mile per hour limit. While Officer Parson advised John of the reason for the stop he noticed an overwhelming odor of pine-scented air freshener and observed that the back of the vehicle appeared to be weighed down. Officer Parson was a bit curious but both passengers insisted that the trunk was empty.

Upon Officer Parson's request, John provided his identification, registration, and proof of insurance. Because John's identification indicated he was from Vermont, Officer Parson inquired about the details of John and Marybeth's journey. Neither provided details with any degree of specificity. Moreover, as Officer Parson continued his questioning, John appeared to become more nervous, evidenced by sweating and dry mouth, and defensive replies.

After running John's name through a routine database to check for outstanding warrants, Officer Parson found out that John had a criminal history involving drug distribution and that a case was pending against him. Officer Parson returned to the vehicle and sought permission to look in the trunk, to which John simply responded "no." Officer Parson told John he could either consent or be detained until a police service dog arrived to conduct a sniff of the vehicle. Until this point, 10 minutes had passed. It took 42 minutes for Officer Lewis to arrive with Dante, the police dog. Dante alerted the officers that something was in the trunk so they opened it and found several pieces of luggage containing what ended up to be 182 pounds of marijuana.

QUESTION:

41. **After John's indictment, he moved to suppress the evidence seized from the car. What is the most probable result?**

    (a) The motion will be granted because the police lacked justification for opening the trunk and the containers therein.

    (b) The motion will be granted because the facts observed by Officer Parson after the initial stop did not amount to a reasonable suspicion of criminal activity.

    (c) The motion will be granted because the detention was unreasonably prolonged by having to wait for a canine unit to arrive.

    (d) The motion will be denied because Officer Parson warned John that if he didn't give his consent to search, he would call for a police dog to search the vehicle.

    (e) The motion will be denied because none of John's constitutional rights were violated.

* * *

While conducting a surveillance of a known narcotics dealer, the police watched the target, Burke, engage in a transaction with two unknown individuals driving a Buick. The officers looked up the license plate number, learning that the car was registered to a man named Hernan. The officers followed the car until it stopped at 40 Richmond Street. The police noted that the vehicle was not registered to the address at which it was stopped. The two men got out of the vehicle and began unloading bags (which the officers saw during the transaction) from the trunk into the garage.

As the police approached Mark in the driveway, the police saw Hernan throw something that looked like a gun under the Buick before running into the house. The police placed Mark in handcuffs before entering the home to find Hernan. Once inside, the police opened a closet door viewing what appeared to be a methamphetamine laboratory. Within moments, Hernan was located and secured and the police recovered the weapon from under the Buick. The police secured the premises and left with Mark and Hernan in the back of their squad car, leaving all but one bag behind due to space and time constraints.

Immediately upon reaching the station, the officers applied for a search warrant of 40 Richmond Street, which turned out to be owned by Mark's sister Clarissa. A magistrate issued the warrant and the officers returned to seize the remaining narcotics in the garage and to obtain evidence about the methamphetamine laboratory. At trial, the prosecution wants to admit the drugs from the transaction the police witnessed as well as the evidence linking both men to the drug laboratory.

QUESTION:

42. **Hernan moves to exclude all of the prosecution's evidence. What is the most accurate and appropriate outcome?**

    (a) The evidence of the initial drug transaction will be excluded because the police could have obtained a warrant; the evidence from inside the home will be admitted because Hernan does not have standing to object to the entry into the home.

    (b) The evidence of the initial drug transaction will be admitted because the police watched the transaction and therefore had probable cause; the evidence from inside the home will be excluded because the police entered the home without a warrant.

    (c) The evidence of the initial drug transaction will be excluded because the police could have obtained an arrest warrant; the evidence from inside the home will be excluded because the police exceeded the bounds of a permissible protective sweep.

    (d) The evidence of the initial drug transaction will be admitted because the officers had probable cause; the evidence from inside the home will be admitted because it was seized pursuant to a valid warrant.

    (e) The evidence of the initial drug transaction will be admitted because the transaction occurred in public; the evidence from inside the home will be excluded because the police were only able to get a warrant based on what they learned while illegally inside of the home.

END OF EXAM III QUESTIONS

ANSWER KEY EXAM I
CRIMINAL PROCEDURE MULTIPLE CHOICE QUESTIONS ANSWER KEY AND EXPLANATIONS

1. **The best answer is (c).** This question is adapted from *Trice v. United States*, 662 A.2d 891 (D.C. Ct. App. 1995). The critical facts have been materially altered since the actual facts make *Trice* a somewhat questionable ruling. On the adapted facts, Trice is in custody and has invoked his right to counsel following receipt of his Miranda warnings. Under such circumstances, the police may not question him unless the questions are not considered interrogation or come within the "public safety" exception of *New York v. Quarles*, 467 U.S. 649 (1984). The questions related to his name, social security number, and medical conditions are not in issue. These questions would not be Miranda-violative since they are arguably booking-type questions. *Pennsylvania v. Muniz*, 496 U.S. 582 (1990). The relevant question relates to the shotgun, and that question falls within the public safety exception. In *Quarles* the Supreme Court concluded that incriminating statements made before Miranda warnings were given were admissible because they were reasonably prompted by concern for public safety. The Court said that if an officer's questions served "an objectively reasonable need to protect the police or public from any immediate danger associated with [a] weapon," then the protection of the public outweighed the need for the prophylactic rule protecting the Fifth Amendment privilege. The facts of this question depart from *Quarles* in two ways. First, in *Quarles*, the question about the gun came before Miranda warnings were given whereas, here, the question about the shotgun came after Miranda warnings were administered and the right to counsel invoked. But federal appellate courts have applied the public safety exception in such circumstances. *See, e.g., United States v. Mobley*, 40 F.3d 688 (4th Cir. 1994), *cert. denied*, 516 U.S. 1135 (1995) (although not applying the exception in the case, the court held that the public safety exception could apply after a suspect has invoked his right to counsel, and therefore excuse a violation of *Edwards v. Arizona*, 451 U.S. 477 (1981), because the danger to the public and to police officers is the same whether the suspect has been Mirandized or not); *United States v. DeSantis*, 870 F.2d 536 (9th Cir. 1989). The court's reason is that the same calculus applied in *Quarles* applies, namely, the need to protect public safety still outweighs the mere prophylactic protections of the Fifth Amendment, and the danger to the public is in no way lessened by a suspect's invocation of Miranda rights. Second, in *Quarles*, the public safety question about the gun was asked immediately during the course of the arrest, whereas here, the question came after the

suspect left his home. The *Quarles* Court stated: "in this case, in the very act of apprehending a suspect, [the police] were confronted with the immediate necessity of ascertaining the whereabouts of a gun . . . ," the question here was still prompted by a contemporaneous and reasonable concern for public safety and not asked as an attempt to elicit testimonial evidence from the suspect. The detective had only just removed Trice from his house; because of the timing, there was strong circumstantial evidence suggesting the gun was in the house and the detective observed that small children were present. **Answers (a) and (b) both err** because they assume that Miranda doesn't apply to the question about the gun because it was either a routine inquiry or an administrative action. Questions about guns and other evidence are within Miranda, and the only question is whether an exception applies. **Answer (d) raises a good point but the categorical assertion that the exception cannot apply once a suspect is taken from his home is overbroad and, hence, wrong.** Generally, courts will not allow statements asked in violation of Miranda if the location has already been secured, nobody remains within, and other people, including the public, have no access to the premises which may contain a weapon. *See, e.g., United States v. Brathwaite,* 458 F.3d 376 (5th Cir. 2006). As the facts indicate however, there are people inside and therefore, *Brathwaite* does not apply. **Answer (e) is also erroneously overbroad.** Suspects may be asked some questions after claiming a right to silence, such as (1) questions that don't "count," like booking questions, (2) reinterrogation if the original invocation was scrupulously honored, or, (3) as here, public safety questions.

- **Additional references**: *See* LaFave, Israel, King & Kerr, Criminal Procedure § 6.7(b) (6th ed. 2017); Whitebread & Slobogin, Criminal Procedure: An Analysis of Cases and Concepts § 16.03(c)(3) (7th ed. 2020).

2. **The best pick is (d).** There is no right to counsel issue here since Trice has not been indicted nor has he faced any formal charge or proceeding. *Kirby v. Illinois,* 406 U.S. 682 (1972). And, in any event, no right to counsel applies to photographic evidence whether formal charges have been laid or not because the suspect is not confronting the state or witnesses against him. *United States v. Ash,* 413 U.S. 300 (1973). But Due Process may limit the use of identification evidence under these circumstances. If the defendant is able to prove that an identification procedure was unnecessary and suggestive and if the defendant is then also able to prove that the identification was unreliable, i.e., created a substantial risk of a mistaken identification, the evidence will be excluded. This is a hard test for defendants to meet. Here the use of a single photo was, by definition, suggestive. It was also arguably unnecessary since there was no emergency or need to act with haste, and the police were not involved in an on-the-scene show-up. But the defendant will not be able to show that the identification is unreliable under the totality of the circumstances. *Manson v. Brathwaite,* 432 U.S. 98 (1977). Green's identification came before the photo, he spoke with certainty, he saw his attacker at close range in broad daylight, and he knew Trice from the neighborhood,

Independent Source Established.

including knowing where he lived. Thus Green made his identification independent of and uninfluenced by the unnecessarily suggestive single photo. And, since the photo identification is admissible, there is no "fruit of the poisonous tree" problem, and the in-court identification will also be admissible. **Answer (a) is wrong** because it reaches the wrong conclusion about the reliability of Mr. Green's identification. As mentioned, he had an independent basis to recognize Mr. Trice and did so under favorable circumstances. **Answer (b)** mistakenly posits a right to counsel and is incorrect. **Answer (c)** starts out well enough but then veers into error. It is true that juries do attach a great deal of significance to in-court identifications, and it is also true that mistakes have been and will be made. Nevertheless, in-court identifications are highly relevant and sometimes crucial pieces of evidence that are routinely and properly relied on at trial. **Answer (e)** is almost always an incorrect answer, and it is wrong here. Under a Due Process analysis, the out-of-court and in-court identifications will usually rise or fall together. If the out-of-court identification was unnecessarily suggestive and unreliable, it means that the in-court identification can only be based on the suggestive actions of the police. It, too, will be unreliable because the witness has no independent basis for making it. Contrariwise, if the out-of-court identification is reliable, the witness, by definition, has an independent basis for fingering the defendant and an in-court identification will be allowed.

- **Additional references:** *See* LAFAVE, ISRAEL, KING & KERR, CRIMINAL PROCEDURE § 7.4 (6th ed. 2017); WHITEBREAD & SLOBOGIN, CRIMINAL PROCEDURE: AN ANALYSIS OF CASES AND CONCEPTS § 17.03 (7th ed. 2020).

3. **The right answer is (e).** The facts of this question are drawn from *United States v. Bogle*, 114 F.3d 1271 (D.C. Cir. 1997). The question rests on the meaning of interrogation *for the purposes of Miranda.* Mr. Bogle invoked his right to silence following receipt of his Miranda warnings. Under those circumstances, police may not reinitiate questioning unless they scrupulously honor his desire not to speak. Typically this will mean honoring the right to silence immediately, introducing some significant period of respite, and returning in a non-threatening mode with a fresh set of warnings. *See Michigan v. Mosley,* 423 U.S. 96 (1975). Since those ingredients are questionable here, Bogle's incriminating statements to Detective Parker must be excluded unless the conversation with Parker was not covered by Miranda. Such is the case here. Even though Bogle was obviously in custody and even though Detective Parker "questioned" Bogle, the questioning was not interrogation but only an ordinary investigative interview. The fact that Bogle was in jail and was charged with a crime did not mean that police could not seek his help in finding out about his brother's murder. There was no need for warnings. The conversation here was akin to an on-the-scene interview, and Bogle's incriminating statements were voluntarily offered in the course of the interview. **Answers (a), (b), and (c)** all falter because they assume Parker's conversation with Bogle was interrogation. **Answer (a)** focuses

on the brief time between the two sessions, **answer (b)** focuses on the failure to rewarn, and **answer (c)** goes fully overboard by stating that further questioning was not allowed without Bogle's attorney. Bogle invoked only a right to silence, not a right to have an attorney present. **Answer (d)** is true enough but misses the controlling issue. The key question here is whether the police could engage in any questioning after Bogle invoked his right to silence.

- • **Additional references**: *See* LaFave, Israel, King & Kerr, Criminal Procedure § 6.7 (6th ed. 2017); Whitebread & Slobogin, Criminal Procedure: An Analysis of Cases and Concepts § 16.03(b) (7th ed. 2020).

4. **The correct choice is (b).** Norma Holloway offered her services to the State and was enlisted, following her proposal, to listen for any incriminating statements Sally Johnson might make. She was, in other words, acting as an agent of the State. Although she was not acting for money, she hoped, and implicitly was promised, that she might get a break on her sentence. In the capacity of an agent and in the expectation of gain, she attempted to elicit incriminating statements by questioning Johnson about her crimes. This scenario parallels *United States v. Henry*, 447 U.S. 264 (1980). In *Henry*, Nichols was approached by the government and asked to listen for any incriminating statements his fellow cellmate, Henry, might make. Nichols, like Holloway here, did not adhere to the instruction to act as a passive listener and prodded the defendant to discuss his crime. The Supreme Court held that this amounted to deliberate elicitation of incriminating statements contrary to the protections of the Sixth Amendment right to counsel. *Id.; see also Massiah v. United States*, 377 U.S. 201 (1964) (noting that post-indictment interrogation by the State or its agent is a critical stage of the prosecution requiring the presence of counsel in the absence of a valid waiver). The *Henry* Court concluded that the government created a situation where Nichols, who stood to gain financially if he "got something," would encourage and stimulate conversations, despite his instructions. As an aside, it should be clear that an accused cannot knowingly and intelligently waive her Sixth Amendment right to counsel when she is unaware that she is being interrogated by the State through an undercover agent or informant. *See, e.g., Patterson v. Illinois*, 487 U.S. 285 (1988). The situation presented here (and in *Henry*) contrasts with the Court's conclusion in *Kuhlmann v. Wilson*, 477 U.S. 436 (1986), where, according to the majority, the informant asked no questions and simply listened to the defendant's unsolicited statements. The Court held that if an informant is merely a listening device and not affirmatively seeking to draw out incriminating statements, there will be no Sixth Amendment violation. On the facts of this question, informant Holloway was more than a listening device because she asked questions relating to the murder. As such, the outcome of this question should be governed by *Henry*. **Answer (e) is wrong** because, as in *Henry*, the government created a situation where the informant was likely to go beyond her instructions in order to gain a lighter sentence. The detective knew or

should have known this was the case and, thus, the State created the situation where, despite the instructions, deliberate elicitation was likely. **Answers (a) and (d)** incorrectly focus on the issue of whether Johnson was pressured to speak. That is irrelevant in assessing whether a surreptitious interrogation violated the Sixth Amendment. The Fifth Amendment concerns itself with issues of compulsion; the Sixth Amendment concerns itself with insuring the defendant has aid of counsel at critical stages of a prosecution, including interrogation, surreptitious or not. **Answer (c) highlights a distinction between this question and *Henry*, but it makes no difference.** Although the government's recruitment of the informant in *Henry* makes it easier to find an agency relationship, the fact that Holloway sought out the police does not negate an agency relationship. Here, the detective agreed that Holloway should report incriminating statements and held out the possibility of gain—a reduced sentence—should she do so. That was enough to create an agency relationship. *If*, however, informant Holloway was not working for the State *at the time the information was obtained from the accused* (for instance, if she went to the police after Johnson made the incriminating remarks and sought to exchange her testimony in Johnson's murder trial for a sentence reduction), *Henry* would no longer apply because there would be no state action implicated in the elicitation. *See, e.g., Maine v. Moulton*, 474 U.S. 159 (1985) (indicating that the government is not precluded from utilizing incriminating statements obtained from the defendant as a result of "luck or happenstance"); *United States v. Kimbrough,* 477 F.3d 144 (4th Cir. 2007) (explaining that the use at trial of an incriminating "statement [that] is 'volunteered' in response to questions or compelling influences emanating from private or other nongovernmental sources" does not implicate the Fifth Amendment's privilege against self-incrimination).

- **Additional references**: *See* LaFave, Israel, King & Kerr, Criminal Procedure § 6.7(c) (6th ed. 2017); Whitebread & Slobogin, Criminal Procedure: An Analysis of Cases and Concepts § 16.04(b) (7th ed. 2020).

5.   **The correct answer is (a).** In *Kansas v. Ventris*, 556 U.S. 586 (2009), the Court, after weighing the costs and benefits, announced that evidence obtained in violation of an individual's Sixth Amendment rights is admissible for impeachment purposes. The Court indicated that the cost of excluding probative impeachment evidence was too high; in other words, excluding the evidence would not pay its way. By excluding the constitutionally-defective evidence in the State's case-in-chief but allowing it to come in for impeachment, the Court has fashioned a rule that deters perjury and simultaneously ensures the integrity of the trial process. If Johnson (and her attorney) wanted to make sure that the evidence derived from the Sixth Amendment violation never made it to the jury (or judge in a bench trial), Johnson should not have taken the stand in her own defense. In fact, one criticism of the rule allowing evidence obtained in violation of constitutional rights to be used for impeachment is that it prevents defendants from testifying because the

defendant will inevitably "open the door" to subsequent impeachment. **Answer (b) is incorrect** because while the police may have acted in good faith, Holloway was acting as a state agent and therefore, her actions are imputed to the State. State actors who, in the absence of a knowing and voluntary waiver, deliberately elicit incriminating statements in violation of the Sixth Amendment right to counsel have violated the Constitution. If state actors could get around this by merely soliciting the assistance of non-state actors, constitutional rights would be eviscerated. Because this type of behavior is something the courts want to deter, irrespective of the state actor's state of mind, good faith will not remedy the underlying constitutional violation. Moreover, police have an interest in making sure their informants adhere to the Constitution so that the State may use the evidence for any purpose, not just for impeachment should the defendant take the stand. **Answer (c) would be correct** *if* **the question was referring to the prosecution's use of the statements in its case-in-chief. However, because the statements are being used for impeachment, the answer is incorrect. Answer (d) is wrong**. Although it is possible that the inevitable discovery doctrine could apply to fruits derived from a statement obtained in violation of the Sixth Amendment, this answer is wrong because the statement is admissible as impeachment evidence. **Answer (e) is also wrong** because the right involved here, the right to be free of uncounseled interrogation, was infringed at the time of the unlawful interrogation by Holloway. It was at that time that Johnson's right to the assistance of counsel was denied. *See Kansas v. Ventris, supra.*

- **Additional references**: *See* LAFAVE, ISRAEL, KING & KERR, CRIMINAL PROCEDURE § 9.6(a) (6th ed. 2017); WHITEBREAD & SLOBOGIN, CRIMINAL PROCEDURE: AN ANALYSIS OF CASES AND CONCEPTS § 16.05(b) (7th ed. 2020).

6.   **The right answer is (d).** In the area of criminal procedure, no less than in any other area involving individual liberties, the United States Supreme Court is the final interpreter of the meaning of the U.S. Constitution, and all governmental bodies, including the states, are bound thereby. We know this as the power of judicial review. But the Supreme Court's rulings are a *floor*, not a *ceiling*. States may interpret their own *state constitutions* in a way that gives greater protections to the criminally accused. Thus a state may, for example, interpret its own state constitution as a prohibition on capital punishment, even though capital punishment is permitted (in limited situations) under the federal constitution. The state is not interpreting the federal constitution, and it is not interpreting its own constitution in a way that falls below what the federal constitution requires. But in any case where the state wishes to provide *greater* protections under its own constitution, it must clearly indicate that it is relying on its own constitution. *Florida v. Powell*, 559 U.S. 50 (2010) (in reversing the Florida Supreme Court, the U.S. Supreme Court explained that because the Florida court did not "indicat[e] clearly and expressly" that state-law sources gave Powell rights distinct from, or broader than, those delineated in Miranda, the decision did not rest on an

independent state ground and therefore, federal law was controlling); *Michigan v. Long*, 463 U.S. 1032 (1983). If the state rests its decision on an independent and adequate state ground, the decision is not reviewable by the Supreme Court for want of a federal question. If, on the other hand, the state court suggests that its ruling is based, even in part, on the federal constitution, the Supreme Court will have the final word on the meaning of the federal constitution. Only answer (d) captures these principles correctly. **Answer (a) is wrong** because the state is not free to apply its own interpretation of the *federal constitution*, even if it is more generous to the accused. Like all governmental entities, the states are bound to follow Supreme Court interpretations of U.S. constitutional law. The state may be more generous if it is interpreting *its own state constitution*. **Answer (b) is similarly wrong but adds an additional dimension of error.** The states are bound by Supreme Court rulings on matters of U.S. constitutional law, but it is not through a supervisory power. There is no general supervisory power over the states. There is the constitutional power of judicial review. *See Marbury v. Madison*, 5 U.S. (1 Cranch) 137 (1803). **Answer (c) goes too far.** The state may interpret its own state constitution to provide greater protections to the criminally accused, but not *fewer*. **Answer (e) fails to acknowledge that the individual liberty protections of the U.S. Constitution are only a floor; states can interpret their own constitutions to enhance the protection of individual rights.**

- **Additional references**: *See* LAFAVE, ISRAEL, KING & KERR, CRIMINAL PROCEDURE §§ 1.4, 2.1 (6th ed. 2017); WHITEBREAD & SLOBOGIN, CRIMINAL PROCEDURE: AN ANALYSIS OF CASES AND CONCEPTS §§ 34.04, 34.05 (7th ed. 2020).

7. **Answer (a) is correct.** Questions 7–8 are drawn from *United States v. LaGrone,* 43 F.3d 332 (7th Cir. 1994). This question looks like a case where an arrestee requested a lawyer but the police, in violation of *Edwards v. Arizona*, 451 U.S. 477 (1981), resumed interrogation without a lawyer being present. When Matt said he wanted to talk to a lawyer, he was in custody, but he was not being interrogated. Courts have held that requesting consent to search is not interrogation because it is not likely to elicit an incriminating response. *See, e.g., United States v. Stevens*, 487 F.3d 232 (5th Cir. 2007) (quoting *United States v. McClellan*, 165 F.3d 535 (7th Cir. 1999) ("[A] request for consent to search is not an interrogation within the meaning of *Miranda* because the giving of such consent is not a self-incriminating statement.") (internal quotations omitted)); *United States v. Bustamante*, 493 F.3d 879 (7th Cir. 2007) ("Though all interrogation must cease once a defendant in custody has invoked his right to counsel, a request to search a vehicle or home is not likely to elicit an incriminating response and is therefore not interrogation."). Therefore, Matt's invocation of his right to counsel came not in connection with interrogation but in connection with giving or withholding consent to search. Furthermore, the Supreme Court has held that invoking a right to counsel for one purpose is not automatically an invocation for Miranda purposes. *McNeil v. Wisconsin*, 501 U.S. 171 (1991). To be an invocation

for Miranda purposes, the suspect must express a desire for the assistance of an attorney in dealing with custodial interrogation by the police. That was not the case here as Matt sought his attorney's advice on whether to consent to the search and "[a] person in custody has no federal constitutional right to consult with an attorney before consenting to a search of his property." *LaGrone, supra. McNeil* makes clear that the *Edwards* initiation requirement kicks in only if Miranda rights are involved, that is, if a suspect makes clear that he or she needs the aid of a lawyer before being subjected to custodial interrogation. Because Matt was not interrogated within the meaning of *Miranda* and because Miranda rights cannot be anticipatorily invoked, the station house questioning was valid. **Answer (d) is wrong** because it assumes that Matt's request to talk to a lawyer before giving consent to search was an invocation of counsel for Miranda purposes. **Answers (b) and (c) are wrong** because neither an officer's lack of knowledge about a prior invocation of counsel at interrogation nor a fresh set of warnings and a waiver will be enough to overcome the rule of *Edwards* and *Oregon v. Bradshaw*, 462 U.S. 1039 (1983) (i.e., after a valid invocation of the right to counsel at interrogation police may not reinterrogate a subject until counsel is present unless he initiates the conversation). **Answer (e) is doubly flawed** because there is no such duty to clarify, and in any event, Matt must invoke his Miranda right to counsel at or near the time he is going to be interrogated, not anticipatorily.

- **Additional references**: *See* LaFave, Israel, King & Kerr, Criminal Procedure § 6.9(g) (6th ed. 2017); Whitebread & Slobogin, Criminal Procedure: An Analysis of Cases and Concepts § 16.03(e)(3) (7th ed. 2020).

8. **The correct answer is (d).** A search conducted pursuant to consent excuses the Fourth Amendment's warrant requirement. *See Schneckloth v. Bustamonte*, 412 U.S. 218 (1973). For consent to be valid, the totality of the circumstances must show that the consent to search was given voluntarily. To be deemed voluntary under the Constitution, the consent must not be a product of coercion or duress, express or implied. The circumstances here do not rise to the level of coercion. There were no threats, Matt was told that he could do what he wanted (implying that he could decline to cooperate), he was advised of his Miranda rights, and he was permitted to call his attorney. The police did enter with guns drawn, but after securing the suspect, the guns were put away. *See United States v. Hidalgo*, 7 F.3d 1566 (11th Cir. 1993) (finding consent was voluntary even though the defendant "was arrested by SWAT team members who broke into his home in the early morning, woke him, and forced him to the ground at gun point"). **Answer (a) is wrong**. Even though a false claim of having a search warrant will render consent involuntary, *Bumper v. North Carolina*, 391 U.S. 543 (1968), and even though baseless threats to get a search warrant *may* be so coercive as to render consent involuntary, *United States v. White*, 979 F.2d 539 (7th Cir. 1992), a genuine statement of an officer's intention to seek a search warrant in the absence of consent does not render subsequent consent involuntary, *United States v. Salvo*,

133 F.3d 943 (6th Cir. 1998). Because the facts do not support a finding that the officer's statement about having sufficient information to obtain a warrant was baseless, the statement did not taint the subsequent consent. **Answers (b) and (c) are wrong** because they convert relevant factors into controlling rules. Denying a suspect a right to consult with an attorney might imply coercion, but all of the facts must be examined. Under all of the facts here, including that the police gave Matt an opportunity to call his lawyer, Matt's consent was not the result of coercion. Similarly, while custodial status may be relevant to voluntariness, it is not determinative. The Supreme Court specifically said that it would be contrary to the totality of the circumstances voluntariness inquiry to "hold that illegal coercion is made out from the fact of arrest." Indeed, courts have found valid consent even where consent was obtained from a suspect in custody at a police station rather than in a public place, like a store. *See United States v. Duran*, 957 F.2d 499 (7th Cir. 1992) (consent voluntary even though suspect was under arrest and at the police station). **Answer (e) is incorrect** because Miranda warnings do not automatically validate consent to search. Other factors must still be weighed.

- **Additional references**: *See* LAFAVE, ISRAEL, KING & KERR, CRIMINAL PROCEDURE § 3.10 (a)–(c) (6th ed. 2017); WHITEBREAD & SLOBOGIN, CRIMINAL PROCEDURE: AN ANALYSIS OF CASES AND CONCEPTS §§ 12.01–12.02 (7th ed. 2020).

9. **Answer (c) is the best choice.** There is no reason to exclude any of Reuben's statements or the video. Reuben's statements during the vehicle stop were either volunteered (his comments while performing the sobriety tests), a response to a question prior to custody (his answer to the question, "where were you coming from"), or a response to non-testimonial physical testing (counting from one to thirty). All are admissible. There is no requirement that suspects be informed that their actions are being videotaped and, hence, **answer (b) is incorrect.** Indeed police are now routinely recording videos of suspected drunk drivers, persons brought into police headquarters, or persons subject to interrogation, and police routinely activate body cameras during encounters with citizens. The fact of the video, without more, and the fact that the suspect is unaware of the video, without more, are insufficient to exclude this evidence. **Answers (a) and (e) are wrong** because an ordinary automobile stop is not custody for Miranda purposes. *Berkemer v. McCarty*, 468 U.S. 420 (1984). Although the motorist is not "free to leave," ordinary roadside detentions do not equal the inherently coercive setting of in-custody interrogation. The driver expects that he will shortly be free to leave, and the stop is usually on a public street. Of course, a traffic stop could become custody if there were words or actions, such as a police-dominated atmosphere, or guns drawn that would lead a reasonable person to believe he or she was under arrest. For answer (e), the question "where are you coming from" *may* have been interrogation, but since there was no custody, Miranda was inapplicable. Alternatively, it is arguable that the responses were *not* prompted by interrogation as asking Reuben to count paces was not likely

to be perceived as calling for an incriminating response or that it was simply a tailored inquiry attendant to legitimate police procedure. From this perspective, the information was "not intended to elicit information for investigatory purposes." *Pennsylvania v. Muniz*, 496 U.S. 582 (1990). **Answer (d) is wrong** because the responses were non-testimonial. Reuben's performance while counting is distinguishable from *Muniz*, where the Supreme Court found Muniz's response to the question of the date of his sixth birthday was testimonial because saying "I don't know" was different from the assertion the trier of fact might reasonably expect a lucid person to provide. In *Muniz*, the Court found that the defendant faced the cruel trilemma, which is the touchstone of self-incrimination analysis. So why is Reuben's case different? *Muniz* does not stand for the proposition that all compelled oral statements are testimonial. To be testimonial, the statement must be an express or implied assertion of fact that can be true or false. Counting from one to thirty cannot be true or false. It is possible to argue that Reuben's responses were simply a form of physical testing. Interestingly, the *Muniz* Court avoided deciding whether two questions—asking Muniz to count while performing a "walk-the-line" test and during a "one leg stand" test—were testimonial. The dissent argued that "[i]f the police may require Muniz to use his body in order to demonstrate the level of his physical coordination, there is no reason why they should not be able to require him to speak or write in order to determine his mental coordination."

- **Additional references**: *See* LAFAVE, ISRAEL, KING & KERR, CRIMINAL PROCEDURE §§ 6.6(e), 6.7(a)–(b) (6th ed. 2017); WHITEBREAD & SLOBOGIN, CRIMINAL PROCEDURE: AN ANALYSIS OF CASES AND CONCEPTS §§ 15.04, 16.02(e)(4), 16.03(a)(1), 16.03(b)(2) (7th ed. 2020).

10. **Answer (d) is the best answer.** This question is drawn from the Supreme Court's opinion in *Colorado v. Connelly*, 479 U.S. 157 (1986), and requires the student to know not only when the rule of that case applies but also when it does not. *Connelly* held that a person who gave incriminating statements to the police under the "coercion" of his own mental illness could not claim a violation of due process of law because there was no state action causally connected to the pressures experienced by the defendant. A violation of due process requires governmental conduct that either coerces the defendant directly or exploits a condition of which the police are aware. Neither was the case here as the facts indicate that Ms. Tiefer appeared "coherent and rational." As in *Connelly*, Ms. Tiefer's statements were voluntary because voluntariness depends on the absence of police misconduct, not on free choice in the broader sense of the word. Thus, the mere use of a statement under such circumstances does not violate any of Ms. Tiefer's constitutional rights. However, the rule of *Connelly* is not dispositive of the question whether Ms. Tiefer validly waived her Miranda rights. A person must be mentally competent to waive her rights, and it does not matter, for waiver purposes, that the police did not cause or exploit the condition of incompetence. In order to find a valid waiver, a defendant must have understood the rights she was

abandoning; in other words, the waiver must be knowing and intelligent. A defendant's mental capacity bears upon the question of whether she understood the meaning of her Miranda rights and the significance of waiving her constitutional rights. *See United States v. Garibay*, 143 F.3d 534 (9th Cir. 1998); *United States v. Aikens*, 13 F. Supp. 2d 28 (D.D.C. 1998) (finding waiver invalid after crediting expert witness who testified that the defendant did not understand his Miranda rights). Just like the expert in *Aikens*, the expert here testified that Ms. Tiefer was too mentally ill to waive her rights. The statements made to the sergeant, however, did not require Miranda warnings or a waiver because Ms. Tiefer was not yet in custody. She went to the police station on her own initiative and volunteered the information regarding her crime. **Answer (a) is wrong** because it would exclude all of Ms. Tiefer's statements as involuntary. And **answer (e) is doubly wrong** because, again, Ms. Tiefer's statements to the sergeant were not involuntary, and there would be no need to advise her that they were. **Answer (c) is incorrect** because it assumes Ms. Tiefer was in custody when questioned by the sergeant. **Answer (b) is also wrong** because it would admit all statements and, again, the statements made to the detective will be excluded because Ms. Tiefer's Miranda rights were not knowingly and intelligently waived.

- **Additional references**: *See* LaFave, Israel, King & Kerr, Criminal Procedure § 6.9(b) (6th ed. 2017); Whitebread & Slobogin, Criminal Procedure: An Analysis of Cases and Concepts §§ 16.02(a)(2), 16.03(a)(3) (7th ed. 2020).

11. **The right answer is (c).** A correct answer to this question depends on knowing the rules of *United States v. Wade*, 388 U.S. 218 (1967), and its companion case, *Gilbert v. California*, 388 U.S. 263 (1967). Only answer (c) captures the *Wade-Gilbert* rules precisely. Absent waiver, a post-indictment line-up conducted without the defendant's lawyer violates the Sixth Amendment right to counsel. The consequences of that violation are two-fold: (1) a *per se* exclusion of the pretrial identification—no matter how fairly conducted; and, (2) a *potential* loss of an in-court identification by the same witness unless the government proves, by clear and convincing evidence, that the in-court identification was not based on the improper line-up. **Answer (a) is wrong** because it applies a *per se* exclusion to the in-court identification. **Answer (b) goes astray** by suggesting that the government might, under some circumstances, be able to admit the line-up identification. That is incorrect; the exclusion is automatic. **Answer (d) is doubly wrong** because it assumes that the line-up identification could be admitted under some circumstances (it cannot), and because it allocates the burden of proof on the reliability of the in-court identification to the defendant (it belongs to the government). **Answer (e) is half right** because it properly states the *per se* exclusion of the pre-trial identification, but there is no requirement that an in-court identification be conducted in a line-up format. This may be good practice, but it is not a constitutional rule.

- **Additional references**: *See* LaFave, Israel, King & Kerr, Criminal Procedure § 7.3(f) (6th ed. 2017); Whitebread & Slobogin, Criminal Procedure: An Analysis of Cases and Concepts §§ 17.02, 18.02 (7th ed. 2020).

12. **The correct answer is (c).** Questions 12 and 13 are developed from *Jordan v. Ducharme*, 983 F.2d 933 (9th Cir. 1993). To answer this question, you need to know the rationale of the Sixth Amendment, *Wade-Gilbert* line-up identification rules. *Wade* and *Gilbert* stressed the need for counsel at a line-up to avert suggestiveness and prejudice and to assure the defendant's right to a meaningful confrontation at trial. Subsequent cases, however, have focused on whether there was *an actual confrontation* between the witnesses and the defendant. If the defendant is *not present*, such as at a photographic display viewed by witnesses, then there is no possibility that the defendant "might be misled by his lack of familiarity with the law or overpowered by his professional adversary," and, therefore, there is no Sixth Amendment right to counsel in that situation. *United States v. Ash*, 413 U.S. 300 (1973). Following from that rationale, lower courts have held that police interviews with witnesses *after* the lineup, that is, after the defendant is *no longer present*, do not trigger the Sixth Amendment right to have counsel present. Thus **(c) is the best answer** and **answer (a), which is essentially the opposite of (c) is wrong. Answer (b) is incorrect** because it assumes that counsel is to play an active, adversarial role at a line-up. That is not the case. Counsel is a passive observer. The point of the lawyer's presence is to detect and note prejudice and suggestive influences, and to use this information to question and cross examine witnesses *at trial*. **Answer (d) is wrong** because the defendant had been "formally charged" with the robbery of Rye Allen prior to the lineup and, therefore, his right to counsel had attached on that charge. **Answer (e) is incorrect** because it identifies the wrong remedy for a violation of one's right to counsel at a line-up. The remedy is not a full opportunity to cross-examine at trial. The remedy is exclusion of the pre-trial identification and potential exclusion of an in-court identification.

  [handwritten margin note: Point of counsel presence.]

  - **Additional references**: *See* LaFave, Israel, King & Kerr, Criminal Procedure § 7.3(c), (e) (6th ed. 2017); Whitebread & Slobogin, Criminal Procedure: An Analysis of Cases and Concepts § 18.02 (7th ed. 2020).

13. **The right answer is (a).** The admission of expert testimony regarding eyewitness identification lies within the sound discretion of the court. While there is currently "near-universal acceptance of the reliability of expert testimony regarding eyewitness identification," *Forensic v. Birkett*, 501 F.3d 469 (6th Cir. 2007), many courts, particularly federal courts, are hostile to such testimony on the ground that it will not assist the trier of fact or that the trial judge can effectively reduce any possible bias by giving cautionary instructions to the jury. *See, e.g., United States v. Carter*, 410 F.3d 942 (7th Cir. 2005). Other considerations include whether this type of testimony touches on the ultimate issue in the case

(on the issue of witness credibility), therefore usurping the jury's role, and whether the jury could more properly evaluate the reliability of eyewitness testimony through cross-examination. *United States v. Smithers*, 212 F.3d 306 (6th Cir. 2000). Furthermore, courts have excluded expert testimony on the reliability of eyewitness identifications when multiple witnesses identify the same person, as is the case here. *See United States v. Williams*, 522 F.3d 809 (7th Cir. 2008). Note, however, that when the case rests on the testimony of a sole eyewitness, or when eyewitness identifications are the only form of inculpatory evidence against a defendant, some courts lean toward admitting the expert testimony. *See, e.g., United States v. Tolliver*, 454 F.3d 660 (7th Cir. 2006) (expert testimony regarding the unreliability of eyewitness testimony was admissible in a criminal prosecution, because the case against the accused was comprised exclusively of eyewitness testimony); *United States v. Smithers, supra.* **Answer (c) is wrong** because it erroneously assumes that there is a categorical constitutional right to admit expert testimony in all cases where identification is a critical issue. As a practical matter, **answer (b) is almost right**, but it states the rule too powerfully. A trial judge's ruling which excludes expert testimony will almost always be upheld, but not always. The standard is abuse of discretion, and it goes too far to answer that the trial judge's ruling "is not subject to reversal." It has actually happened, although quite rarely. *United States v. Stevens*, 935 F.2d 1380 (3d Cir. 1991) (reversing and remanding for new trial partially because of the trial judge's exclusion of expert testimony on the reliability of witness identifications); *State v. Chapple*, 135 Ariz. 281, 660 P.2d 1208 (1983). A more common result is that an appellate court will find that the exclusion of expert testimony was an abuse of discretion but will then find that the error was harmless. *See United States v. Smith*, 736 F.2d 1103 (6th Cir. 1984). **Answer (e) is wrong** because trial court errors in excluding the evidence are not "*always* deemed harmless." **Answer (d) is incorrect** because it assumes that an appellate court will review the exclusion to exclude the witness *de novo*. The appellate court will show deference to the trial judge's ability to manage the trial and will thus examine the exclusion question with deference to the trial court's view. This deference is built into the abuse of discretion standard.

- **Additional references**: *See* LAFAVE, ISRAEL, KING & KERR, CRIMINAL PROCEDURE § 7.5(a)–(b) (6th ed. 2017); WHITEBREAD & SLOBOGIN, CRIMINAL PROCEDURE: AN ANALYSIS OF CASES AND CONCEPTS § 17.06 (7th ed. 2020).

14. **The best answer is (e).** Let's begin by discussing the manner of the entry into the Mathis residence. The facts clearly indicate that the knock and announce principle, which is part of the Fourth Amendment reasonableness analysis, *Wilson v. Arkansas*, 514 U.S. 927 (1995), was properly followed. The police waited "minutes" before knocking down the door, much longer than the 15–20 seconds in *United States v. Banks*, 540 U.S. 31 (2003) (15–20 seconds is not an unrealistic time period for someone to dispose of drugs). Although the police were mainly looking for documents, files (whether paper or electronic) can be destroyed within a

matter of moments and therefore, waiting for "minutes" was entirely reasonable. As such, **answer (b) is incorrect**. Answer (b) also errs because a violation of the knock-and-announce requirement does not justify exclusion of evidence found in a subsequent search of the premises. *Hudson v. Michigan*, 547 U.S. 586 (2006) (The interests protected by the knock and announce rule are different from the interests in preventing the government from seeing or seizing property *inside* the house, and, in any event, the costs of exclusion outweigh the deterrent value of applying the rule). In analyzing the manner of entry, we must now examine the police conduct in entering the home with weapons drawn. The facts here show that the officers were reasonably entitled to believe that the drawing of weapons was necessary in order to gain control of an uncertain situation. *See Michigan v. Summers*, 452 U.S. 692 (1981) ("The risk of harm to both the police and the occupants is minimized if the officers routinely exercise unquestioned command of the situation."). Here, the officers could not be sure of how many people were in the house (the facts suggest that people came in and out frequently) and they knew that Dr. Mathis was affiliated with a dangerous gang. Now, let's move on to the second big issue in the question: whether the detention of Janet and Melissa was reasonable under the Fourth Amendment. (**Answer (a) is wrong** because it fails to account for this second issue and is therefore incomplete.) The police were permitted to detain Janet and Melissa because the Supreme Court has held that officers may "detain an occupant of the place to be searched," *Michigan v. Summers*, *supra*, and may use "reasonable force to effectuate the detention," *Muehler v. Mena*, 544 U.S. 93 (2005) (holding that a two-hour detention in handcuffs of a person present at an address being searched for weapons related to gang activity was reasonable). While handcuffing is a demonstration of force, there is nothing in the facts that suggests that the handcuffing of Janet or Melissa was particularly offensive. *Cf. Williams v. Kaufman County*, 352 F.3d 994 (5th Cir. 2003) (holding that detaining club patrons in handcuffs for three hours after subjecting them to strip searches and warrant checks was unlawful); *Bailey v. United States*, 568 U.S. 186 (2013) (determining taking an individual back to his home for detention during a search warrant after the individual has left the premises is unlawful). Moreover, although the warrant authorized only the seizure of documents or other records, the nature of the other facts (violent gang, drug trafficking, heavy foot traffic in and out of the home, etc.) suggests that the detention was reasonable and therefore renders **answer (d) incorrect**. *Cf. Unus v. Kane*, 565 F.3d 103 (4th Cir. 2009), *cert. denied*, 558 U.S. 1147 (2010) (rejecting distinction between warranted search for contraband and warranted search of documents in a civil case claiming government misconduct). **Answer (c) states a potential ground for denying the motion but the issue of the warrant's sufficiency is answered by the warrant targeting "twenty separate categories of documents and things" related to money laundering, tax evasion, and documentation of cocaine sales.**

- **Additional references**: *See* LaFave, Israel, King & Kerr, Criminal Procedure § 3.4(i) (6th ed. 2017); Whitebread & Slobogin, Criminal Procedure: An Analysis of Cases and Concepts §§ 3.02(d), 5.05(e) (7th ed. 2020).

15. **The best answer is (d).** It is quite true that *Illinois v. Gates*, 462 U.S. 213 (1983) and *United States v. Leon*, 468 U.S. 897 (1984) have made it very easy for courts to admit evidence obtained pursuant to a search warrant. According to *Gates*, a search warrant is sufficiently grounded on probable cause if the magistrate, accorded all due deference, had a substantial basis to conclude that there was a fair probability that evidence of a crime would be found in a particular place. According to *Leon*, even if probable cause under such a lenient standard is lacking, evidence seized pursuant to a warrant may still be admissible if an officer's reliance on the probable cause determination and the technical sufficiency was "objectively reasonable." *See, e.g., United States v. Paull*, 551 F.3d 516 (6th Cir. 2009) (holding that even though the information about Paull's possession of child pornography was dated, the warrant did not "clearly lack" probable cause because the officer had experience in child pornography investigations that caused her to believe the evidence was still on the premises: "even when an officer's experience provides too little evidence to establish probable cause, it suffices to make the affidavit not bare bones by providing a reasonable connection between the defendant and the alleged crime."); *United States v. Marion*, 238 F.3d 965 (8th Cir. 2001) (reasonableness of officers' reliance on invalid warrant may include information known to officers but not presented to issuing magistrate). In spite of the breadth of the good faith exception, *Leon* indicates that a warrant may be so deficient and so lacking in probable cause that reliance on it may be unreasonable. *See, e.g., Messerschmidt v. Millender*, 565 U.S. 535 (2012) (Reliance on the warrant is unreasonable when it is obvious that no reasonably competent officer would have concluded that a warrant should be issued); *United States v. West*, 520 F.3d 604 (6th Cir. 2008) (affidavit merely reiterated uncorroborated hearsay and was accordingly bereft of facts that suggested any connection between the victim's disappearance and any evidence likely to be found at the defendant's residence or in his van; reliance on warrant unreasonable). In the instant case, reliance on the warrant was unreasonable. The tip contains no facts from which inferences may be drawn, and there is no basis to assess its credibility. Though fervently pressed, the anonymous tip offers nothing but a bare assertion. And the police "corroboration" consists of nothing more than readily observable facts. Not only are the fancy house and nice cars not suspicious, it would be strange indeed if it were otherwise since top executives of major foundations are usually paid handsome sums. To make things worse, the affidavit seeks *any* documents, in the suspect's business or home, that may be related to mail or wire fraud, which, under the circumstances, is essentially a fishing expedition and seeks just what the drafters of the Fourth Amendment sought to prevent: general search warrants. It must be remembered that the analysis is not to be influenced by what the police

actually found because this would eviscerate Fourth Amendment protections. **Answer (b) is wrong.** Deference is one thing, but there must be more than a bare bones, anonymous tip to warrant deference. **Answer (c) is not a good choice.** Although the affidavit is ordinarily physically attached to the warrant, the fact that it was not does not defeat the existence of probable cause so long as the warrant and the affidavit actually support and refer to each other. Sometimes the failure to attach or incorporate by reference the affidavit and the warrant will spell trouble. Such was the case in *Groh v. Ramirez*, 540 U.S. 551 (2004). There a warrant failed to describe "the persons or things to be seized" as required by the Fourth Amendment. This deficiency was not cured by the particularity in the application for the warrant since the warrant and the application did not accompany each other, nor did the warrant incorporate by reference the application. That is not the case here, however. **Answer (e) is incorrect**. An affidavit usually stands as the sole basis for the warrant, and the magistrate is not obliged to ask any questions. Of course, if the magistrate does not even bother to read the affidavit (assuming this could be proven), then we would have a different case.

- **Additional references**: *See* LaFave, Israel, King & Kerr, Criminal Procedure §§ 3.1(c), 3.3 (6th ed. 2017); Whitebread & Slobogin, Criminal Procedure: An Analysis of Cases and Concepts §§ 2.03(c)(1), 5.03 (7th ed. 2020).

16. **Answer (a) is the best answer.** This problem puts two issues in play: what is the justification for a valid frisk and when does a detention begin and end. This problem is loosely drawn from the facts of *Reittinger v. Commonwealth*, 260 Va., 232, 532 S.E. 2d 25 (Sup. Ct. 2000). *Terry v. Ohio*, 392 U.S. 1 (1968), requires reasonable, individualized suspicion that a person is armed and dangerous before a search for weapons can be conducted. Often this suspicion will arise in the context of a police encounter with someone suspected of a crime, but it need not happen that way. An officer may be validly in a person's presence when there is no suspicion of criminal activity by that person. For example, an officer may ask or be asked a question, or she may offer assistance to someone in distress. If, in the circumstances of that or any other lawful encounter, articulable facts arise to create a reasonable suspicion that the person is armed and dangerous, a frisk is permissible even if there is no reasonable suspicion of criminal activity. The test for determining whether an interaction with the police is a stop (requiring reasonable suspicion of criminal activity) or a consensual encounter (requiring no justification because it is not a Fourth Amendment seizure) is often stated as: whether, under all of the circumstances an innocent person reasonably believed he or she was (or was not) free to leave. *United States v. Mendenhall*, 446 U.S. 544 (1980); *INS v. Delgado*, 466 U.S. 210 (1984). Alternatively the Supreme Court has stated that a stop occurs when police conduct "communicate [s] to a reasonable person that the person [is] not free to decline the officers' requests or otherwise terminate the encounter." *Florida v. Bostick*, 501 U.S. 429 (1991). However, even though many people may not feel free to ignore questions put to them by an officer, the

Supreme Court has made clear that neither the "free to leave" standard nor the "free to terminate the encounter" standard is violated simply by an officer approaching a person and politely, briefly, and without coercion, asking questions. **Answer (b) is wrong** because there is no automatic right to frisk any person who exits a vehicle after a stop. The Supreme Court has held than an officer may automatically order a driver out of the vehicle, *Pennsylvania v. Mimms*, 434 U.S. 106 (1977), concluding that being ordered out of a car was a *de minimis* intrusion since the driver was already stopped. Even the dissent did not appear to dispute this proposition. The Court extended *Mimms* in *Maryland v. Wilson*, 519 U.S. 408 (1997), holding that an officer making a traffic stop may order passengers out of the car as well. That there is an automatic right to order drivers and passengers out of the vehicle during a traffic stop does not mean that there is an automatic right to frisk those ordered out of the vehicle. In other words, the Court has not abandoned its case-by-case analysis of whether reasonable suspicion provided a basis to frisk. As the Court explained in *Arizona v. Johnson*, 555 U.S. 323 (2009), "to justify a patdown of the driver or a passenger during a traffic stop . . . just as in the case of a pedestrian reasonably suspected of criminal activity, the police must harbor reasonable suspicion that the person subjected to the frisk is armed and dangerous." **Answer (c) is wrong** because the officer told the driver he was free to leave and did not engage in any coercive behavior signaling the contrary. Without some show of force or coercion, this officer's question to a motorist on the side of a road is not a stop. Moreover even if the original stop, which was justified, was construed to continue through to the question about drugs or guns, the action would still be within the definition of brief investigative action and thus valid. *Ohio v. Robinette*, 519 U.S. 33 (1996) (questions asked after citation given valid; some continued detention permissible beyond dealing with the traffic violation). **Answer (d) is incorrect** because it assumes that a frisk requires reasonable suspicion that a suspect is engaged in criminal activity. Rather, the frisk is valid so long as an officer is lawfully confronting someone and, then and there, develops reasonable, articulable suspicion that the person is armed and dangerous. That is the case here based on the driver's whispering to the passengers, the pocket bulge, and the attempt to conceal the bulge. **Answer (e) goes astray** because it requires that an officer have a *duty* to be in a person's presence and questionably assumes there was no such duty here. An officer need only be lawfully in a person's presence, such as responding to a person's question, coincidentally standing next to a person in the court house, or finding a person on premises to be searched.

- **Additional references**: *See* LaFave, Israel, King & Kerr, Criminal Procedure § 3.8 (6th ed. 2017); Whitebread & Slobogin, Criminal Procedure: An Analysis of Cases and Concepts §§ 11.02–11.05 (7th ed. 2020).

17. **Answer (d) is the best answer.** The facts of this problem are drawn loosely from *McDaniel v. State*, 337 Ark. 431, 990 S.W.2d 515 (Sup. Ct. 1999) decided by the Arkansas Supreme Court. The first key is

appreciating that the officer developed probable cause to believe ("a fair probability that . . . ") that marijuana was contained in the vehicle. He had detected the odor of marijuana and, crucially, Yasmin admitted she had just been smoking a joint. It was a fair inference that marijuana was located in the vehicle. This conclusion is similar to the Supreme Court's view of the facts in *Wyoming v. Houghton*, 526 U.S. 295 (1999). There a police officer spotted a hypodermic syringe in the pocket of a driver whom he had pulled over for an equipment violation. The driver's admission that he used the syringe to inject illegal drugs gave rise to probable cause to believe there were drugs in the car. The second key is appreciating that, once probable cause arose to believe that evidence of a crime was in the vehicle, an officer was permitted to search all containers in the vehicle— no matter who owned them—where that evidence could be found. *Wyoming v. Houghton, supra*; *United States v. Ross*, 456 U.S. 798 (1982). Of course, a search would include a pat down, even a vigorous one as performed here. Indeed the vigorous "pat down" is actually a red herring in this problem. **Answer (a) is wrong** because it assumes Officer Brig's probable cause was limited to the cab of the truck; in fact, the smell of marijuana and Yasmin's admission were sufficient to raise a fair probability that drugs were located somewhere in the vehicle or within its contents. **Answer (b) is incorrect** because the probable cause ran to any container in the vehicle which could harbor illegal drugs. Officer Brig did not have to believe Yasmin's statement that Betty "was a good kid," etc. As the Court noted in *Wyoming v. Houghton, supra*, law enforcement officers would be unduly impeded by a rule that exempted vehicle containers from a lawful search based on ownership, especially since a passenger with knowledge of the activities of the driver may well be pursuing the same activities as the driver or permitting the driver to hide contraband in her belongings. **Answer (c) is irrelevant to these facts.** Although it is true that a vigorous manipulation of one's bags counts as a Fourth Amendment intrusion, *Bond v. United States*, 529 U.S. 334 (2000), this is not a case about reasonable suspicion or proportionality. It is a case about probable cause and the scope of a vehicle search. **Answer (e) is incorrect** based on the Court's ruling in *Bond*. There the Court ruled that a bus passenger retained a Fourth Amendment reasonable expectation of privacy in opaque, soft-side luggage which was placed in an overhead bus bin accessible to other passengers who might touch, push, or otherwise handle it. A passenger "does not expect that other passengers or bus employees will, as a matter of course, feel the bag in an exploratory manner." Therefore, the "agents' physical manipulation of petitioners' bag [without justification] violated the Fourth Amendment." Here, Betty retained her reasonable expectation of privacy, but there was probable cause to overcome it.

- **Additional references**: *See* LAFAVE, ISRAEL, KING & KERR, CRIMINAL PROCEDURE § 3.7 (6th ed. 2017); WHITEBREAD & SLOBOGIN, CRIMINAL PROCEDURE: AN ANALYSIS OF CASES AND CONCEPTS § 7.04 (7th ed. 2020).

18. **The best answer is (c).** This question tests your knowledge of the exigent circumstances doctrine, particularly what has been called the "emergency aid exception." Although warrantless home intrusions are presumptively unreasonable, there are a few specifically delineated exceptions obviating the need for a warrant. One such exigency, the emergency aid exception, has been fleshed out in recent years by the Supreme Court. *Michigan v. Fisher*, 558 U.S. 45 (2009) (*per curiam*); *Brigham City v. Stuart*, 547 U.S. 398 (2006). Under this doctrine, a warrantless entry into a home is reasonable, and thus permissible, if police officers have an objectively reasonable basis for believing that a person within the house is in need of immediate aid. In both *Brigham* and *Fisher*, the police encountered individuals with minor injuries and witnessed situations where there was either a fight or an individual acting out of control. In the instant case, police encountered a calm individual outside of the home and did not view any suspicious behavior. However, in spite of the lack of blood or gunfire, the report the police received, from an identified 911 caller, provided them with an objectively reasonable justification to enter the home without a warrant. As the Court in *Fisher* made clear, "[o]fficers do not need ironclad proof of a likely serious, life-threatening injury to invoke the emergency aid exception." Here, police have credible information that an unnatural death has or may have occurred. As such, they may act to aid the victim and may act in view of knowledge that the 911 caller's report of a death could be inaccurate and that a spark of life remains. This explains why **answer (a) is incorrect.** Although the caller said that the victim had been murdered, courts routinely find it reasonable for police to believe that the layperson's account could be wrong. In sum, if police reasonably fear for the safety of someone inside the premises, exigent circumstances justify a warrantless entry and a search consistent with the safety concern. There is no indication from the facts here that the police exceeded the permissible scope of the search. Because the police were lawfully inside of the house, the contraband they saw in plain view could be seized without a warrant. *Horton v. California*, 496 U.S. 128 (1990). **Answer (e) is wrong** because it would allow the exigency to turn on the subjective state of mind of the officers, and subjective belief, even a good faith subjective belief, cannot justify a warrantless entry. The test is objective; that is, would the circumstances as they appeared at the time, lead a reasonable, experienced officer to believe that someone inside the house required immediate assistance. **Answer (b) is also wrong** *not* because it is an error to consider whether an alternative to a warrantless entry is available—that can be a factor—but because the "alternative" given is not responsive to the nature of the emergency. Either there is an objective basis to believe immediate action is required or not. If there is no such need, then securing the premises is probably irrelevant. **Answer (d) is on to something but is incorrect** in its conclusion. It is true that a report of a death or impending injury must be credible and that anonymous calls *may* lack credibility. *Cf. Florida v. J.L.*, 529 U.S. 266 (2000); *United States v. Copening*, 506 F.3d 1241 (10th Cir. 2007) (noting

that where 911 calls were made from an unblocked number, the caller was no longer anonymous). However, it doesn't necessarily follow that if a caller does provide a name, then police must act immediately. The named caller's information could be completely unbelievable, as in reporting that space aliens have captured the President and are threatening to electrocute him.

- **Additional references**: *See* LaFave, Israel, King & Kerr, Criminal Procedure § 3.6(f) (6th ed. 2017); Whitebread & Slobogin, Criminal Procedure: An Analysis of Cases and Concepts § 9.03 (7th ed. 2020).

19. **Answer (c) is correct.** This question is based on *United States v. Argent Chemical Laboratories*, 93 F.3d 572 (9th Cir. 1996). The Fourth Amendment protects against intrusions caused by civil inspections as well as intrusions caused by conventional law enforcement methods. This was not always the case. In *Frank v. Maryland*, 359 U.S. 360 (1959), the Court upheld a warrantless nuisance abatement inspection of premises, saying that municipal health, fire, and housing inspections are essentially outside of Fourth Amendment protections. However, the Court repudiated *Frank* in *Camara v. Municipal Court of San Francisco*, 387 U.S. 523 (1967), saying that "administrative searches . . . are significant intrusions upon the interests protected by the Fourth Amendment. . . ." At the same time, the Court also decided that the Fourth Amendment applied to inspections of the non-public areas of commercial premises as well as to private homes. *See v. City of Seattle*, 387 U.S. 541 (1967). This turnabout explains why **answer (a) is incorrect** because it posits that inspection of commercial premises are not protected. They are protected, but the applicable rules are not the same as those applicable to criminal law enforcement and not even precisely the same as those applicable to civil inspections of homes. For non-consensual, regulatory inspections of homes, the Court requires a warrant, but the warrant need not be supported by traditional probable cause in the nature of individualized suspicion of wrongdoing. Rather, it is enough to have "area-wide" probable cause, a finding that an entire area requires inspection because of neutral factors such as the age of buildings, the periodic and systematic checking of homes section by section, or the passage of time. The Court requires the same type of a warrant for inspections of non-public areas of commercial premises *unless* the commercial activity is considered a "closely regulated business." If we are dealing with a closely regulated business, such as a business dealing in guns, liquor, mining, automobile parts, or other extensively regulated activities, then no warrant is needed so long as three criteria are met. First, the government must have a substantial interest in the activity regulated—a fact specified in this question. Second, warrantless inspections must be necessary to further the regulatory scheme. And third, the government's statute or regulatory program must be a constitutionally adequate substitute for a warrant by providing notice to businesses that their properties are subject to inspection and by identifying the criteria and scope of inspections. *Donovan v. Dewey*, 452 U.S. 594 (1981); *New York v. Burger*, 482 U.S. 691

(1987). All of these requirements are met here. As the facts disclose, the drug industry is "closely regulated." And the government has a very significant interest in assuring properly manufactured and labeled drugs; unannounced, warrantless inspections are critical to deterrence, and they insure swift action to remove misbranded drugs from circulation; and, in terms of the certainty and regularity of its application, the regulatory scheme is a constitutionally adequate substitute for a warrant. **Answer (b) is close, but overstates the applicable principles.** Warrantless inspection of commercial premises is not automatically permissible in routine inspections. The business must be closely regulated and meet the other three criteria of *Donovan v. Dewey* and *New York v. Burger*. **Answer (d) is wrong** because a warrantless inspection also permits a warrantless seizure of contraband discovered during the inspection. *United States v. Argent Chemical Laboratories, supra.* **Answer (e) is incorrect** because it is the nature of the inspection and not the existence or not of an emergency or an opportunity to get a warrant that permits warrantless inspection of closely regulated industries.

- **Additional references**: *See* LAFAVE, ISRAEL, KING & KERR, CRIMINAL PROCEDURE § 3.9 (6th ed. 2017); WHITEBREAD & SLOBOGIN, CRIMINAL PROCEDURE: AN ANALYSIS OF CASES AND CONCEPTS § 13.03 (7th ed. 2020).

20. **Answer (b) is the best.** Police do not need *probable cause* to believe a suspect is at home in order to execute an arrest warrant in the home. Nor do they need to allege that a suspect is at home in order to secure an arrest warrant. They do, however, need *reasonable suspicion* to believe the suspect is present at his residence at the time they enter to arrest. *Payton v. New York*, 445 U.S. 573 (1980). Here, the boarded up windows, high grass, and conversation with the neighbors all pointed to the suspect's absence. Under the circumstances, the officers could not reasonably believe that Mr. Vander was inside his house at the time they entered to arrest. **Answer (a) is wrong**. Police may use all reasonable force to execute a warrant, including forcing their way through a door if they are denied admittance or if the door poses a barrier to entry. **Answer (c) is incorrect**. There is no constitutional right to prevent the government, acting through the police, to have access to government records, such as a driver's license application. When information is voluntarily disclosed to the government, just as when it is handed to a third-party such as a bank, *California Bankers Association v. Shultz*, 416 U.S. 21 (1974), the government's lawful use of the information is not a search. The government is the owner of the data and may use it as it sees fit. Even in those jurisdictions where the government has barred various private parties from having access to drivers' license information, there is always an exception for access on behalf of law enforcement personnel. As against the government, there is no reasonable expectation of privacy in one's driver's license application. **Ordinarily answer (d) would be correct, but it is not** under these facts because the police have facts strongly pointing to Mr. Vander's departure. Because of this information, they acted unreasonably in entering the home to carry out the arrest. If the

officers possessed a *search* warrant, the police action would be deemed reasonable (and if, for some reason, the State wanted an additional argument, they could argue that Mr. Vander had abandoned the property). **Answer (e) is wrong.** Perhaps the police did act in good faith, and they certainly were acting pursuant to an arrest warrant, but that is insufficient here. They also needed reasonable suspicion to believe that Mr. Vander was at home.

- **Additional references**: *See* LaFave, Israel, King & Kerr, Criminal Procedure § 3.6(a) (6th ed. 2017); Whitebread & Slobogin, Criminal Procedure: An Analysis of Cases and Concepts § 3.04(b) (7th ed. 2020).

21. Although all of the answers are helpful in establishing valid consent, **answer (a) is the best pick among the choices.** It is well understood that a person may waive her expectation of privacy and consent to a police search. To be valid, consent must be voluntary, that is, it must "not be coerced, by explicit or implicit means, by implied threat or covert force." *Schneckloth v. Bustamonte*, 412 U.S. 218 (1973). Since the court will examine the "totality of the circumstances" to ascertain voluntariness, all of the answers, **answers (c), (d), and (e),** are relevant because they suggest the absence of force (i.e., a well-lighted area, a modest police presence, and the absence of any racial tension). But, under the circumstances, they are less a factor in negating coercion than the fact that Marcella was informed of her right to refuse consent. At first blush this may seem odd since the Supreme Court has specifically held that there is no constitutional *obligation* that police inform a person of her right to refuse consent. *Schneckloth v. Bustamonte, supra.* Nevertheless, one's awareness of the right to refuse consent is a critical factor in the voluntariness calculation. Thus while the failure to warn is unlikely to invalidate consent, giving a warning is almost always deemed "highly relevant" in finding consent. *United States v. Mendenhall*, 446 U.S. 544 (1980). In this question, the police have not stopped or obstructed Marcella, and they appear to have behaved peaceably. The fact that Marcella was actually warned that she need not give consent will almost surely lead to a finding of valid consent. **Answer (b) is least relevant** because competence to consent is a very minimal requirement. The courts will consider age, illness, emotional state, and low intelligence, but there must be marked dysfunction, almost bordering on incompetence to negate voluntariness. The fact that Marcella has a college degree does speak to the issue of capacity, but since that issue is so readily overcome, it is most important to pick the answer that most strongly overcomes a claim of coercion, and here that is answer (a).

- **Additional references**: *See* LaFave, Israel, King & Kerr, Criminal Procedure § 3.10(b) (6th ed. 2017); Whitebread & Slobogin, Criminal Procedure: An Analysis of Cases and Concepts § 12.02 (7th ed. 2020).

22. **The right answer is (a).** This question tests your understanding of the reach of the exclusionary rule. Under the Fourth Amendment, a valid in-

home arrest requires probable cause and, absent an emergency or other exigency, a warrant. *Payton v. New York*, 445 U.S. 573 (1980); *Kirk v. Louisiana*, 536 U.S. 635 (2002) (*per curiam*). Here, there was no exigency: although Cruella was a wanted felon, there is no reason to think Cruella was in the process of destroying evidence, that Cruella posed a danger to others, and although the police had probable cause to arrest Cruella and were in fact sitting outside of her house, there was no "hot pursuit." *Cf. Welsh v. Wisconsin*, 466 U.S. 740 (1984). Given the lack of exigent circumstances, the arrest was unjustified without a warrant. **Answer (e) is wrong precisely because it assumes that this was a valid warrantless arrest.** The crucial question is thus: what consequences flow from the fact that the arrest was improper? As a threshold matter, it matters why the arrest is alleged to be improper. If the arrest was improper for want of probable cause, then all statements and other evidence which are proximately obtained as a result of that illegal arrest are inadmissible as fruits of the poisonous tree. Thus, in *Taylor v. Alabama*, 457 U.S. 687 (1982), the Supreme Court held that a confession obtained six hours after an arrest without probable cause was inadmissible and that even the giving of Miranda warnings was not sufficient to purge the taint of the illegal arrest. Furthermore, in *Kaupp v. Texas*, 538 U.S. 626 (2003) (*per curiam*), which involved far more egregious facts, the Court indicated that proving the purgation of the primary taint of the unlawful invasion includes the following considerations: (1) the observance of *Miranda*, (2) the temporal proximity of the arrest and confession, (3) the presence of intervening circumstances, and (4) the purpose and flagrancy of the police conduct. Although the defendant in *Kaupp* had received Miranda warnings, the Court noted that Miranda warnings alone and per se cannot always break, for Fourth Amendment purposes, the causal connection between the illegality and the confession. If, on the other hand, an arrest is based on probable cause but there was a failure to get a warrant, then we follow the approach set out by the Court in *New York v. Harris*, 495 U.S. 14 (1990). Harris was arrested in his home. The police had probable cause but no warrant. Harris confessed to his crimes at the station house approximately one hour after the warrantless in-home arrest. Harris argued that the confession was close enough in time and circumstance to the warrantless arrest that it should be excluded as a product of the warrantless arrest. The Supreme Court refused to follow the fruit of the poisonous tree approach saying that a confession made outside of the home can never be the product of a warrantless in-home arrest. An arrest without a warrant, the Court said, does not create unlawful custody. A warrantless in-home arrest is properly viewed as a form of illegal search of the home, not an illegal arrest. And, as an illegal search of the home, it is a harm that is fully completed when the police leave the home, and there is no necessary connection between this invasion or search of the home and a subsequent confession given outside of the home. Of course, if the illegal entry into the home—for lack of a warrant—turns up evidence *in the home*, that evidence is excluded as a fruit of the illegal invasion into the home. So, in this question, the statements made by Cruella in the home are connected to and are the fruit of the illegal invasion into the home. They are inadmissible. The statements made in the cruiser, however, have occurred after the invasion into the home is over, and there can be no connection between the two. They are otherwise in compliance with *Miranda* and are voluntary and therefore, admissible. **Answer (b) contradicts the rule of *Harris* and is incorrect.** As indicated, the Court views the warrantless entry into the house as an illegal entry and search of the home, not as an illegal arrest. Here custody was legal because it was based upon probable cause; the statements in the cruiser are admissible. **Answer (c) correctly states that the Officer acted in bad faith but that fact is irrelevant.** It doesn't matter why Officer Dithers did not get the warrant. The only question is, what is the consequence of his failure—for whatever reason—to get the warrant. According to *Harris*, the consequence is a loss of evidence obtained as a result of the illegal entry into the house, and that is all. **Answer (d) assumes that a warrantless arrest in the home should be treated as an illegal arrest; this is a mistake according to *Harris*.** If this were an illegal arrest, i.e., an arrest without probable cause, the problem would have to be evaluated under *Taylor* and *Kaupp*. But, again, this is an arrest with probable cause and the only error is failure to get a warrant to enter the home. The illegal entry into the home is over once the police depart the home, and statements made thereafter are not causally connected to the interests of maintaining the security and privacy of the home.

- **Additional references**: *See* LaFave, Israel, King & Kerr, Criminal Procedure § 3.1 (6th ed. 2017); Whitebread & Slobogin, Criminal Procedure: An Analysis of Cases and Concepts § 2.04(b)(3) (7th ed. 2020).

23. **The best answer is (e).** Although even the "most outrageous behavior by a private party seeking to secure evidence against a defendant does not make that evidence inadmissible under the Due Process Clause," *Colorado v. Connelly*, 479 U.S. 157 (1986), the police are not free to exploit the coercion exerted by a private party in circumstances where they are under a duty to intervene, as here, or where they have arguably encouraged or become responsible for the private party's conduct. The facts here disclose that the police set up the encounter between the father and the son and that they "looked on" while the father repeatedly beat the son. Among the choices given, answer (e) offers the most convincing basis for excluding the in-home statements. If the physical force of the father can be attributed to the police, Due Process will clearly prohibit the use of statements obtained by force or violence. **Answer (a) is not the strongest argument** because there is no custody and Miranda is not applicable. **Answer (b) is factually in error.** The facts simply indicate that the police were admitted to the home, and only once inside did they make a false representation to the father. Therefore, there is no basis to argue that the police gained entry on false pretenses. **Answer (c) wrongly assumes that the police needed probable cause to**

approach Johnny and his father at home. Police may seek the voluntary cooperation of witnesses and suspects and, so long as they do not arrest or search, they do not need probable cause to take actions that are the staple of police work. It is true that a valid in-home arrest ordinarily requires probable cause and a warrant. *Payton v. New York*, 445 U.S. 573 (1980). Here there was no warrant. But the police were already legally in the home by virtue of the consensual entry and therefore, no warrant was necessary. And, although the police did not have probable cause to arrest Johnny when they first entered the home, Johnny's blurted admissions provided enough to establish a "fair probability" that a crime was committed and that he committed it. *Illinois v. Gates*, 462 U.S. 213 (1983). **Answer (d) is not the strongest answer** because, although it is true that the police misrepresented the evidence they had against Johnny, they made the false statement to *Johnny's father*. A false statement about evidence ("we have your fingerprints," "an eyewitness has identified you," etc.) is ordinarily not enough to render a suspect's incriminating statements involuntary. Interrogation manuals routinely include such tactics, police routinely use them, and courts applying the voluntariness test frequently permit them. *See, e.g., Frazier v. Cupp*, 394 U.S. 731 (1969) (maintaining that the use of "false friend" and "game is up" tactics, while relevant to the due process inquiry, were insufficient to render confession involuntary). As such, a false statement made to someone other than the suspect is certainly not a basis to exclude Johnny's incriminatory statements made in the house.

- **Additional references**: *See* LaFave, Israel, King & Kerr, Criminal Procedure §§ 3.6(a), 6.10(b) (6th ed. 2017); Whitebread & Slobogin, Criminal Procedure: An Analysis of Cases and Concepts §§ 3.4(b), 16.03(d) (7th ed. 2020).

24. **The best answer is (a).** The threshold issue here is whether the statements in the police station are products of the earlier violation in the home; whether they are, in other words, the "fruit of the poisonous tree." That depends on the nature of the violation in the home. If the violation was only a disregard of Miranda safeguards, then the fruit of the poisonous tree doctrine does not apply except in very narrow circumstances. This is because the Miranda warnings, although constitutionally based, *Dickerson v. United States*, 530 U.S. 428 (2000), do not draw after them the full scope of exclusionary rules. Rather a confession made after a Miranda-violative confession will be inadmissible but only if the officers were acting in bad faith and the second set of incriminating statements proceeded directly from the first. *See Missouri v. Seibert*, 542 U.S. 600 (2004). If, however, the violation in the home was an involuntary confession and a violation of Due Process of law, then the exclusionary rule will apply not only to the evidence obtained in violation of Due Process but also to the "fruits," or products, of that evidence. The question then is whether the giving of Miranda warnings, of itself, would be enough to "purge the taint" of the earlier illegality. Here the initial statements were obtained coercively when Johnny's father beat the admissions out of him, and the police effectively employed the father as

[margin note: Voluntary cooperation]

their agent. This was a violation of Due Process of law, not a violation of Miranda. To know its effect on the subsequent confession, all of the facts have to be examined, and the giving of Miranda warnings, while relevant, is not *per se* determinative. *See Oregon v. Elstad, supra; Brown v. Illinois,* 422 U.S. 590 (1975). This is the correct rule and is stated in answer (a). **Answers (b) and (e) are wrong** because both assume that the giving of Miranda warnings would be sufficient to disconnect the first set of statements from the second. **Answer (c) is incorrect** because it doesn't consider all of the relevant factors, such as the time elapsed between the two sets of statements or the egregiousness of the beating, to determine whether the stationhouse statements were a fruit of the original illegality. **Answer (d) is simply wrong on the facts** because all of Johnny's incriminating statements were not only not volunteered, i.e., not independently offered to the police, they were involuntary.

- **Additional references**: *See* LaFave, Israel, King & Kerr, Criminal Procedure § 9.5 (6th ed. 2017); Whitebread & Slobogin, Criminal Procedure: An Analysis of Cases and Concepts § 16.05 (7th ed. 2020).

25. **The answer is (b).** Jackie was arrested pursuant to a valid arrest warrant and given Miranda warnings, which she understood. In order to invoke the right to silence, the suspect must do so unambiguously and unequivocally. Jackie did not do that here, rather, she just didn't respond to most of the police's questions. *Berghuis v. Thompkins,* 560 U.S. 370 (2010). This explains why **answer (c) is wrong. Answer (a) is wrong** because *Davis v. United States,* 512 U.S. 452 (1994), says that if a suspect makes a statement regarding counsel that is ambiguous or equivocal, the police are not required to end interrogation, and they are not obligated to ask clarifying questions to see whether the suspect wants to invoke her Miranda rights. Jackie's passing reference to her hope that her father would retain decent counsel was not a valid invocation of her right to an attorney. *Cf. Hyatt v. Branker,* 569 F.3d 162 (4th Cir. 2009) (suspect whose "daddy wanted him to call a lawyer" insufficient invocation of right to counsel). Thus, because there was no invocation of Jackie's right, none of the protections arising from a valid invocation come into play. Because Jackie never explicitly invoked any of her Miranda rights, the police were not required to secure waiver before they continued questioning Jackie, so long as a waiver was ultimately secured. *Berghuis v. Thompkins, supra.* Here, Jackie waived her rights by giving a voluntary and uncoerced confession to the police. Remember, the *Berghuis* Court, citing *North Carolina v. Butler,* 441 U.S. 369 (1979), said that a waiver can be inferred from the actions and words of the person. In essence, there is no formalistic procedure to waive Miranda rights and thus, a waiver can be implied from all of the circumstances, including an eventual confession. **Answer (d) is wide of the mark** because it contradicts the facts. The police did begin an interrogation, as is evidenced by their use of familiar tactics, such as lying about the evidence and admonishing the suspect that she was in trouble and the best thing for her to do would be to confess. *See Rhode Island v. Innis,* 446 U.S. 291 (1980) ("[T]he term "interrogation"

under *Miranda* refers not only to express questioning, but also to any words or actions on the part of the police (other than those normally attendant to arrest and custody) that the police should know are reasonably likely to elicit an incriminating response from the suspect."). **Answer (e) is incorrect** because police are allowed to continue to seek a knowing and voluntary waiver if a suspect does not explicitly invoke her Miranda rights.

- **Additional references**: *See* LaFave, Israel, King & Kerr, Criminal Procedure § 6.9 (6th ed. 2017); Whitebread & Slobogin, Criminal Procedure: An Analysis of Cases and Concepts § 16.03(d)–(e) (7th ed. 2020).

26. **The correct answer is (a).** In this question, the police secure incriminating statements through an undercover agent at a time when the suspect is not in custody (a prerequisite for the application of Miranda) and has not been formally charged with the crime of securities fraud (a prerequisite for the attachment of the right to counsel). Consequently the statements are admissible, and no Fifth or Sixth Amendment rights have been violated. The fact that Bugsy retained an attorney and preemptorily notified the police that she did not want to answer any questions makes no difference. Fifth Amendment rights must be asserted at the time of interrogation and not anticipatorily. *McNeil v. Wisconsin*, 501 U.S. 171 (1991). **Answer (b) is wrong** because although false-friend questioning would not violate Miranda (the suspect has to be aware of the pressures of interrogation), it could violate one's right to counsel. If the false friend is an agent of the government and is deliberately trying to elicit incriminating statements about a crime after the prosecution has begun, then such behavior could violate the defendant's right to counsel. Thus the statement in answer (b) that "neither the 5th or 6th Amendments protect a person from a 'false friend,'" is inaccurate. **Answer (c) could be correct if the right to counsel had attached, but it didn't and so this response is wrong. Answer (d) is creative but incorrect.** Although a person may not be compelled to incriminate herself before a grand jury, the government need not stop its investigative efforts, including securing a potential defendant's own admissions. The Fifth Amendment is inapplicable because there is no custody, and the Sixth is inapplicable because an investigation by a grand jury is not the commencement of a criminal case and does not trigger the right to counsel. **Answer (e) is wrong on the facts.** The informant did more than merely listen to Bugsy. She was directed to elicit incriminating statements about the securities fraud matter and engaged in conversations with Bugsy toward that end.

- **Additional references**: *See* LaFave, Israel, King & Kerr, Criminal Procedure § 6.9(g) (6th ed. 2017); Whitebread & Slobogin, Criminal Procedure: An Analysis of Cases and Concepts § 16.03(e)(3) (7th ed. 2020).

27. **Answer (b) is best.** Simone was validly arrested. There was probable cause, and the police, by virtue of being lawfully in the house pursuant to

the search warrant, did not need an arrest warrant. Although it is true that police need a warrant to make an in-home arrest, *Payton v. New York*, 445 U.S. 573 (1980), if the police are already in the home lawfully, either because of an emergency, or consent, or having *a valid search warrant*, then no arrest warrant is necessary. And, with a valid arrest, police may automatically conduct a search incident to the arrest, *United States v. Robinson*, 414 U.S. 218 (1973). Such a search includes a search of the person and the area, including drawers, immediately surrounding the person. Such a search was conducted here, and both the gun and the pendant were recovered in that search. **Answer (c) is wrong** because, as discussed above, no arrest warrant was needed. **Answer (a) sounds sensible, but it is an overstatement and not appropriately responsive to the facts of the question.** If officers have a valid search warrant, they may, of course, search everywhere in the place they are authorized to search and search everywhere the particularly described items can be found. *See United States v. Ross*, 456 U.S. 798 (1982). But they are not always entitled to search every person who is present at the place to be searched. *See Ybarra v. Illinois*, 444 U.S. 85 (1979) (tavern patrons not automatically subject to search during the execution of a search warrant of the tavern). And, in any event, the facts more readily align with a search incident to an arrest, rather than execution of a search warrant. **Answer (d) is off track** because the police, after discovering the pendant in Simone's pocket, searched "further" as part of a search incident to an arrest. Thus, whatever the proper scope of a search for the pendant may have been, the search incident to Simone's arrest allowed them to continue the search beyond her person and to include all objects within her "wingspan" area. **Answer (e) has some appeal but, on the facts, should be rejected.** In *Richards v. Wisconsin*, 520 U.S. 385 (1997), the Supreme Court explained that the knock and announce requirements of common law and similar mandates found in federal statute 18 U.S.C.A. § 3109, are also constitutional requirements under the Fourth Amendment. That is, when executing a search or an arrest warrant at a home, police must knock and announce their presence, unless they have reasonable suspicion that such action would be dangerous or result in the destruction of evidence. *Richards v. Wisconsin, supra*. But here the police *did* knock and announce. And they waited several minutes for a response. Getting none, they were entitled to use all reasonable means to effect a lawful search. Consent is not necessary. And, in any case, violation of the knock and announce rule does not require exclusion of evidence found within the house. *Hudson v. Michigan*, 547 U.S. 586 (2006).

- **Additional references**: *See* LaFave, Israel, King & Kerr, Criminal Procedure § 3.5 (6th ed. 2017); Whitebread & Slobogin, Criminal Procedure: An Analysis of Cases and Concepts § 6.04 (7th ed. 2020).

28. **The best answer is (c).** The gun is admissible against Raul. It was found as part of a lawful search incident to Simone's arrest. Such a search includes the "grab space" around the arrestee, including drawers and closed containers. Once the police found the gun in the coffee table drawer,

both Simone and Raul, seated on the living room couch, were closely enough connected to it to give rise to probable cause of illegal (constructive) possession. The marijuana is not admissible against Raul. The search incident doctrine does not permit searches beyond the immediate area of the arrested person, *Chimel v. California*, 395 U.S. 752 (1969). The only other basis to be in the other rooms would be the search warrant. That warrant might have allowed searching the shaving kit in the upstairs bureau since a stolen pendant could be found there. However, the warrant permitted a search only for that one specific item and, once it was recovered, the police had no basis for any further intrusion. (**The opposite conclusion reached in answer (e) is, therefore, wrong.**) Raul had standing to object to the search because he has a reasonable expectation of privacy in his own property, namely, his shaving kit. **Answer (a) is incorrect** because Raul's proximity to the gun raised a "fair probability" that he had illegal possession of the gun. A "fair probability" or probable cause, *Illinois v. Gates*, 462 U.S. 213 (1983), is not proof beyond a reasonable doubt or a preponderance of the evidence. It is just a common sense assessment that the suspect may be involved in criminal activity. **Answer (b) stumbles on two grounds.** First, it mistakenly assumes that the police needed an arrest warrant to arrest Simone. They were already lawfully in the house and, therefore, no arrest warrant was needed. Second, Raul would have no standing to claim that Simone's arrest was illegal (but it wasn't). **Answer (d) goes too far** because, although there are standing issues on the facts, it is overbroad to say that Raul "had no standing to complain of any search inside Simone's house." As indicated, he has standing to complain of searches involving his own property and his person. He may even succeed to the standing of an overnight guest since he was not temporarily on the premises and was more than a casual visitor or a person briefly on the premises to conduct a business transaction. *Compare Minnesota v. Olson*, 495 U.S. 91 (1990) (person who slept over one night and was never alone in the apartment had standing to object to his warrantless arrest there) *with Minnesota v. Carter*, 525 U.S. 83 (1998) (persons in an apartment for a few hours to bag cocaine and who had no previous relationship with the lawful occupants had no standing to object to a search of the premises). But that need not be argued here since Raul plainly had a reasonable expectation of privacy in his own possessions, namely, the shaving kit where the marijuana was discovered.

- **Additional references**: *See* LaFave, Israel, King & Kerr, Criminal Procedure §§ 3.5(b), 9.1(b) (6th ed. 2017); Whitebread & Slobogin, Criminal Procedure: An Analysis of Cases and Concepts § 6.04 (7th ed. 2020).

29. **The correct answer is (b).** The courts have rarely applied the exclusionary rule in proceedings other than in the guilt adjudication stage of a criminal trial. This is not surprising given the Supreme Court majority's evident distaste for the rule. *See Hudson v. Michigan*, 547 U.S. 586 (2006) (in a case deciding that the exclusionary rule does not apply to mere violations of the knock and announce requirement, the Court took

the opportunity to question the continued vitality of the exclusionary rule). The Court applies the rule only where, applying a loose and easily manipulated balancing test, the need to deter police misconduct plainly outweighs the loss of probative evidence and any procedural disruption the rule will cause. *See Hudson v. Michigan, supra.* Thus, for example, the rule is inapplicable in proceedings such as grand jury proceedings, *United States v. Calandra*, 414 U.S. 338 (1974) (serious disruption of the grand jury's investigative functions and little deterrence value), federal habeas corpus proceedings, *Stone v. Powell*, 428 U.S. 465 (1976) (interference with truth finding and little deterrence since police are not likely to be thinking about a procedure that comes long after a criminal trial), parole revocation proceedings, *Pennsylvania v. Scott,* 524 U.S. 357 (1998) (interference with the flexible and administrative nature of parole proceedings, and parole officers are not adversaries of the parolee), civil deportation proceedings, *INS v. Lopez-Mendoza,* 468 U.S. 1032 (1984) (heavy social costs of freeing illegal aliens, severe burden on deliberately simple deportation proceedings, and little likely deterrence because Fourth Amendment challenges are rare and INS has its own scheme to remedy misbehavior). Thus, Raul will not be able to invoke the rule in his parole revocation or deportation proceedings, even assuming it would be applicable in a criminal case against him. **Answers (a), (c), and (d) are all bad choices** because they assume that the exclusionary rule will apply to either of the proceedings or to both. **Answer (e) is wrong** because the Fourth Amendment applies to persons legally residing in this country. The Fourth Amendment protects even non-citizen persons who have a substantial and voluntary attachment to the country, as opposed to someone merely being held in detention in this country. *See United States v. Verdugo-Urquidez,* 494 U.S. 259 (1990) (upholding U.S. agents' search of Mexican home of Mexican citizen already in U.S. custody; suspect had no voluntary attachment or connection to the community of the United States).

- **Additional references**: *See* LAFAVE, ISRAEL, KING & KERR, CRIMINAL PROCEDURE § 3.1(g) (6th ed. 2017); WHITEBREAD & SLOBOGIN, CRIMINAL PROCEDURE: AN ANALYSIS OF CASES AND CONCEPTS § 2.03 (7th ed. 2020).

30. **The right answer is (d).** Despite the facts relating to probable cause or the extent of the search, the key to finding the best answer among the choices given is to focus on the matter of timing. Officer Fallon had probable cause to believe that there were drugs at Donnie's house based on the informant's personal observations, made reliable by an accurate prediction of a future narcotics sale, Officer Fallon's own corroboration of the predicted facts, and the observed behavior being consistent with the modus operandi for drug dealing. This would surely be enough under the test of *Illinois v. Gates*, 462 U.S. 213 (1983); that is, whether, under the totality of the circumstances, there was a "fair probability" that evidence of a crime, in this case illegal drugs, would be found in a particular place. However, Officer Fallon waited approximately eight months to bring the information to a magistrate and, by then, it was fatally stale. Remember

that "the facts in an affidavit supporting a search warrant must be sufficiently close in time to the issuance of the warrant and the subsequent search conducted so that probable cause can be said to exist as of the time of the search and not simply as of some time in the past." *United States v. Grubbs*, 547 U.S. 90 (2006). Staleness, however, will be judged on a case by case basis. The question is whether there is probable cause to believe that evidence of a crime is *then* at the place to be searched. Although evidence of ongoing criminal activity will generally defeat a claim of staleness, *United States v. Greene*, 250 F.3d 471 (6th Cir. 2001), that is not the case here. The search at issue here is not a search for stolen equipment used in a business or a search for a personal child pornography collection that may be kept for years. Rather, it appears to be a search based on two, perhaps isolated, instances of drug transactions. The facts are similar to those in *United States v. Grant*, 108 F. Supp. 2d 1172 (D. Kan. 2000), where the court found that evidence of two drug transactions occurring six months and four-and-a-half months prior to the application for a warrant did not establish continuous and ongoing activity. The court noted "there is no indication, for instance, that defendant had recently kept a supply of drugs at his house or that he was receiving more contraband in the future or that he was continuing to use or sell illegal drugs or that it was likely that he still kept records or other evidence of drug sales at his house." Answer (a) is wrong because it assumes, apart from the matter of timing, that there was no probable cause for the warrant. But there were the personal observations of criminality by the tipster, reliability established by predicting, accurately and hence reliably, future drug dealing, and the officer's own observations which were consistent with the illegal drug transactions. **Answer (b) is wrong** because there is no obligation for the police to obtain an arrest warrant once probable cause to arrest arises. If the police have probable cause and a search warrant to search the premises, they may enter and search even if they could have also obtained an arrest warrant. If the search had been proper under the facts, Donnie's arrest would also have been proper. **Answer (c) mistakenly characterizes the scope of a permissible search.** If the search warrant was valid, the police would have been permitted to search anywhere on the premises where the object of the search, in this case drugs, could be found. Obviously, drugs could be secreted in guitar cases, and thus, the search was within its proper scope. **Answer (e) mistakenly assumes that there is some obligation to disclose the informant's identity to the magistrate.** There is no such rule.

- **Additional references**: *See* LAFAVE, ISRAEL, KING & KERR, CRIMINAL PROCEDURE § 3.3(g) (6th ed. 2017); WHITEBREAD & SLOBOGIN, CRIMINAL PROCEDURE: AN ANALYSIS OF CASES AND CONCEPTS §§ 4.05, 5.05(a) (7th ed. 2020).

31. **The right answer is (c).** Amy invoked her right to counsel under *Miranda*, and under the bright line, categorical rules laid down in *Edwards v. Arizona*, 451 U.S. 477 (1981), and *Minnick v. Mississippi*, 498 U.S. 146 (1990), Detective Henderson was not permitted to interrogate

Amy unless her counsel was present or Amy initiated the conversation with the police under *Oregon v. Bradshaw*, 462 U.S. 1039 (1983). As *Bradshaw* held, when an accused has invoked her right to have counsel present during custodial interrogation, a valid waiver of that right cannot be established by showing only that she responded to further police-initiated interrogation even if she has been advised of her rights. Here, Detective Henderson impermissibly initiated interrogation without Amy's counsel's presence. Even though Amy actually conferred with counsel, her valid invocation of her right to counsel means that the absolute bar on police-initiated interrogation remains in place. *Minnick* makes this last proposition crystal clear and is best understood to be a prophylactic rule protecting the bright line rule of *Edwards*. Thus, if the suspect's counsel is not present, the police may not reinitiate questioning, even if their objective is only to see if the suspect would like to waive the right to have counsel present. The rule is a stiff, suspect-protective approach that avoids inquiry into whether the suspect's consultation was effective and posits that a single consultation with a lawyer may be insufficient to fend off repeated attempts to interrogate or to relieve the pressures inherent in the custodial situation. **Thus answer (d) is in error** because it argues for inadmissibility based on a lack of a knowing and voluntary waiver. The waiver here was knowing and voluntary, but a knowing and voluntary waiver is insufficient if police initiate interrogation in the absence of counsel. **Answer (a) is wrong** because it rests on the Sixth Amendment which is not applicable in this case. Amy has only been arrested and jailed. There has been no indictment or information filed nor any other indication that a formal prosecution has begun. **Answer (b) is wrong on the facts and irrelevant**. Amy invoked her right to an attorney and not her right to remain silent. Invoking the right to silence does not cut off all future opportunities to question a suspect. It requires that the police scrupulously honor the right not to speak by, then and there, ceasing questioning. The police may, however, come back to a suspect after a sufficient interval and in a manner, preferably respectful and with fresh Miranda warnings, that conveys to the suspect that her rights will be honored. *Michigan v. Mosley*, 423 U.S. 96 (1975). This more lenient rule is permitted because the Court believes that a suspect is saying different things when she invokes the right to silence and the right to counsel. By not speaking, the suspect is simply saying, "I don't want to talk at this time," but later, she may want an opportunity to talk. In contrast, by invoking the right to an attorney, the suspect is saying, "I feel unable to face an interrogation situation without the aid of my lawyer," and there is no reason to think that the sense of disability will change. This is not a question about the right to silence, but, if it were, the facts show that the police *did* scrupulously honor the right to remain silent. **Answer (e) is incomplete**. Yes, Amy's invocation of counsel was clear and unequivocal under *Davis v. United States*, 512 U.S. 452 (1994), but the evidence will be suppressed, not because of that alone, but because the police attempted to question her again without her counsel being present.

- **Additional references**: *See* LaFave, Israel, King & Kerr, Criminal Procedure § 6.9(f) (6th ed. 2017); Whitebread & Slobogin, Criminal Procedure: An Analysis of Cases and Concepts § 16.03(e)(4) (7th ed. 2020).

32. **The correct answer is (d).** Even with abundant probable cause, a valid phone tap requires a warrant. *Katz v. United States,* 389 U.S. 347 (1967); 18 U.S.C. §§ 2510–2522. Since there was no warrant here, the essential question is who has standing to object. Standing requires that a person have a reasonable expectation of privacy in the invaded place or premises. *Rakas v. Illinois*, 439 U.S. 128 (1978). Nick, as the owner of the phone, has such an expectation of privacy, as do Marlene and Janice, as the participants in the phone conversation. Only Tony, who had neither an ownership or possessory interest nor was a participant in the conversation, lacks standing. **Answers (a), (b), and (c) are incorrect** because they identify too many persons having standing or too few. **Answer (e) is wrong** about standing and wrong about the inevitable discovery exception to the exclusionary rule. As to standing, Nick, Marlene, and Janice still have standing and "can object," even though, on the merits, they might lose. As to the exclusionary rule, the inevitable discovery doctrine does not permit the police to forego a warrant by simply saying that they could have gotten one eventually. Such a rule would completely eviscerate the warrant requirement since police could always say that, eventually, they could have or would have sought a warrant. And one main benefit of the warrant is a *prior* determination by a neutral and detached officer that, in fact, probable cause exists and a *particularly described* search or seizure may take place. *See United States v. Mejia,* 69 F.3d 309 (9th Cir. 1995). Even courts that have accepted that the exclusionary rule can apply to primary evidence as well as derivative evidence have not gone so far.

   - **Additional references**: *See* LaFave, Israel, King & Kerr, Criminal Procedure §§ 3.2(a), 9.1 (7th ed. 2017); Whitebread & Slobogin, Criminal Procedure: An Analysis of Cases and Concepts § 4.04 (7th ed. 2020).

33. **The best answer is (e).** This question tests your understanding of the exigent circumstances doctrine. Ordinarily, unconsented entry into a home requires probable cause and a warrant. As the Court enunciated in *Payton v. New York*, 445 U.S. 573 (1980), the Fourth Amendment draws a firm line at the entrance to the house. However, exigent circumstances can provide a basis to overcome the traditional rule that a warrant is required prior to entering a house. Remember that although exigent circumstances excuse the need for a warrant, probable cause remains necessary for an entry conducted pursuant to an exigency. The existence of exigent circumstances is determined in a highly fact specific, totality of the circumstances inquiry. The facts must show that immediate action was reasonably necessary to (1) prevent flight of a suspect, (2) safeguard the police or the public, or (3) protect against the loss of evidence. The Supreme Court has not spelled out the precise boundaries of the

destruction of evidence exigency, but the essence of the exception is the prospect of imminent or immediate destruction of evidence. Proving that evidence was actually in the process of destruction is not necessary. However, the mere presence of illegal drugs or other destructible evidence inside the premises does not in itself justify such immediate entry into a home. *United States v. Santa*, 236 F.3d 662 (11th Cir. 2000). The relevant focus is whether the facts, as they appeared at the moment of entry, would lead a reasonable, experienced police officer to believe that evidence might be destroyed or removed before a warrant could be secured. *United States v. Andrews*, 442 F.3d 996 (7th Cir. 2006). Here, although the nature of the evidence is such that it could easily be destroyed or removed from the premises, and although the open door suggests that someone may have been at home, the facts say that the house was "quiet" and that no one answered the officer's knock on the door. The Supreme Court pointed out in *Kentucky v. King*, 563 U.S. 452 (2011), "[p]ersons in possession of valuable drugs are unlikely to destroy them unless they fear discovery by the police." In this problem, there is no indication in the facts that the residents were alerted to the police officer's presence, so there is no way a reasonable police officer could believe that the evidence would be destroyed before a warrant could be secured. The officer here could have called for assistance to secure the area, and, if the owners showed up, the officer could have kept the individual out of the home while a warrant was approved. *See Illinois v. McArthur*, 531 U.S. 326 (2001). Moreover, the officer could have applied for a warrant over the telephone. Fed. R. Crim. Pro. 41(d)(3). Given the day and time, there appears to be no special obstacle to frustrate a prompt issuance of a warrant. There was no immediate danger that evidence would be lost. **Answer (c) is wrong** because it reaches the opposite conclusion. But, our work is not done. We also need to note that the officer entered an area where he was lawfully entitled to be, namely, the front entrance where guests, peddlers, post office employees, and all others have access. From this legal vantage point, he acquired a view that gave him probable cause to believe that evidence of a crime, the marijuana, was in the house. He could use this evidence to establish probable cause to secure a warrant; thus, the correct answer is (e). The opposite conclusion—that the front entrance is protected as curtilage—is wrong precisely because the front door area is open to the public and readily accessible to anyone who wants to come up the steps and knock on the door. However if the officer entered the cartilage area to gather evidence, that is a search and a Fourth Amendment violation. *Florida v. Jardines,* 569 U.S. 1 (2013). But here the officer entered the curtilage area to say hello, not gather evidence. **Thus, answer (d) is incorrect. Answer (a) goes astray** because it posits that plain view dispenses with the need for a warrant. Not so. In order to seize something in plain view (1) the incriminating character must be immediately apparent (satisfied here) and (2) the officer must be (a) legally in the place where he can see the object (also satisfied here) and (b) must have lawful right of access to the place because he either (i) possesses a warrant or (ii) there is a valid exception to the warrant

[margin handwritten note: Standard for Emergent or Exigency Exist.]

(neither of which is the case here.). *Horton v. California*, 496 U.S. 128 (1990). While plain view here provides probable cause to secure a warrant, it does not eliminate the need for a warrant because the officer does not have lawful right of access to the marijuana plant. **Answer (b) is incomplete**. Although the owners of the marijuana may have sacrificed their reasonable expectation of privacy with respect to the plant by leaving it where it could easily be observed from a legal vantage point, they have not sacrificed their reasonable expectation of privacy with respect to the entry into the home.

- **Additional references**: *See* LAFAVE, ISRAEL, KING & KERR, CRIMINAL PROCEDURE §§ 3.2(c), 9.1(b) (6th ed. 2017); WHITEBREAD & SLOBOGIN, CRIMINAL PROCEDURE: AN ANALYSIS OF CASES AND CONCEPTS §§ 4.03(f)(4), 6.04(b)(3), 9.03, 10.02 (7th ed. 2020).

34. **The best answer is (a).** In order to seek redress for a constitutional violation, a person must have a personal stake, or standing, in the matter. To claim standing to raise a Fourth Amendment violation, a person must have a legitimate expectation of privacy in the property subject to a search or seizure. *Rakas v. Illinois*, 439 U.S. 128 (1978). A legitimate expectation of privacy requires a subjective expectation of privacy in the property, and the subjective expectation must be one society is prepared to deem reasonable. *Katz v. United States*, 389 U.S. 347 (1967). Ordinarily a person will have a reasonable expectation of privacy in property that he owns or rents, in property that he possesses or uses with the permission the owner, and in property, such as a house or an apartment, where he is staying as an overnight guest or is authorized to control. A person even has standing to complain of a stop of a rental car where he is not on the rental agreement but permitted to drive by the renter. *Byrd v. United States*, 548 U.S. ___, 138 S.Ct. 1518 (2018). Conversely, a person will not have a reasonable expectation of privacy, and hence no standing to complain about Fourth Amendment intrusions, in property which he does not own or rent, property which he has no authority to possess or be present upon, (think of a thief in a car or house), property where he is present only as a transient guest (such as a visitor to your home or a passenger in a car), or property of another. Thus, even if a person is the "target" of an unlawful search of the property of another, such as the illegal ransacking of a relative's house, if the suspect has no reasonable expectation of privacy in that property, he has no standing to complain. *United States v. Payner*, 447 U.S. 727 (1980) (defendant denied standing to raise the intentional theft of accountant's files which contained incriminating evidence against him). Moreover, the burden rests on one who claims a Fourth Amendment violation to prove, by a preponderance of the evidence, that he has standing to raise the claim. *Rawlings v. Kentucky*, 448 U.S. 98 (1980). In the current problem, Kramer has standing to raise the unlawfulness of the search of his backpack. Even though he is in Jerry's apartment, he is the owner of the backpack, and there is no evidence that he abandoned it or otherwise disassociated himself from it. **Thus, answer (c), which asserts that Kramer has no standing to object to the search is incorrect.** What he lacks is standing to object to the search of Jerry's apartment, where although he is a frequent and presumably welcome guest, he is not an overnight guest nor is he entitled to exercise dominion and control or exclude others from the apartment. **Hence answer (b), which asserts standing to object to the search of the apartment, is also wrong.** Of the possible answers to this question, answer (a) is correct because it states the general burden Kramer faces in raising a Fourth Amendment violation to exclude the gun found in his backpack. **Answer (d) incorrectly allocates the burden of proof to the government. Answer (e) is wrong** because it relies on a now discredited basis to find standing to object to an unlawful search or seizure, namely that one is "legitimately on the premises" of another. That test was rejected as overly broad, allowing even a "casual visitor who has never seen, or been permitted to visit the basement of another's house, to object to the search of the basement if the visitor happened to be in the kitchen of the house at the time of the search." *Rakas v. Illinois, supra.*

- **Additional references**: *See* LaFave, Israel, King & Kerr, Criminal Procedure §§ 3.2(c), 9.1(b) (6th ed. 2017); Whitebread & Slobogin, Criminal Procedure: An Analysis of Cases and Concepts § 4.04(d) (7th ed. 2020).

35. **The best answer is (d).** This question tests your understanding of how *Arizona v. Gant*, 556 U.S. 332 (2009) interacts with earlier precedent arising under the automobile exception. Here, the police have probable cause to arrest the occupants of the car based on the parking lot attendant's descriptions and the immediate and geographically proximate sighting of the car and persons who match those descriptions. The search of the trunk is not a problem here because there is also probable cause to believe that the car contains evidence of the crime such as the proceeds and the guns. Once probable cause extends to a car, the police may look everywhere in the car where the suspected evidence could be, including the locked trunk, *United States v. Ross*, 456 U.S. 798 (1982), and any containers in the locked trunk, *California v. Acevedo*, 500 U.S. 565 (1991). **Answer (b) is wrong** because it says that it was error to enter the trunk. **Answer (c) is incorrect** because it assumes that the police need a warrant to search containers within cars. When the police have probable cause to believe there is evidence of a crime in a car, they may search the entire vehicle, including any container capable of hiding the evidence, without a warrant. *Chambers v. Maroney*, 399 U.S. 42 (1970). This so-called "automobile exception" to the warrant requirement is based on the mobility of the car and the diminished expectation of privacy courts recognize in vehicles. *California v. Carney*, 471 U.S. 386 (1985). **Answer (e) is close, but is not the best answer** because the facts align more closely with a search conducted pursuant to probable cause than a search incident to arrest. Two things should be pointed out here. First, under *Arizona v. Gant, supra,* the police may search the passenger compartment of a vehicle (even when recent occupants cannot access the interior at the time of the search) when it is "reasonable to believe" that evidence of the crime of arrest is in the car. Here, it would have been reasonable to believe

that evidence of the robbery was in the car, but the police had a higher level of individualized suspicion, namely, probable cause. Second, the relevant search incident to arrest precedent, *New York v. Belton*, 453 U.S. 454 (1981) and *Gant*, prohibits searches of trunks. However, it should be noted that if there is a legal search incident to arrest of the passenger compartment that gives the police the additional information they need for probable cause, the police could then search the trunk, without a warrant, pursuant to the automobile exception. **Answer (a) is wrong** because it assumes that this is a search incident to arrest. Although answer (a) correctly states how *Gant* changed *Belton* with respect to police authority to search the car incident to arrest when there is no reason to think evidence of the crime of arrest is contained therein, here there was probable cause that evidence of the robbery would be in the car.

- **Additional references**: *See* LAFAVE, ISRAEL, KING & KERR, CRIMINAL PROCEDURE § 3.7 (6th ed. 2017); WHITEBREAD & SLOBOGIN, CRIMINAL PROCEDURE: AN ANALYSIS OF CASES AND CONCEPTS § 6.04(c) (7th ed. 2020).

36. **The right answer is (e).** In *Gerstein v. Pugh*, 420 U.S. 103 (1975), the Supreme Court held that the Fourth Amendment requires a judicial or grand jury determination of probable cause for any significant pretrial restraint on a person's liberty. There is no risk to the state in requiring this determination because the defendant is already in custody, and there is no danger of escape or the commission of further crimes. At the same time, the suspect's need for a neutral evaluation of the legality of his detention grows more urgent. The suspect faces serious consequences from prolonged detention including loss of employment and disruption of family life. The requirement of a judicial post-arrest determination of probable cause does not apply, however, if the defendant was arrested pursuant to a warrant. With a warrant, there has already been a judicial determination that probable cause existed. The rule also does not apply if the defendant has been indicted. If there has been an indictment, a neutral and detached body, namely the citizens comprising the grand jury, has already made a determination that probable cause exists. But if the arrest is without a warrant and there has been no indictment, the defendant faces continued detention without an objective, disinterested finding of probable cause. **Thus answer (c) misses the point** because the judgment of the police, no matter how sound it may appear to be, is no substitute for judicial oversight of the probable cause decision. In addition, as the Court stated in *Gerstein*, it is no answer that the prosecutor files an information that recites facts sufficient to establish probable cause: "Although a conscientious decision that the evidence warrants prosecution affords a measure of protection against unfounded detention, we do not think prosecutorial judgment standing alone meets the requirements of the Fourth Amendment." **Hence answer (a) is wrong. Answer (d) is not the best choice.** The defendant is entitled to a "prompt" judicial determination of probable cause as a prerequisite to an extended pretrial detention following a warrantless arrest. Prompt means within forty-eight hours. *County of Riverside v. McLaughlin*, 500

U.S. 44 (1991). Theoretically, the preliminary hearing could meet this test, but it is unlikely to do so. Moreover, even though a *Gerstein* hearing can be waived, there is no clear evidence here of the defendant's actual waiver. In the end, answer (e) is the better choice. **Answer (b) has some potential but is not the crisply correct response available in (e).** Answer (b) indicates that the defendant has been released from jail, although he is wearing a monitoring bracelet and is confined to his home. The probable cause determination of *Gerstein* only comes into play if the defendant remains subject to a "significant pretrial restraint on liberty." The Supreme Court has never specified what restraints short of incarceration are "significant" but commentators argue that any restraint, including bail and conditions of release, should count as infringements on liberty protected by the Fourth Amendment.

- **Additional references**: *See* LaFave, Israel, King & Kerr, Criminal Procedure §§ 3.5(a), 12.3(d) (6th ed. 2017); Whitebread & Slobogin, Criminal Procedure: An Analysis of Cases and Concepts § 20.02 (7th ed. 2020).

37. **The correct answer is (a).** This question tests your understanding of the difference between the Fifth and Sixth Amendment invocations of the right to counsel. To answer this question, we first need to get a precise fix on the significance of the defendant's appearance before the Magistrate. The right to counsel attaches with the commencement of formal proceedings against the defendant. Precisely when that occurs is not always crystal clear. Here, charges have been filed with the court, meaning either the filing of a complaint or an information. The defendant has also appeared, and the charges have been read. We may confidently say that the right to counsel attaches when an indictment issues or when a preliminary hearing is held. *Brewer v. Williams*, 430 U.S. 387 (1977) ("[T]he right to counsel . . . means at least that a person is entitled to the help of a lawyer at or after the time that judicial proceedings have been initiated against him—'whether by way of formal charge, preliminary hearing, indictment, information or arraignment.'"). Also, it is fairly settled that the right to counsel does not attach when a person is still simply a suspect, even if the police have begun to "focus" on him, indeed, even if he is arrested. The uncertainty tends to lie in circumstances where a complaint has been filed with the court. Whether that marks the beginning of the prosecution, and the conversion of a suspect into an "accused," depends on the purpose of the complaint in the specific case and in the specific state procedural system. If the complaint is simply a step in obtaining an arrest warrant, then that step, without more, does not mark the beginning of the prosecution. *See, e.g., United States v. Boskic*, 545 F.3d 69 (1st Cir. 2008); *United States v. Alvarado*, 440 F.3d 191 (4th Cir. 2006). If, however, the complaint is filed by the government as a *charging document,* especially if the defendant appears in court on these "charges," then this does signal that the government has "committed itself to prosecute, and . . . the adverse positions of the government and the defendant have solidified." *Kirby v. Illinois*, 406 U.S. 682 (1972); *see also Rothgery v. Gillespie Cty., Texas*, 554 U.S. 191 (2008) ("[A] criminal

[handwritten margin note: How is 6th Amend Right to Counsel triggered]

defendant's initial appearance before a judicial officer, where he learns the charge against him and his liberty is subject to restriction, marks the start of adversary judicial proceedings that trigger attachment of the Sixth Amendment right to counsel."). Here, it is safe to say that formal charges have been initiated against Henderson. So, Henderson's Sixth Amendment rights have attached. Next, note that Henderson invoked his right to counsel during his initial appearance, not in the context of custodial interrogation, which explains why **answer (e) is wrong**. When a suspect validly invokes the Miranda right to counsel during custodial interrogation, all further police-initiated interrogation of the suspect must cease unless the defendant initiates the conversation or counsel is present. *Edwards v. Arizona*, 451 U.S. 477 (1981). Remember, *McNeil v. Wisconsin*, 501 U.S. 171 (1991), says that Miranda rights cannot be invoked anticipatorily and to get the protection of *Edwards*, the right to counsel must be invoked in the Miranda context. This means that an invocation at an initial appearance does not suffice to trigger Miranda because there is no interrogation. Thus, when the police approached Henderson several days later, they secured a valid waiver of Miranda, and the subsequent interrogation was entirely lawful. The important case for understanding all of this is *Montejo v. Louisiana*, 556 U.S. 778 (2009). *Montejo* explicitly overruled *Michigan v. Jackson*, 475 U.S. 625 (1986), which held that if a defendant requested counsel at arraignment or a similar proceeding, the police could not attempt to interrogate the accused. The *Montejo* Court thought this rule was superfluous because Miranda and its progeny sufficiently protect the right to counsel. This means that there are different rules for the Miranda and Sixth Amendment invocations of the right to counsel. Once the Miranda right is invoked, *Edwards* kicks in and the police cannot initiate further questioning. But, if a charged defendant invokes his Sixth Amendment right to counsel outside the context of custodial interrogation, like Henderson here, the police remain free to approach him and seek a knowing and voluntary waiver. This is why, even though they attached, Henderson's Sixth Amendment rights were not violated. *Montejo* explains that Miranda warnings sufficiently appraise the accused of his Sixth Amendment right to counsel, so a waiver of Miranda rights is a knowing waiver of the Sixth Amendment right to counsel. So, if the Sixth Amendment right is invoked, police still must give Miranda warnings prior to custodial interrogation. If the defendant invokes the counsel right after the warnings, the protections of *Edwards* and its progeny apply. **Answer (c) is also wrong** because the presumption of coercion was the underlying rationale for the *Jackson* rule, and this rule was specifically rejected in *Montejo*. **Answer (b) is incorrect.** The first proposition of answer (b) is correct: Henderson certainly had the right to the presence of counsel during interrogation, because interrogation by the State is a critical stage of the prosecution, *Montejo*; *Massiah v. United States*, 377 U.S. 201 (1964), but this right is waivable. The defendant's decision to waive the right to counsel's presence does not depend on whether or not the defendant is already represented and the decision to waive need not itself be counseled. *Michigan v. Harvey*, 494 U.S. 344 (1990). Answer (b) is incorrect because Henderson's invocation of his right to counsel was definitely clear and unequivocal under *Davis v. United States*, 512 U.S. 452 (1994). But *Davis* is about the clarity needed to invoke the protections of *Edwards* and is thus irrelevant in the present context. **Answer (d) is intriguing but incorrect**. It is intriguing because a defendant, if he is to be held in custody after a warrantless arrest, has a Fourth Amendment right to a judicial determination of probable cause within 48 hours. *County of Riverside v. McLaughlin*, 500 U.S. 44 (1991). But if there is no such determination, and it later turns out that there was probable cause, there appears to be very little effect on the criminal prosecution itself. Courts have not set aside convictions, have not freed defendants from custody, and have not excluded incriminating statements made prior to the determination of probable cause. *See Powell v. Nevada*, 511 U.S. 79 (1994) ("[W]hether a suppression remedy applies . . . remains an unsolved question."). Furthermore, given that the exclusionary rule is primarily to deter police misconduct, it seems unlikely that the Supreme Court would apply the rule when the police are not at fault (and, it is fair to say that police officers do not control court calendars). Thus, answer (d) is not the best of the answer choices given.

- **Additional references**: *See* LaFave, Israel, King & Kerr, Criminal Procedure § 6.4 (6th ed. 2017); Whitebread & Slobogin, Criminal Procedure: An Analysis of Cases and Concepts §§ 31.03, 16.04 (7th ed. 2020).

38. **The correct answer is (d).** The facts of this problem are a close cousin to the case of *Maine v. Moulton*, 474 U.S. 159 (1985). Jules has been indicted for fraud, and as a result of this formal charge, his Sixth Amendment right to counsel has attached. *Maine v. Moulton, supra* held that, after the attachment of the defendant's Sixth Amendment rights, the police may not "knowingly exploit" an "opportunity to confront the accused without counsel being present." Here, as in *Moulton,* the police knew that the defendant and his co-defendant were going to meet to discuss their upcoming trial on the fraud charges. The police knew or must have known that they would be privy to incriminating statements on the crime charged. As a result, they "deliberately elicited" defendant's incriminating statements, and these statements cannot now be used by the prosecution at his trial. It doesn't matter whether the police were acting to investigate other crimes, even crimes that may affect the trial of the crime already charged. Of course they may continue to investigate such crimes, try to prevent them, and use whatever statements they obtain concerning those (uncharged) crimes in a separate prosecution. But they may not use the statements which incriminate the defendant on the fraud charge. **Hence, answers (b) and (c) are wrong.** The Court in *Moulton* specifically rejected the idea that police could use statements concerning the crime charged if they were in good faith pursuing evidence of other crimes. Such an approach would invite the police to lie about what they were actually trying to do and would create too broad an exception to Sixth Amendment protections. The Court said: "To allow the admission

[margin handwritten note: trigger of 6th Amendment]

of evidence obtained from the accused in violation of the Sixth Amendment rights whenever the police assert an alternative, legitimate reason for their surveillance invites abuse by law enforcement personnel in the form of fabricated investigations and risks the evisceration of the Sixth Amendment right recognized in *Massiah v. United States,* 377 U.S. 201 (1964)." It also doesn't matter that it was the defendant and not the police who set up the meeting with the co-defendant. For a Sixth Amendment violation, it is sufficient to establish that the police knew of the circumstances of the meeting and deliberately exploited the opportunity to obtain the incriminating statements. Since the police actively deputized the co-defendant to go forward with the conversations knowing their likely content, it was irrelevant who arranged the encounter. **Thus, answer (a) is wrong. Answer (e) is not the best answer** because, although it states the right result, it rests on finding that the police acted with a bad motive. In *Moulton,* the Court ignored motive and looked, instead, to the natural consequences of the actions taken by the police.

- **Additional references**: *See* LAFAVE, ISRAEL, KING & KERR, CRIMINAL PROCEDURE § 6.4 (6th ed. 2017); WHITEBREAD & SLOBOGIN, CRIMINAL PROCEDURE: AN ANALYSIS OF CASES AND CONCEPTS § 16.04 (7th ed. 2020).

39. **The best answer is (a), though answer (b) is a close second choice.** This question is similar to the facts in *United States v. Allen*, 159 F.3d 832 (4th Cir. 1998). There are two bases on which the police might justify their search of the black duffel bag: abandoned property and inevitable discovery. But neither ground can do the trick on these facts. As to abandonment, the Supreme Court has recognized that police may inspect items cast off by their owners without any Fourth Amendment consequences. However, the item must truly be abandoned, that is, the owner must have manifested an intention to give up all claim to the object. Abandonment has been found, for example, where a suspect checked out of his hotel room and left behind incriminating evidence in a wastebasket. Police seizure of that evidence was not a Fourth Amendment violation because the property was abandoned. *Abel v. United States*, 362 U.S. 217 (1960). But there is no abandonment when the owner of property tries to conceal it from the police or stashes it when prompted by illegal police pursuit or seizure. *Rios v. United States*, 364 U.S. 253 (1960). There is also no abandonment when the police separate a person from his property and give him no opportunity to claim it. Here the police removed Opperman from the bus, and he had no chance to lay claim to the duffel. Opperman never manifested any intention to relinquish his claim to the bag. **Thus, answer (c), which states that the bag was abandoned, is incorrect.** The next issue is whether the search of the bag was nevertheless permissible because the police would have inevitably discovered the cocaine by legal means. In *Nix v. Williams*, 467 U.S. 431 (1984), the Court ruled that information actually obtained by illegal means (as here) is nevertheless admissible if "the prosecution can establish by a preponderance of the evidence that the information ultimately or

4

inevitably would have been discovered by lawful means." In *Nix*, the Court permitted the victim's body to be used as evidence even though they learned its location from statements illegally obtained from the defendant. Because there was a search party at work in the area where the body was discovered, the government was able to prove that it would have inevitably found the victim anyway. Under such circumstances, the Court reasoned, "the deterrence rationale [of the exclusionary rule] has so little basis that the evidence should be received." Here the facts are just not strong enough to make out a case of inevitable discovery. Although the police do have drug sniffing dogs "available," their pattern is to use these dogs "sometimes" and only to sniff the outside luggage compartment of the bus or luggage left on the walkway leading to the bus. There is no indication that they would bring the dogs on board. And if the police had asked Opperman whether the duffel bag was his, it is entirely speculative whether they would have subjected the bag to a dog sniff simply because he did not consent to a search. **Answer (d), which asserts that the inevitable discovery doctrine does apply here, is incorrect. Answer (e) is wrong** because it rests on the search incident to arrest doctrine. First, it is not even clear that Opperman is under arrest (he may only be detained while the police calm things down). Second, even if he were under arrest, that arrest is arguably illegal because police lacked probable cause to believe that Opperman was committing a crime (his tantrum on the bus may be upsetting or, perhaps, thrilling, but we have no clear basis to conclude that it is illegal). And third, a search incident to arrest encompasses only the area immediately surrounding the arrestee, and since Opperman has been moved out of the bus, that area no longer includes the interior of the bus. **Answer (b) has appeal but is not better than (a).** As indicated, it is not clear that Opperman has actually been arrested. His removal from the bus may only be a brief detention. A reasonable person in Opperman's circumstances may likely believe that, once things have calmed down, he would be free to go on his way. If Opperman had been arrested, (uncertain under these facts) then it might be possible to view all subsequent activity as derivative of that illegality. But the chain of uncertainties grows too long and, therefore, under the choices given, answer (a) is plainly better.

- **Additional references**: *See* LaFave, Israel, King & Kerr, Criminal Procedure §§ 3.2(h), 9.3(d) (6th ed. 2017); Whitebread & Slobogin, Criminal Procedure: An Analysis of Cases and Concepts § 2.04 (7th ed. 2020).

40. The right answer is (d). In this question, the police obtained incriminating statements from the defendant without giving the required Miranda warnings. If that was all they did, then, although the government could not use the evidence in its case-in-chief, it could use the statements to impeach the defendant after he testified in his own behalf. *Harris v. New York*, 401 U.S. 222 (1971)(after defendant testified that he never made a sale of heroin to an undercover officer, prosecution allowed to impeach through statements obtained in violation of Miranda); *accord Oregon v. Hass,* 420 U.S. 714 (1975)(allowing the government to use

Miranda-violative statements to impeach the defendant even where the incriminating statements were obtained by ignoring the suspect's request for an attorney). The point of the impeachment exception is to deprive the defendant of the opportunity to use Miranda as a sword, instead of only as a shield. As the Supreme Court put it, a failure to give Miranda warnings is not "true" compulsion to speak, a violation of Miranda should not enable the defendant to commit perjury, and the police will remain sufficiently deterred from violating Miranda since the government will still lose the statements in its case in chief. Even though Miranda itself seemed to say that statements obtained contrary to its rules could not be used for any purpose, *Harris* illustrates that this principle has not taken root. **Answer (c) is, therefore, wrong.** In this question, however, the police did more than violate the rules of Miranda. The police also yelled at the suspect and threatened that, unless he confessed, he would be set up to be attacked by other inmates. In a similar context, the Supreme Court accepted the trial court's conclusion that the defendant's incriminating statements were involuntary and obtained in violation of Due Process of law. *Arizona v. Fulminante,* 499 U.S. 279 (1991) (government agent posing as an inmate with organized crime contacts presses the defendant to tell him about the murder of a child because, otherwise, he was not sure he could protect him from inmate violence in connection with the death). The Miranda impeachment exception is *not* available when a confession is involuntary. Indeed statements obtained in violation of Due Process voluntariness standards are not admissible for any purpose. *Mincey v. Arizona,* 437 U.S. 385 (1978). This is true coercion and a direct violation of Due Process of law, not a mere transgression of Miranda rules. So an involuntary statement may not be used, period. And this is true even if the statement is reliable (i.e., other evidence corroborates it) and even if the defendant may get away with perjury. **It follows that answers (a) and (b) which would allow the statements to be used if they were reliable or would expose perjury are incorrect. Answer (e) is contrary to the facts and is not a good pick.** The statement is reliable. As the facts state, the suspect gave full details "providing ample and unmistakable corroboration of his guilt."

- **Additional references**: *See* LaFave, Israel, King & Kerr, Criminal Procedure §§ 9.1, 9.6 (6th ed. 2017); Whitebread & Slobogin, Criminal Procedure: An Analysis of Cases and Concepts § 16.02 (7th ed. 2020).

41. **The right answer is (c).** Some basic courses in criminal procedure include the topic of bail. Others do not. If you have covered this, here is a question. If not, here is a brief exposure. The Eighth Amendment provides, "Excessive bail shall not be required." There is no absolute right to bail. There is only a guarantee that "bail shall not be excessive in those cases where it is proper to grant bail." *Carlson v. Landon,* 342 U.S. 524 (1952). Judges are given wide discretion in setting conditions on a defendant's pretrial release, and they may conclude that no conditions are adequate. But adequate for what? In other words, what are the legitimate purposes of setting conditions? For a long time, the courts acted as if the

singular purpose of setting bail was to assure the defendant's presence at trial. *E.g., Stack v. Boyle*, 342 U.S. 1 (1951) ("Since the function of bail is limited, the fixing of bail for any individual defendant must be based upon standards relevant to the purpose of assuring the presence of that defendant."). But, more recently, courts have also recognized that the pretrial release decision may be based on a determination that the defendant's release poses a danger to the community or to witnesses. **(Hence answer (d) is wrong.)** In *United States v. Salerno*, 481 U.S. 739 (1987), the Supreme Court upheld the federal Bail Reform Act of 1984 saying that pretrial detention to prevent harm to others was permissible. In so holding, the Court rejected the idea that pretrial detention was "punishment" under substantive due process. The objective of the detention was to protect the public (almost like a quarantine), and unlike prison inmates, detained defendants were held for relatively brief periods, usually in facilities and under conditions separate from and more agreeable than prisoners. Pretrial detention was, therefore, a regulatory not a punitive act. Nevertheless, the Court agreed that the government must have a compelling reason to restrict a defendant's freedom in this way and that there must be a hearing and a specific showing of a need to detain a defendant prior to trial. This is where the Massachusetts law falters. The statute automatically assumes that someone like Benny, charged with aggravated sexual battery on a minor, is a danger and may be detained. That is impermissible. Although rebuttable presumptions may be used, an individual determination needs to be made and a hearing held. Sometimes courts will not detain a defendant prior to trial but will impose a bail amount that the defendant is not able to meet. That is the case for Andy in this question. But if the bail is set for a proper purpose, such as assurance that the defendant will appear at trial, it will be upheld so long as it is rational. Here the court may properly conclude that the defendant's lack of community ties, unemployment, and the nature of the case against him require bail in the amount of $10,000. This is no more of a punishment than pretrial detention and, thus, **answer (b) is a poor choice.** (While not directly relevant to the correct answer, students should note that this question is about *constitutional* violations. If the question was about a *statutory* violation the result would differ. The facts indicate that the Massachusetts statute at issue is modeled after the Federal Bail Reform Act of 1984. Section 3142(c)(2) of the federal act actually does instruct courts that they may not impose financial conditions on the accused that result in pretrial detention.) Nor is bail set in an amount to assure the defendant's appearance at trial "excessive" under the Eighth Amendment. Bail "is not excessive merely because the defendant is unable to pay it." *Hodgdon v. United States*, 365 F.2d 679 (8th Cir. 1966). **Accordingly, answer (a) is wrong.** Nor is bail a fundamental right like a right to a lawyer or a right to a first appeal on an equal basis. Equal protection is not violated so long as the determination of bail is not irrational and the individual circumstances of each case are assessed (as opposed to a simple schedule of bail applied in a one-size-fits-all fashion. *See Ackies v. Purdy*, 322 F. Supp. 38 (S.D. Fla.

1970)(setting bail simply according to the nature of the offense is irrational)). **Thus, answer (e) has a good ring, but it overstates the equal protection standard for bail determinations.**

- **Additional references**: *See* LAFAVE, ISRAEL, KING & KERR, CRIMINAL PROCEDURE §§ 12.1–12.3 (6th ed. 2017); WHITEBREAD & SLOBOGIN, CRIMINAL PROCEDURE: AN ANALYSIS OF CASES AND CONCEPTS § 20.03 (7th ed. 2020).

42. **At least as of now the best answer is (d).** This question is based on *United States v. Arnold*, 533 F.3d 1003 (9th Cir. 2008) *cert. denied*, 555 U.S. 1176 (2009). The key to understanding this problem is having a working knowledge of the border search doctrine and the amount of individualized suspicion that is required for different types of border searches, namely, searches of people and searches of property. First, it is necessary to point out that searches of international passengers at American airports are considered border searches because they occur at the "functional equivalent of a border." *Almeida-Sanchez v. United States*, 413 U.S. 266 (1973) ("For . . . example, a search of the passengers and cargo of an airplane arriving at a St. Louis airport after a non stop flight from Mexico City would clearly be the functional equivalent of a border search."). Second, border searches are analyzed pursuant to the reasonableness clause of the Fourth Amendment because there is a per se special need (and therefore, no warrant is required). *United States v. Flores-Montano*, 541 U.S. 149 (2004) ("The Government's interest in preventing the entry of unwanted persons and effects is at its zenith at the international border."); *United States v. Ramsey*, 431 U.S. 606 (1977) ("[S]earches made at the border, pursuant to the longstanding right of the sovereign to protect itself by examining persons and property crossing into this country, are reasonable simply by virtue of the fact that they occur at the border."). The United States' inherent authority to protect its territorial integrity means that those who enter the country "must establish the right to enter and to bring into the country whatever he may carry." *Torres v. Puerto Rico*, 442 U.S. 465 (1979). This includes containers. **Answer (a) is wrong** because "[t]he luggage carried by a traveler entering the country may be searched at random by a customs officer . . . no matter how great the traveler's desire to conceal the contents may be." *United States v. Ross*, 456 U.S. 798 (1982). A caveat: the Supreme Court has also indicated that reasonable suspicion is required when the Fourth Amendment interests of human dignity are implicated, such as a search of a person's "alimentary canal." *United States v. Montoya de Hernandez*, 473 U.S. 531 (1985). As for searches of property at the border, however, no individualized suspicion is required unless the search reaches a certain threshold of offensiveness or destructiveness, neither of which is present here. *Cf. Flores-Montano* (holding that complete disassembly and reassembly of a car gas tank did not require particularized suspicion). The Court in *Arnold* rejected the argument that the search of the laptop required reasonable suspicion because they saw the search as a routine inspection of a container at a border and rejected that a sliding scale should be used depending on how "intrusive" the search of the property is.

[handwritten margin note: Scarcem Requirement of cell phone]

It should be noted, however, that the recent case of *Riley v. California*, 573 U.S. 373 (2014) (warrant needed to search contents of cell phone in search incident to arrest) may cast some doubt on this conclusion. The degree of intrusion into the wealth of personal data on a computer might be so extensive that the Court will require some particularized suspicion even in a border search. Here, nothing suggests that the search of Ashton's property was any more offensive to the Fourth Amendment than searches of other containers at the border. Thus, **answer (b) is wrong. Answer (c) is incorrect**. Although law enforcement agents usually need a warrant to seize personal property, containers may be seized pending issuance of a warrant if the agents have probable cause to believe that it holds contraband or evidence of a crime. *United States v. Place*, 462 U.S. 696 (1983). Here, the agents possessed probable cause and had a reasonable fear that allowing Ashton to leave with the computer would result in the destruction of evidence. **Answer (e) is also incorrect** because there is no expectation of privacy in contraband on a laptop during a border search, and it did not matter that Ashton did not take any affirmative measures to protect his privacy.

- **Additional references**: *See* LAFAVE, ISRAEL, KING & KERR, CRIMINAL PROCEDURE § 3.9(f) (6th ed. 2017); WHITEBREAD & SLOBOGIN, CRIMINAL PROCEDURE: AN ANALYSIS OF CASES AND CONCEPTS § 13.05 (7th ed. 2020).

ANSWER KEY EXAM II
CRIMINAL PROCEDURE MULTIPLE CHOICE QUESTIONS ANSWER KEY AND EXPLANATIONS

1. **Answer (a) is the best answer.** The essential question is whether Swaggart was in custody during his first visit to the police station. Once a suspect is in custody and is subject to interrogation, the requirements of *Miranda v. Arizona*, 384 U.S. 436 (1966) come into play. Under Miranda and its progeny, particularly *Edwards v. Arizona*, 451 U.S. 477 (1981), once a suspect requests counsel, as Swaggart unequivocally did here, all questioning must cease, and any incriminating statements obtained in the absence of counsel are inadmissible. But Miranda is inapplicable because Swaggart was not in custody. To determine whether a suspect is in custody, courts view the totality of the suspect's circumstances and ask whether, from an objective point of view, a reasonable person would have understood himself to be under arrest. An accused is in custody when, even in the absence of formal arrest, law enforcement officials act or speak in a manner that conveys the message that they will not permit the suspect to leave and that he will be held in confinement. Contrariwise, questioning during a chance encounter is not custody for Miranda purposes. *See Bobby v. Dixon*, 565 U.S. 23 (2012). Important factors include the place of the interrogation, the length and nature of the questioning, and the demeanor of the officers. Although the questioning here took place in a small room, Swaggart initiated contact with the police and went voluntarily to the station. Most crucially, Swaggart was specifically told that he was not under arrest, and he did, in fact, leave the police station unhindered. Similar facts proved determinative in *Oregon v. Mathiason*, 429 U.S. 492 (1977). There the defendant voluntarily came to the police station, answered questions for about half an hour, and gave incriminating statements in response to false statements that police found his fingerprints at the crime scene. The Supreme Court found no custody and relied heavily on the fact that the defendant was informed that he was not under arrest and that he did, in fact, leave at the end of the interview. **Answer (b) is incorrect.** Interrogation for the purposes of Miranda includes questions and any words or actions which police know or should know are reasonably likely to elicit an incriminating response. *Rhode Island v. Innis*, 446 U.S. 291 (1980). Admonishing a suspect to "just tell the truth" is a classic interrogation technique and amounts to questioning for the purposes of Miranda. **Answer (c) is incomplete and, hence, wrong** because although the Detective's actions in allowing Swaggart to leave confirm the view that there was no custody, the issue of custody requires a look at all of the circumstances. A key ingredient

here was the fact that the police told Swaggart, at the outset, that he was not under arrest. **Answer (d) is wrong,** because, as with any other non-Miranda interview, the police can continue to talk with a suspect even if he states that he wants to talk to a lawyer. Of course, disregarding the suspect's request may be a factor in proving a Due Process (coercion) violation, but the facts are simply not strong enough here. **Answer (e) is incorrect,** because telling a suspect factual lies about the evidence against him is not, without more, enough to exclude an incriminating statement as involuntary and a violation of Due Process of law.

- **Additional references**: *See* LAFAVE, ISRAEL, KING & KERR, CRIMINAL PROCEDURE § 6.6(d) (6th ed. 2017); WHITEBREAD & SLOBOGIN, CRIMINAL PROCEDURE: AN ANALYSIS OF CASES AND CONCEPTS § 16.03(a)(3) (7th ed. 2020).

2. **The right answer is (b).** The Supreme Court has held that once a suspect has waived his Miranda rights and is answering questions, police need not cease questioning simply because the suspect makes equivocal references to a lawyer. *See, e.g., Davis v. United States*, 512 U.S. 452 (1994) (finding "maybe I should talk to a lawyer" insufficient to trigger the invocation of counsel prophylactic rule outlined in *Edwards v. Arizona*, 451 U.S. 477 (1981)); *United States v. Havlik*, 710 F.3d 818 (8th Cir. 2013) ("I guess you better get me a lawyer, then"—held insufficiently specific); *United States v. Wysinger*, 683 F.3d 784 (7th Cir. 2012) ("Do you think I should have a lawyer at this point?" was not an explicit invocation, but "Can I call one now?" was). The burden is on the suspect to clearly and unequivocally assert his right to have counsel present during interrogation. Although the Supreme Court has indicated that it is good practice for the police to clarify an ambiguous reference to counsel, they are not constitutionally obligated to do so. This explains why **answer (d) is incorrect**. In this question, when the suspect raised the matter of getting a lawyer, it was unclear whether he just wanted an attorney to discuss giving body samples or whether he wanted an attorney before answering any more questions. The police did then attempt to clarify what the suspect meant—even though they need not have done so. **Answer (a) is wrong** because it is irrelevant. Ascertaining whether a decent interval exists between two interrogation sessions matters in three situations. In the first situation, the interval length comes into play when there is a Miranda-defective confession and then the police seek to obtain a second confession after Miranda warnings are given. *Oregon v. Elstad*, 470 U.S. 298 (1985); *Missouri v. Seibert*, 542 U.S. 600 (2004). The second situation is a situation where a suspect has invoked a right to silence in the first encounter. Police are permitted to try later if they "scrupulously honor" the suspect's invocation. *Michigan v. Mosley*, 423 U.S. 96 (1975). Lastly, the length of the interval between interrogation sessions matters when the suspect has invoked the right to counsel. Police may reinterrogate a suspect after the suspect has invoked counsel if the suspect waives his Miranda rights and there has been a 14 day break in custody. *Maryland v. Shatzer*, 559 U.S. 98 (2010). None of these situations is applicable, so answer (a) has no bearing on this question. **Answer (c) is incorrect**

because it, too, is irrelevant. The issue in this question is whether there was a sufficient invocation of counsel and not whether any problem with the first encounter carried over to the second. Problems with one interrogation session may carry over into a second session. But here, there was no custody in the first encounter. **Answer (e) is incorrect** because, again, there was no custody in the first encounter, and it is ineffective for Miranda purposes to invoke a right to counsel prior to actual in-custody interrogation. A suspect may not invoke the Miranda right to counsel before custodial interrogation has begun or is imminent. *Montejo v. Louisiana*, 556 U.S. 778 (2009); *McNeil v. Wisconsin*, 501 U.S. 171 (1991); *United States v. Wyatt*, 179 F.3d 532 (7th Cir. 1999) (suspect could not invoke his Miranda right to counsel when he was not yet in custody; thus, there was no violation of *Edwards* when police officers initiated interrogation, administered warnings, and the defendant confessed voluntarily). Therefore, there could be no carry-over of the reference in the first, non-custodial situation to the second, custodial situation. In this question, the suspect's Miranda right to counsel rises or falls depending solely upon his actions in the second encounter.

- **Additional references**: *See* LAFAVE, ISRAEL, KING & KERR, CRIMINAL PROCEDURE § 6.9(g) (6th ed. 2017); WHITEBREAD & SLOBOGIN, CRIMINAL PROCEDURE: AN ANALYSIS OF CASES AND CONCEPTS § 16.03(e)(3)–(e)(4) (7th ed. 2020).

3. **The correct answer is (d).** Questions 3–5 are based directly on *United States v. Turner*, 157 F.3d 552 (8th Cir. 1998), and question 6 is based on the facts of *Turner,* although the issue posed was not resolved in that case. This question is a straightforward test of the appropriate standard of appellate review of the question of Miranda waiver. Although this issue is sometimes given short shrift, it is of considerable practical importance. A defendant's chance of overturning a trial court's ruling admitting a confession may turn on the applicable standard. As a general proposition, appellate courts defer to trial courts on findings of fact but make independent judgments on questions of law. Waiver questions, like the question of the voluntariness of confessions generally, present *mixed* questions of fact and law. For example, the defendant may say he was threatened to sign a waiver card; the police may deny any threats. This is a factual question. Even if everyone agrees, however, on what the police said or did, the parties may still argue over whether whatever was said or done rendered a waiver involuntary. This is a question of law. Only answer (d) states the standard of review accurately and completely. **Answer (a) is wrong** because it makes no distinction between the review of facts and the review of law. Factual conclusions will be sustained unless clearly erroneous, but questions of law are subject to *de novo* evaluation. **Answer (b) is similarly in error** because it, too, draws no distinction between appellate review of the facts and appellate review of the law. Again, questions of law are decided *de novo*, but questions of fact are entitled to deference. **Answer (c) is backwards.** Rather than evaluating the facts in a light most favorable to the defendant, appellate courts must show deference to the trial court's factual conclusions. **Answer (e) is**

wrong because it goes too far—appellate courts are not required to defer to the trial court's conclusions of law.

- **Additional references**: *See* LAFAVE, ISRAEL, KING & KERR, CRIMINAL PROCEDURE § 6.9 (6th ed. 2017); WHITEBREAD & SLOBOGIN, CRIMINAL PROCEDURE: AN ANALYSIS OF CASES AND CONCEPTS § 16.03(d) (7th ed. 2020).

4. **Answer (b) is correct.** To answer this question, you must understand that a valid Miranda waiver has two distinct dimensions. First, the waiver must be voluntary, that is, the product of a free and deliberate choice rather than the result of intimidation, coercion, or deception. Second, and independently, the waiver must be knowing and intelligent, that is, made by the suspect with awareness of the nature of the right being abandoned and the consequences of abandoning it. *Colorado v. Spring*, 479 U.S. 564 (1987). Although it is true "that coercive police activity [or state action] is a necessary predicate to the finding that a confession is not 'voluntary,'" *Colorado v. Connelly*, 479 U.S. 157 (1986), police coercion has no bearing on whether a waiver is knowing or intelligent. **Thus, answer (a) is wrong** because the issue of whether the suspect was competent to waive his Miranda rights does not depend on actions by the police. A suspect may be too young, too drunk, or too mentally impaired to understand the Miranda warnings, and the fact that the police did nothing to cause this incompetence is irrelevant. At the same time, the fact that police officers sought a waiver at a time when they *thought* a suspect was incompetent is also irrelevant to whether he was, in fact, competent to waive his rights. **Answer (e) is, therefore, also wrong**. What is relevant is whether, at the time of waiver, based on the totality of the circumstances, the suspect understood that he could remain silent, was entitled to have a lawyer present, and that anything he did say could be used against him. A full and complete appreciation of all of the consequences flowing from the nature and quality of the evidence in the case or anything beyond a simple understanding of the Miranda rights themselves is not required. Moreover, low intelligence, injury, intoxication, or any other condition does not *per se* invalidate a waiver—the condition must render a suspect incompetent to understand the Miranda rights. On the facts of the question, although Turner may have been impaired by PCP at the time of his confession and although he later exhibited bizarre behavior, the evidence shows that he possessed the mental capacity, *at the time*, to understand the Miranda warnings. **Answer (c) is incorrect** because, although Turner's initialing of the warnings is an indication that he was competent to understand them, it is not determinative and, therefore, not as complete an answer as choice (b). **Answer (d) is wrong** because neither PCP intoxication nor any other intoxication is *automatically* determinative—the suspect's actual competence must be judged under all of the circumstances.

- **Additional references**: *See* LAFAVE, ISRAEL, KING & KERR, CRIMINAL PROCEDURE § 6.9 (6th ed. 2017); WHITEBREAD & SLOBOGIN,

CRIMINAL PROCEDURE: AN ANALYSIS OF CASES AND CONCEPTS § 16.03(d) (7th ed. 2020).

5.   **Answer (b) is the right response.** Although Turner was in custody when he blurted out his personal information, not all statements made while in custody are products of interrogation. Interrogation is express questioning or words or actions that the police know or should know are reasonably likely to elicit an incriminating response. *Rhode Island v. Innis*, 446 U.S. 291 (1980). A voluntary statement made by a suspect, not in response to interrogation, is not barred by Miranda. Indeed Miranda specifically notes that volunteered statements are not within its strictures. In fact, knowing this, police sometimes say nothing to a suspect and happily take note of any information or statements a suspect feels an urge to share. In this question, the officer was merely driving away from the scene. Turner had previously been asked for his driver's license and registration and whether he was under the influence of alcohol or drugs. There was no further questioning and no attempt by the police to elicit further information. Turner's statements were spontaneous and, therefore, outside of the scope of Miranda. **Answer (a) could be correct but is not responsive to this question.** Routine booking questions are generally outside of Miranda's requirements, but there were no booking questions, as such, propounded on these facts. **Answer (c) has superficial appeal but should be rejected.** First, questions about one's name, age, height, social security number, and so on are outside of Miranda not because they are about "basic information which each individual constantly exposes to the public," but because such questions are not intended to elicit information for investigatory purposes. Second, again, there were no questions put to Turner; he volunteered his statement. **Answer (e) may be true as far as it goes, but it is an inadequate answer.** Even if someone first refuses to cooperate with the police, he or she may later validly volunteer information, as was the case here.

- **Additional references**: *See* LaFave, Israel, King & Kerr, Criminal Procedure § 6.7(d) (6th ed. 2017); Whitebread & Slobogin, Criminal Procedure: An Analysis of Cases and Concepts § 16.03(b) (7th ed. 2020).

6.   **Answer (b) is correct.** Under Fourth Amendment doctrine, a search incident to arrest of a vehicle is permissible in three situations. First, police may search a vehicle incident to arrest in those *rare circumstances* where they are unable to secure the arrestee. *Arizona v. Gant*, 556 U.S. 332 (2009). Second, if the individual is secured and has no way to access the vehicle at the time of the search, police may search the passenger compartment of a vehicle when it is reasonable to believe that evidence of the offense of arrest might be found in the vehicle. Probable cause is not required because courts deem vehicles to involve a diminished expectation of privacy. *Gant; California v. Carney*, 471 U.S. 386 (1985). Lastly, the Court in *Gant* reaffirmed that if police have reasonable suspicion that an individual (whether or not the arrestee) is dangerous and might access

the vehicle and gain control of weapons, they may search the car under *Michigan v. Long*, 463 U.S. 1032 (1983). Here, the first and third situations do not apply. Turner was in the police vehicle at the time of the search, and there is no indication the police thought he posed a danger. The question then is whether the search was permissible under the second justification: that police reasonably believed there was evidence of the offense of arrest in the vehicle. Although Turner was stopped for driving erratically, this was not the offense of arrest, **which explains why answer (d) is wrong**. Because the underlying offense of arrest was suspicion of drug use, it was reasonable to believe that the officers would find an illegal substance somewhere in the vehicle. The scope of the officer's search here was permissible because it did not extend beyond the passenger compartment. Remember, *Gant* does not authorize the search of a trunk, but only allows police to search the passenger compartment. Moreover, the police were authorized to search the bag because the drugs could have been stowed in there for safekeeping. *See United States v. Ross*, 456 U.S. 798 (1982). **Answer (e) is wrong** because the police did not need probable cause to search the bag. (The part of answer (e) that says the police lacked reasonable suspicion that Turner was armed and dangerous is correct.) **Answer (c) seems plausible but should be rejected**. Not only does the search incident doctrine more completely justify the officer's actions in this case, but stopping a person for driving erratically does not provide a reasonable suspicion to think that the individual is armed and dangerous—the necessary justification for a frisk. **Answer (a) errs** because the protective sweep doctrine "is a quick and limited search of a premises, incident to an arrest and conducted to protect the safety of police officers or others." *Maryland v. Buie*, 494 U.S. 325 (1990). Although the protective sweep doctrine is generally applied in a building, such as a home or office, for the narrow purpose of inspecting places in which a person may be hiding, the Supreme Court applied a similar protective search doctrine to vehicles in *Michigan v. Long*, 463 U.S. 1032 (1983) ("*Terry* permits limited examination of an area from which a person, who police reasonably believe is dangerous, might gain control of a weapon."). The police action here does not comfortably fit within this type of search because there is no indication that the officers thought Turner was armed and dangerous.

- **Additional references**: *See* LAFAVE, ISRAEL, KING & KERR, CRIMINAL PROCEDURE § 3.7(a)–(b) (6th ed. 2017); WHITEBREAD & SLOBOGIN, CRIMINAL PROCEDURE: AN ANALYSIS OF CASES AND CONCEPTS § 6.04(c) (7th ed. 2020).

7. **The correct choice is (c).** *Massiah v. United States*, 377 U.S. 201 (1964) stands for the proposition that police may not, consistent with the Sixth Amendment right to counsel, deliberately elicit incriminating statements from defendants without their lawyers present. Statements so obtained will be inadmissible as to the crime charged, and it does not matter that the police may have been acting pursuant to a valid warrant or that they were investigating other crimes as well. *Maine v. Moulton*, 474 U.S. 159 (1985). However, this Sixth Amendment exclusionary rule applies only to

statements relating to the crime charged, not to any other crimes which have not yet led to the filing of formal charges. As the Court expressed it, "The Sixth Amendment right is, however, offense specific." *McNeil v. Wisconsin*, 501 U.S. 171 (1991). Moreover, even if the mail fraud charge and the drug charge were somehow part of a single overall criminal scheme—for example if Mia were using the proceeds of the fraud to buy drugs—these would still be different offenses under the Court's narrow view of what is an "offense charged" under the Sixth Amendment. In *Texas v. Cobb*, 532 U.S. 162 (2001), an offense charged would include only that offense, a lesser included crime of that same offense, or any charge based on the same act. It would not include crimes "closely related to" or "inextricably bound up with" the offense charged. In this question, Mia has been indicted only on the mail fraud charge. She is simply a suspect in the drug distribution ring, and no Sixth Amendment right has attached to that crime yet. Thus, the incriminating statements about the mail fraud are inadmissible, but the statements related to the drug distribution ring are admissible. **Answer (a) is wrong and odd, all at the same time.** The facts say a valid tap was obtained. That means the invasion was valid without anyone's consent. The statements relating to the drug ring are admissible. **Answer (b) is wrong.** Even if the tap was valid, that satisfies only Fourth Amendment requirements. The Sixth Amendment must still be complied with. With probable cause and a warrant, the police were certainly authorized to listen in on the conversations, but the prosecutor may not use statements relating to the mail fraud charge. **Answer (d) would extend the protections of the Sixth amendment too far.** The protections of the Sixth are specific to the offense charged. Mia has only been charged with the mail fraud crime. No Sixth Amendment right has attached on the drug distribution matter because the state has not yet formally committed itself to prosecute her on that charge. She is not yet an "accused." **Answer (e) is silly.** Maybe there is some down-the-road issue that might arise in connection with the speedy trial guarantee, but that has no connection to whether the statements can or cannot be used.

- **Additional references**: *See* LAFAVE, ISRAEL, KING & KERR, CRIMINAL PROCEDURE § 6.4(b), (d) (6th ed. 2017); WHITEBREAD & SLOBOGIN, CRIMINAL PROCEDURE: AN ANALYSIS OF CASES AND CONCEPTS §§ 14.03, 16.04 (7th ed. 2020).

8. **The correct answer is (b).** The facts of this question are loosely drawn from *United States v. Mobley,* 40 F.3d 688 (4th Cir. 1994), *cert. denied*, 516 U.S. 1135 (1995). This question presents a close call, but among the choices offered, (b) is the best pick. The FBI agents obviously have Mobley in custody and, in response to his Miranda warnings, he has plainly invoked his right to counsel. Questioning him thereafter violates Miranda unless Mobley volunteers information or initiates further conversation about the criminal matter, neither of which is applicable here. So his statement about the gun will be inadmissible *unless* the "public safety exception" of *New York v. Quarles*, 467 U.S. 649 (1984), applies. In *Quarles* the police chased a suspect into a grocery store, apprehended him, cuffed and frisked him, and discovered that the gun holster he wore was empty.

Without administering Miranda warnings, they asked him where the gun was. The Supreme Court held that, "the need for answers to questions in a situation posing a threat to the public safety outweighs the need for the prophylactic rule protecting the Fifth Amendment's privilege against self-incrimination." The statements and the gun were admissible under the "public safety exception" to Miranda. Exactly when the exception applies is sometimes hard to know. In *Quarles*, the Court used words suggesting a narrow application ("The police in this case, in the very act of apprehending a suspect, were confronted with the immediate necessity of ascertaining the whereabouts of a gun . . . " and, "In recognizing a narrow exception" . . . police will act "instinctively," etc.), but lower courts have sometimes given the doctrine a broader reach. As the *Quarles* Court stated, however, there must be "an objectively reasonable need to protect the police or the public from any immediate danger." Here, as the majority of the Fourth Circuit said in *United States v. Mobley, supra*, there was no immediate danger. Mobley was under arrest, being led from the house, and the police had satisfied themselves that he was completely alone. "There is nothing that separates these facts from those of an ordinary and routine arrest scenario," the Fourth Circuit said. And, we could add, the fact that police officers would come later and conduct a search of the premises, and possibly find weapons, was also entirely routine. **Answer (a) presents an intriguing alternative but should be rejected.** The public safety exception in *Quarles* arose before any Miranda warnings were given. Here the warnings *were given* and the suspect asked for counsel. Does the public safety exception apply in those circumstances as well? There are several lower court opinions on point, and they say "yes." *See, e.g., United States v. Mobley, supra; United States v. DeSantis,* 870 F.2d 536 (9th Cir. 1989); *Trice v. United States,* 662 A.2d 891 (D.C. 1995). These courts conclude that the reasoning of *Quarles* applies with equal force even after Miranda rights are invoked and that the dangers faced by the police and the public could be equally as acute. **Answer (c) misstates the premise of the public safety exception and is wrong.** The exception does not depend on the actual motivations of the police or on the existence, or not, of their *subjective* safety concerns. The exception applies based on whether a reasonable police officer *in those circumstances* would have instinctively asked the questions in order to protect his safety or the safety of others. **Answer (d) is not completely unappealing, but it is not the best pick.** Some courts have recognized something like a spontaneous question exception to Miranda, such as the startled policeman, with suspect in tow, seeing body parts on the stove and exclaiming (and thereby asking) "My God, what is all of this!" But we have no equivalent facts here. **Answer (e) is well wide of the mark.** It suggests that there is a Miranda-free zone if the police are asking about firearms. No such rule exists.

- **Additional references**: *See* LaFave, Israel, King & Kerr, Criminal Procedure § 6.7(b) (6th ed. 2017); Whitebread & Slobogin, Criminal Procedure: An Analysis of Cases and Concepts § 16.03(c)(3) (7th ed. 2020).

9. **The correct answer is (b).** This question presents a scenario at the hinge of the "protective sweep" doctrine of *Maryland v. Buie,* 494 U.S. 325 (1990), and the line-drawing doctrine separating plain view observations from improper searches in *Arizona v. Hicks,* 480 U.S. 321 (1987). In *Buie,* the Court said that the police, incident to an arrest, may conduct a quick and limited search of the premises to protect the safety of the police officers or others. This action is limited to "a cursory visual inspection of those places in which a person might be hiding." And the sweep is not automatic. The police must have "reasonable, articulable suspicion that the house is harboring a person posing a danger to those on the arrest scene." Here the reasonable suspicion is a bit flimsy but could rest on the crime of arrest, namely, conspiracy to distribute drugs—obviously a dangerous enterprise involving at least one other person. But the focus of the question is on scope, not justification. The sweep could properly put the agent in Mobley's bedroom, but it could not justify a look into the drawer as no person could be hiding there. However, since a sweep properly put the agent in the bedroom, it enabled him to have a plain view look at the open drawer with the betting slips. If the agent had truly seen the slips without any other intrusion, they would be properly admissible. But this is where *Arizona v. Hicks* comes in. There police were properly inside a squalid apartment and, from their perspective, they could see stereo equipment that looked new and out of place in the circumstances. This view was insufficient to determine if the equipment was stolen, and the police then lifted the equipment and moved it around in order to be able to see the serial numbers. This action is analogous to the agent here pulling open the drawer. That movement, like the movement in *Hicks,* went beyond plain view and constituted a search. And since there was no probable cause to conduct the search at that point, it was impermissible. **Answer (a) is incorrect** because it posits that the justification for a protective sweep is probable cause. That is too strong. Reasonable suspicion is adequate. **Answer (c) is perhaps sensible sounding but it's wrong.** One assumes the risk that the police will see what is exposed to public view, but nothing more. Here, Mobley had the drawer open, true enough, but the agent had to pull it out in order to observe the contents. There was no assumed risk of *that.* **Answer (d) is wrong** because it contradicts the facts as they are given in the problem. Here is where careful reading pays a dividend. The facts say that the agent could see some papers protruding out of the night stand but adds, "pulling the drawer slightly open, was able to see betting slips . . ." Thus the agent had to manipulate the drawer to gain a view of what was inside. This is not the stuff of protective sweeps. **Answer (e) twists the protective sweep into a search for weapons and is thereby mistaken.** The police are allowed to sweep for people, not things.

- **Additional references**: *See* LaFave, Israel, King & Kerr, Criminal Procedure § 3.6(d), (f) (6th ed. 2017); Whitebread & Slobogin, Criminal Procedure: An Analysis of Cases and Concepts §§ 6.04(b), 10.03 (7th ed. 2020).

10. **The correct answer is (a).** Assuming, as this question does, that the statements about the whereabouts of the gun were illegally obtained and inadmissible, then the gun itself would be derived therefrom and, arguably, inadmissible as "fruit of the poisonous tree." *See Wong Sun v. United States*, 371 U.S. 471 (1963). However the Supreme Court has been steadily severing "mere" Miranda violations from derivative evidence rules. An early and leading case is *Oregon v. Elstad*, 470 U.S. 298 (1985). There the police secured incriminating statements from the defendant prior to giving him Miranda warnings. Later the police administered the warnings and obtained a second confession. The Supreme Court held that the initial statements were inadmissible but that the second confession was not tainted by the earlier Miranda violation and was admissible. In other words, a "mere" violation of Miranda, unaccompanied by actual coercion or involuntariness, could be "cured" by later warnings and a voluntary statement. Then in *New York v. Quarles*, 467 U.S. 649 (1984), the Court held that considerations of public safety outweighed a mere failure to give Miranda warnings and admitted both the unwarned statement and the physical evidence (a gun) derived therefrom. The majority did not specifically confront Justice O'Connor's separate view that courts should never suppress physical evidence derived from a mere Miranda violative statement. That changed in *United States v. Patane*, 542 U.S. 630 (2004). There a majority of five, though disagreeing in the rationale, ruled that failure to warn a suspect of his Miranda rights did not require suppression of physical evidence derived from his voluntary statements. That rule covers even this case where the Miranda violation was not simply a failure to warn, but a failure to end interrogation after invocation of counsel. Unless the interrogation after invocation amounts to securing an involuntary confession, there is still no violation of the Self-incrimination Clause (and hence nothing to deter according to the plurality) and, still, on balance, no need to keep reliable, probative, physical evidence from fact-finders (according to the concurring opinions of Justices Kennedy and O'Connor). **Answer (b) would have been the best choice** if derivative evidence rules applied to Miranda violations, but, after *Patane*, they do not. **Answer (c) focuses on the wrong issue and is an incorrect pick.** The issue is not voluntariness, *per se*, but the consequences of a Miranda violation. If the agents violated Miranda by asking questions, and if Mobley not only incriminated himself in response but also led them to physical evidence, the only question is whether and to what extent the exclusionary rule will apply to the gun. **Answer (d) sounds good but, after *Patane*, is wrong.** This answer tracks the reasoning of the principal dissent in *Patane*. **Answer (e) is right but incomplete.** It is correct to say that it was a violation of Miranda rules to ask Mobley questions after he requested counsel (assuming, for the moment, no public safety exception). But the key issue is what exclusionary consequences flow from this, and, after *Patane*, physical evidence derived from Miranda violative statements will not be excluded.

• **Additional references**: *See* LAFAVE, ISRAEL, KING & KERR, CRIMINAL PROCEDURE § 9.5 (6th ed. 2017); WHITEBREAD & SLOBOGIN,

EXAM PRO ON CRIMINAL PROCEDURE

CRIMINAL PROCEDURE: AN ANALYSIS OF CASES AND CONCEPTS § 16.05(c) (7th ed. 2020).

11. **The right choice is (a).** This question requires that you know the basic rules concerning so-called harmless errors. Not every criminal procedure course covers this matter, although some exposure is a good idea. Nevertheless, if you haven't covered it, consider this your very, very brief introduction. To begin, we note that it is possible for a legal system to follow a rule of automatic reversal whenever an appellate court determines that there was an error in the proceedings below. In fact, the United States once had such a system in place. Eventually, however, the Supreme Court determined that automatic reversal was extremely wasteful and unnecessarily time consuming, especially in circumstances where the evidence against the defendant was otherwise so overwhelming or in situations in which the error had no effect on the outcome of the trial. *See Chapman v. California*, 386 U.S. 18 (1967). States do vary in how they resolve the problem under state law. But if the error is based on the federal constitution, then a federal standard must be applied. Under federal law, there are two approaches to constitutional errors depending on the nature of the error. The first group of errors is comprised of errors that are "structural" in nature. Structural simply means that the error pervasively affects the trial itself. Structural errors include things like biased judges, *Tumey v. Ohio*, 273 U.S. 510 (1927), a total deprivation of the right to counsel at trial, *Gideon v. Wainwright*, 372 U.S. 335 (1963), and improper jury instructions on the prosecutor's burden of proof, *Sullivan v. Louisiana*, 508 U.S. 275 (1993). With structural errors there is a *per se* rule of reversal; in other words, courts do not assess the harmlessness of the error. "Trial" errors are the second group of constitutional errors. An example of a trial error is improperly admitted evidence (think of evidence gathered in violation of the Fourth Amendment). Because trial errors do not pervasively influence the entire trial proceeding and are more easily pinpointed than structural errors, the harmless error rule applies. The harmless error rule is premised on the idea that an appellate court can determine the level of harm caused by the error below. Trial errors are reversible on appeal *unless* the government can prove that the error was harmless beyond a reasonable doubt. *Chapman v. California, supra.* Precisely what harmless beyond a reasonable doubt means is not perfectly clear. The factors include: whether the other evidence was overwhelming, *Carella v. California*, 491 U.S. 263 (1989)), whether the dichotomy between structural and trial errors is appropriate, and whether, even if appropriate, certain issues should fall on one side or the other. Each of these factors has been vigorously contested among the Supreme Court justices. *See, e.g., Arizona v. Fulminante*, 499 U.S. 279 (1991) (5–4 opinion holding that admission of an involuntary confession was not *per se* reversible but, rather subject to harmless error analysis). In the instant case, the mistaken admission of evidence is a trial error, not a structural error. Therefore, the harmless error analysis applies and only answer (a) states the correct standard. **Answer (b) is incorrect** because it assumes that all constitutional errors

are *per se* reversible, but no such rule exists. **Answer (c) treats the error as pervasive but misapprehends what that means in terms of the applicable doctrine.** Despite how evidence was obtained, using it is still just a matter of the improper admission of evidence. And the Court deems such a problem to be a "trial error." Again, *Arizona v. Fulminante, supra,* is instructive. There, the four dissenters argued, among other things, that some errors, like the admission of evidence of an involuntary confession, must be grounds for *per se* reversal because they offend our basic notions about how police may gather evidence. The majority looked past such a rationale saying that the cause of the error was not determinative. The only question was whether the error was of such a nature that we should assess its impact in the context of the entire trial or whether, contrariwise, it was so pervasive as to infect the entirety of the proceedings. If the error was of the former kind, which the majority ruled it was (while noting, however, that because of the impact that confessions have at trial, erroneous admissions of confessions will rarely be harmless), then it was subject to harmless error analysis. **Answers (d) and (e) state the wrong test and misallocate the burden of proof.**

- **Additional references**: *See* LAFAVE, ISRAEL, KING & KERR, CRIMINAL PROCEDURE § 27.6 (6th ed. 2017); WHITEBREAD & SLOBOGIN, CRIMINAL PROCEDURE: AN ANALYSIS OF CASES AND CONCEPTS § 29.05 (7th ed. 2020).

12. **The right answer is (d).** The key issue in this question concerns Officer Hunter's return to the house to retrieve the gun. Based on the homeowner's report and their own observations at the open window of the Mayberry house, Officers Gunny and Gander had probable cause to think that the fleeing burglars entered the window of the house and were then inside. In addition, the officers were excused from getting a warrant either because of hot pursuit of fleeing felons or, perhaps less persuasively, because the house may have been the residence of others who might then be in immediate danger. Thus, once inside, the two officers were in a place they were lawfully entitled to be, and they saw the gun in plain view on the table. They had probable cause to seize it then and there, but they asked that another officer pick it up later. The later entry into the house came after the emergency had ended, and there are no other facts offering an exception to the general requirement that police need a warrant to enter a home. **Answer (a) is fine as far as it goes, but it is inadequate** because it doesn't grapple with Officer Hunter's subsequent entry into the house without a warrant. It is that entry that renders seizure of the gun unlawful. **Answer (b) is effectively a restatement of (a) and is also wrong. Answer (c) fails** because it underestimates the strong evidence of probable cause. The fresh complaint and information provided by the neighbor together with the incriminating evidence found at the base of the open window, including a TV, gave rise to a fair probability that the burglars had just entered the house. **Answer (e) is wrong** because it suggests a course of action that would be appropriate in the absence of an emergency, but here there was an emergency sufficient to justify a warrantless entry.

- **Additional references**: *See* LaFave, Israel, King & Kerr, Criminal Procedure § 3.7(f) (6th ed. 2017); Whitebread & Slobogin, Criminal Procedure: An Analysis of Cases and Concepts § 10.02 (7th ed. 2020).

13. **Answer (d) is the right response.** As the incorrect answers demonstrate, there is no Fourth, Fifth, or Sixth Amendment violation here, nor any Due Process errors relating to the eye witness identification. The photo was validly taken of an arrestee in custody, and the identification was neither unnecessarily suggestive nor likely to lead to mistaken identification. **Answer (a) is wrong** because, although there was a violation of Kenny's Miranda rights when officers questioned him after his request for counsel, there was no connection between that error and any other evidence gathered by the police including the pretrial identification; to apply the exclusionary rule to the pretrial identification would not vindicate any rights of Kenny's and would simply be a windfall for him. **Answer (b) is wrong** because the identification procedure was not suggestive. There are no facts indicating that the police did anything other than make a neutral presentation of photos (i.e., no comments like, "take a good look at the picture on the end"). There were multiple photos, and the persons in the photos had the same general features as Kenny. And even if the identification was suggestive (which it was not), the identification evidence would still be admissible because it was arguably reliable under the factors set out in *Manson v. Brathwaite*, 432 U.S. 98 (1977). Although the circumstances were not ideal because Bobbie had only a brief and traumatic opportunity to view Kenny, she did see him in afternoon light, gave an accurate description, displayed a high level of certainty upon viewing the photos, and there was only a brief period of time between the crime and the identification. **Answer (c) is mistaken** because Kenny had no right to have counsel present when Bobbie viewed the photos. Kenny had not been formally charged, and his Sixth Amendment right to counsel had not yet attached. *Kirby v. Illinois*, 406 U.S. 682 (1972). In any event, Kenny was not present at the identification, and so, even if the Sixth Amendment had attached (but it had not), Kenny was not present and, therefore, there was no confrontation between Kenny and the state requiring the assistance of counsel. *United States v. Ash*, 413 U.S. 300 (1973). **Answer (e) is wrong** because whether Kenny consents to having his photo taken is irrelevant. He is properly in custody and the taking of a photo works no additional intrusion under the Fourth Amendment; a photo is a display of physical characteristics and non-testimonial and, therefore, no Fifth Amendment right is implicated, and no Sixth Amendment right to counsel has yet attached. Kenny has no rights to waive, and his consent matters not at all.

    - **Additional references**: *See* LaFave, Israel, King & Kerr, Criminal Procedure § 7.4 (6th ed. 2017); Whitebread & Slobogin, Criminal Procedure: An Analysis of Cases and Concepts § 18.04 (7th ed. 2020).

14. **The correct answer is (a).** The rule here is straightforwardly set out in *Edwards v. Arizona*, 451 U.S. 477 (1981): "... when an accused has invoked his right to have counsel present [as is the case in this problem] ... a valid waiver of that right cannot be established by showing that he responded to further police-initiated custodial interrogation even if he has been advised of his rights. ... [H]aving expressed his desire to deal with the police only through counsel, [an accused] is not subject to further interrogation by the authorities until counsel has been made available to him, unless the accused himself initiates further communication [not the case here]." Once Kenny invoked his right to counsel under Miranda, police were not permitted to reinterrogate him, no matter how amiable the atmosphere, whether he was reread his rights, or whether the officers knew of his invocation. **Answer (b) states the right result but offers the wrong reason.** Miranda does not require that police ask only about the charges under which the suspect was arrested, and police need not give a suspect notice of the matters they plan to ask about. *Colorado v. Spring*, 479 U.S. 564 (1987). If, after proper Miranda warnings, Kenny had waived his rights, the questioning could properly include unrelated offenses. The problem here, of course, is that Kenny did not waive his rights. **Answer (c) is incorrect.** Although truly volunteered statements are always admissible under Miranda, answers given in response to police questioning, as here, are not volunteered. There is a distinction between voluntary statements, which are statements obtained by the police without *undue* pressure, i.e., statements which are not coerced in violation of Due Process of law, and volunteered statements which are simply offered up to the police on the suspect's own initiative. Here, even though the atmosphere was not hostile, Kenny was responding to police questioning when he made incriminating statements and, hence, his statements were not volunteered. **Answer (d) is wrong** because, under cases interpreting the requirements of Miranda, it is irrelevant that the officers who questioned Kenny were unaware that he had requested counsel. The burden is on the officer seeking to interrogate to determine if a request for counsel has been made. Once counsel is requested, the Court has applied a bright line, categorical rule: no further interrogation unless the suspect initiates conversation or counsel is present. *Minnick v. Mississippi*, 498 U.S. 146 (1990). **Answer (e) is incorrect** because it assumes that Miranda protections apply only to the charges on which the suspect was arrested. This is a mistake. Fifth Amendment Miranda rules are not specific to the charges of arrest in the same way as Sixth Amendment right to counsel rules are specific to the offense charged. Once a suspect is in custody, he is in custody, and if the police seek to interrogate, Miranda rules must be followed.

- **Additional references**: *See* LAFAVE, ISRAEL, KING & KERR, CRIMINAL PROCEDURE § 6.9(f) (6th ed. 2017); WHITEBREAD & SLOBOGIN, CRIMINAL PROCEDURE: AN ANALYSIS OF CASES AND CONCEPTS § 16.03(e)(2) (7th ed. 2020).

15. **The right answer is (e).** A correct response to this question requires that you know the different ways that the Fifth and Sixth Amendments

apply to interrogation of suspects and defendants. The Sixth Amendment right to counsel arises upon formal charge, which is the case here since Bugsy was "arraigned" on the charge of grand larceny. After the right to counsel has attached, the government may not attempt to elicit incriminating responses from the accused surreptitiously through undercover agents. *Massiah v. United States*, 377 U.S. 201 (1964). So, it might seem that the government's attempts to elicit incriminating responses related to a possible kidnapping charge against Bugsy would violate her Sixth Amendment rights. But they don't. This is because Sixth Amendment rights are "offense specific." That is, the right to counsel is the right to have a lawyer at your side in critical confrontations with the government, including interrogations, but only as to those charges where the government has signaled, through formal charges, that it is prepared to prosecute you. It is only as to those matters actually charged that you and the government have become adversaries, entitling you to have counsel to meet the case against you. *McNeil v. Wisconsin*, 501 U.S. 171 (1991). Since Bugsy's right to counsel attached only with respect to the charge of grand larceny, the Sixth Amendment was not violated by any attempts to secure incriminating statements on the uncharged crime of kidnapping. **Both answers (a) and (c) are wrong** because they state that Bugsy's Sixth Amendment rights were violated. Fifth Amendment rights are not offense specific. Once a suspect in custody indicates that he or she desires a lawyer, no questioning related to the crime of arrest *or any other crime* may occur in the absence of counsel. The Supreme Court has said that a suspect facing custodial interrogation who requests counsel is saying that she feels unable to face an interrogation alone and that that insecurity relates to the pressures and compulsions of interrogation, irrespective of the crimes inquired about. So, it might seem that the government's attempts to secure incriminating statements from Bugsy about a kidnapping, while she was in custody and after she requested counsel at her arraignment, would violate her Miranda rights. But they don't. There are several reasons why Miranda does not apply to this set of facts. First, the request for counsel at an arraignment is not equivalent to requesting counsel when facing interrogation. Under similar facts, the Court has held that a person charged with a crime may be seeking representation with respect to that crime but that that request says nothing about what they are willing to do *when actually faced with interrogation. McNeil v. Wisconsin*, 501 U.S. 171 (1991). Miranda counsel rules only apply when the suspect expresses a desire for counsel when actually faced with custodial interrogation by the police. That was not the case here. Second, Bugsy was not aware that she was talking to a government agent. In similar circumstances, the Court said that Miranda is not applicable "when the suspect is unaware that he is speaking to a law enforcement officer." *Illinois v. Perkins*, 496 U.S. 292 (1990). In such circumstances, the custodial pressures identified in Miranda, the "interplay" of custody plus interrogation, are simply not at work. Third, being held in jail or prison is not necessarily custody *for the purposes of Miranda*. Of course a person in jail or prison is actually in custody in the very real sense, but, depending on the particular circumstances, the mere fact of actual imprisonment is not determinative of the Miranda issue. *Cf. Maryland v. Shatzer*, 559 U.S. 98 (2010) ("Without minimizing the harsh realities of incarceration, we think lawful imprisonment imposed upon conviction of a crime does not create the coercive pressures identified in *Miranda* . . . suspects who have previously been convicted of crime live in prison."). Otherwise, any question to a prisoner regarding criminal activity would trigger Miranda. Although prisoners do have a right to be warned when the government is investigating a crime (or crimes) unrelated to the crime of incarceration, there is no *per se* finding of custody; rather, the inquiry is whether the prison officials' (or other government agents') conduct would cause a reasonable person to believe that his or her freedom of movement had been further diminished. *Mathis v. United States*, 391 U.S. 1 (1968) (custody found when prisoner was subjected to direct questioning about a criminal offense). **Hence answer (b) is incorrect.** Bugsy's Fifth Amendment rights were not violated because he had no idea that he was being interrogated and thus, the pressures inherent in custodial interrogation were not present. *Illinois v. Perkins, supra.* **Answer (d) is wrong because there is no issue of compulsion raised by the facts**.

- **Additional references**: *See* LAFAVE, ISRAEL, KING & KERR, CRIMINAL PROCEDURE §§ 6.4–6.6 (6th ed. 2017); WHITEBREAD & SLOBOGIN, CRIMINAL PROCEDURE: AN ANALYSIS OF CASES AND CONCEPTS § 16.04 (7th ed. 2020).

16. **The best answer is (a).** The right answer emerges when the facts related to the eyewitness identification are isolated from the other circumstances presented in the question. First, although Hunter asked for a lawyer at the line-up, none was constitutionally required. Hunter had only been arrested, not formally charged, and his Sixth Amendment right of counsel had not yet attached. *Kirby v. Illinois*, 406 U.S. 682 (1972). Thus **answer (c) which assumes Hunter's request for counsel was relevant, and answer (b) which assumes there was a right to counsel but it was waived, are both wrong.** Second, even though police should have stopped questioning Hunter when he invoked his right to have counsel present, placing Hunter in a line-up was not a form of interrogation, *Montejo v. Louisiana*, 556 U.S. 778 (2009), nor was the line-up identification in any sense derivative of the prior questioning. Not only did the police learn nothing, but a mere violation of Miranda, unaccompanied by any "real" coercion, was not in any way causally connected to the line-up. One may also offer the argument, though it is debatable, that there is no violation of Miranda until illegally obtained statements are obtained and used and, since no statements were obtained here, there is no wrong for the line-up to be derivative of. **Hence answer (d) is incorrect.** Finally, it is well settled that obtaining a suspect's voice prints or requiring him to speak words in a line-up is a display of physical characteristics, and like all displays of physical characteristics, is not "testimonial" and thus, not protected by the Fifth Amendment privilege against self-incrimination. *United States v. Wade*, 388 U.S. 218 (1967); *see*

also Schmerber v. California, 384 U.S. 757 (1966). **Thus, answer (e) is not a sensible pick**.

- **Additional references**: *See* LAFAVE, ISRAEL, KING & KERR, CRIMINAL PROCEDURE §§ 7.2(b), 7.3(b) (6th ed. 2017); WHITEBREAD & SLOBOGIN, CRIMINAL PROCEDURE: AN ANALYSIS OF CASES AND CONCEPTS §§ 17.02(b), 17.04(b) (7th ed. 2020).

17. **The correct choice is (e).** The issue of counsel is irrelevant in this question. First, the identification was not custodial interrogation; therefore, the Fifth Amendment right to counsel did not apply. Second, there were no formal charges filed against Hunter yet and, therefore, the Sixth Amendment right to counsel did not apply. The only question is whether this identification amounted to a violation of Hunter's due process rights. Identifications which are unnecessarily suggestive and which, under the totality of the circumstances, are substantially likely to lead to irreparable misidentification are unfair and offend due process of law. *See Foster v. California*, 394 U.S. 440 (1969). Here, the identification was unnecessarily suggestive because there was no exigency or emergency. Moreover, the witness viewed only one suspect thus pointing the finger of guilt at him. The Supreme Court has made clear that the question for admissibility under the Due Process Clause is whether the witness or victim had an accurate picture of the accused in his or her mind *before* the suggestiveness occurred. *Neil v. Biggers*, 409 U.S. 188 (1972). Here, the identification will be admitted *if* a court is satisfied that Mr. Jackson had an accurate picture of Hunter in his mind prior to the impermissibly suggestive techniques utilized by the police. *See Manson v. Brathwaite*, 432 U.S. 98 (1977) (reaffirming the totality of the circumstances approach to assess reliability of the identification and reiterating the factors, initially laid out in *Biggers*, to be considered). Only answer (e) captures the right test to be applied in such circumstances. **Answer (c) is a mistake** because it posits that the identification was necessary. Although courts have ruled that on-the-scene, one person show-ups (which involve bringing the victim or witness to view the suspect near the time of the criminal act) are necessary (and therefore not a violation of due process), the identification must be close in time to the criminal act. *See, e.g., Brisco v. Ercole*, 565 F.3d 80 (2d Cir. 2009) (show-up immediately after the crime was not unnecessarily suggestive: "If no identification was made at the showup, the officers could resume their search for the offender"); *United States v. Martinez*, 462 F.3d 903 (8th Cir. 2006) ("Police officers need not limit themselves to station house line-ups when an opportunity for a quick, on-the-scene identification arises. Such identifications are essential to free innocent suspects and to inform the police if further investigation is necessary. Absent special elements of unfairness, prompt on-the-scene confrontations do not entail due process violations."). An identification more than two or three hours past the event, or as here, the next day, is too long to come within the rule (or its rationale). **Answers (a), (b), and (d) are all wrong** because, in one way or another, they assume that a right to counsel was or, under better circumstances, could have been applicable. However, because formal

proceedings had not been initiated, the right to counsel had not yet attached.

- **Additional references**: *See* LAFAVE, ISRAEL, KING & KERR, CRIMINAL PROCEDURE § 7.4(f) (6th ed. 2017); WHITEBREAD & SLOBOGIN, CRIMINAL PROCEDURE: AN ANALYSIS OF CASES AND CONCEPTS § 18.03 (7th ed. 2020).

18. **The right answer is (c).** Hunter was in custody, and the remarks of Detective Maddie were interrogation because they were in the nature of an accusation, and thus, words the police should have known were likely to elicit an incriminating response. *Rhode Island v. Innis*, 446 U.S. 291 (1980). Therefore, Miranda was applicable, and given that Hunter had already invoked his right to counsel, police were permitted to interrogate Hunter only with his counsel present. **Answer (a) is a trap.** It may be true that Hunter *could* argue that the words were not incriminatory, but he doesn't want to be in that position. And according to Miranda, he doesn't have to be. As *Miranda* explicitly states, "no distinction may be drawn between inculpatory statements and statements alleged to be merely 'exculpatory.' If a statement made were in fact truly exculpatory it would, of course, never be used by the prosecution." **Answer (b) is partly right but, consequently, partly wrong.** There was no right to have a lawyer at the line-up because the right to counsel had not yet attached. That's the right part (and the reason why **answer (d), which reaches the opposite conclusion, has no redeeming value).** But answer (b) portrays Detective Maddie's comments as inconsequential remarks. That's the wrong part. The detective's comments were the functional equivalent of interrogation. **Answer (e) stumbles** because it erroneously assumes the line-up was unconstitutional when, in fact, it was fine.

- **Additional references**: *See* LAFAVE, ISRAEL, KING & KERR, CRIMINAL PROCEDURE § 6.7 (6th ed. 2017); WHITEBREAD & SLOBOGIN, CRIMINAL PROCEDURE: AN ANALYSIS OF CASES AND CONCEPTS § 16.03(b) (7th ed. 2020).

19. **The best answer is (c).** Once a suspect becomes a defendant, the right to counsel attaches on the crime charged. When a defendant faces the government's decision to prosecute, "whether by way of formal charge, preliminary hearing, indictment, information, or arraignment," he faces "the prosecutorial forces of society, and [becomes] immersed in the intricacies of substantive and procedural criminal law." *Massiah v. United States*, 377 U.S. 201 (1964). He is entitled to meet his adversary, the State, with a lawyer at his side. However, waiver is possible. Waiver at trial or trial-type proceedings requires a stringent application of the voluntary, knowing, and intelligent standard. *Faretta v. California*, 422 U.S. 806 (1975). But waiver in the context of police-initiated questioning is easier. In *Patterson v. Illinois*, 487 U.S. 285 (1988), the Supreme Court considered waiver in the situation where a defendant had been indicted but did not have counsel and had not requested counsel. In that circumstance, the Court said, waiver was effective where police informed the defendant that he had been indicted and read him the Miranda

warnings. Since the defendant did not then invoke his right to a lawyer and agreed to talk to the police, his Sixth Amendment right was deemed waived. Here, however, Hunter requested counsel on two different occasions. How do those invocations affect the outcome here? Well, they don't—the waiver is valid. The first time Hunter invoked his Fifth Amendment or Miranda right to counsel, he was in custodial interrogation. However, by the time Officer Riley and Hunter conversed on the street, Hunter was no longer in custody. Although Hunter was unmistakably interrogated, he was not interrogated while in custody. Miranda and the prophylactic rules protecting the Miranda right only come into play when a suspect is subjected to custodial interrogation. Once the inherently coercive pressures of custodial interrogation are removed, there is no need to continue protecting the suspect in the same fashion. The aforementioned explains why **answer (d) is wrong**. Hunter's second invocation of counsel (at his arraignment) has no bearing on the issue because, after *Montejo v. Louisiana*, 556 U.S. 778 (2009), police may approach accused individuals who have requested an attorney at their arraignments or other similar proceedings and seek a knowing and voluntary waiver. That is precisely what happened here. Because Hunter was not in custody, the inherently coercive pressures that worried the Miranda Court simply did not exist and new Miranda warnings were not required. **Answer (b) is incorrect.** Whether or not Hunter was represented, Hunter validly waived his right to have counsel present. Represented defendants may waive their right to counsel, and this decision need not be counseled. *Michigan v. Harvey*, 494 U.S. 344 (1990). **Answer (e) is wrong** because the case supporting this answer, *Michigan v. Jackson*, 475 U.S. 625 (1986), was specifically overruled by *Montejo*. Police may deliberately elicit information from an accused provided a valid waiver is ultimately found. **Answer (a) is incorrect** because "decent intervals" in this context refers to how long the police must wait before they may reinitiate questioning after a suspect has invoked his right to silence under the Fifth Amendment. There is no Fifth Amendment issue here as Hunter was not in custody.

- **Additional references**: *See* LAFAVE, ISRAEL, KING & KERR, CRIMINAL PROCEDURE § 6.4(f) (6th ed. 2017); WHITEBREAD & SLOBOGIN, CRIMINAL PROCEDURE: AN ANALYSIS OF CASES AND CONCEPTS § 16.04 (7th ed. 2020).

20. **The right answer is (a).** At the time Hunter spoke to Officer Riley, there was no formal charge or commencement of formal proceedings on that charge, and therefore, no Sixth Amendment right to counsel had attached *on that charge*. The Sixth Amendment right is specific to the offense charged. *McNeil v. Wisconsin*, 501 U.S. 171 (1991). And, at the time Hunter spoke to Officer Riley, he was out on bail and no longer in custody, and therefore, no Miranda issue was presented. **All of the remaining answers are in error** because each, in its own way, erroneously assumes that either the Fifth or Sixth Amendment is implicated on these facts.

- **Additional references**: *See* LAFAVE, ISRAEL, KING & KERR, CRIMINAL PROCEDURE § 6.4(e) (6th ed. 2017); WHITEBREAD & SLOBOGIN, CRIMINAL PROCEDURE: AN ANALYSIS OF CASES AND CONCEPTS § 16.04 (7th ed. 2020).

21. **The best answer is (a).** This question is answered by the Supreme Court's ruling in *Arizona v. Gant*, 556 U.S. 332 (2009). In that case, the Court set out to clarify the scope of the search incident to arrest doctrine as applied to automobile searches. The Court altered the once bright-line rule of *New York v. Belton*, 453 U.S. 454 (1981), which permitted police, pursuant to the arrest of a recent occupant, to search a vehicle (but not the trunk) regardless of whether the arrestee could access the interior of the automobile. *Gant* held that *Belton* "does not authorize a vehicle search incident to a recent occupant's arrest after the arrestee has been secured and cannot access the interior of the vehicle." This makes sense in light of the origin of the search incident to arrest doctrine, which was designed to protect police safety and prevent the destruction of evidence. *Chimel v. California*, 395 U.S. 752 (1969). The *Gant* decision further held that because of "circumstances unique to the automobile context," police may search incident to arrest "when it is reasonable to believe that evidence of the offense of arrest might be found in the vehicle." In the instant case, Barney was safely secured in the back of the patrol car and thus, could not reach anything in the car, including the gun in the glove compartment. Moreover, there is no evidence at all that Barney was drinking in the car. In fact, he said that he had just departed a party where there was a lot of liquor. Thus, neither justification permitting a search incident to arrest was present, making **answer (d) incorrect**. (The fact that there was no evidence that Barney was drinking in the car also explains why **answer (e) is off the mark**. Given the facts provided, there was no reason to think that liquor could be found in the car.) **Answer (b) errs in its scope.** If the police are justified in conducting a search incident to arrest, the police may search the passenger compartment, all containers found in the passenger compartment, the glove compartment and similar spaces, whether locked or not, in the passenger compartment. **Answer (c) could be right if the facts were different** (which, to quote former Chief Justice Rehnquist, is like saying if my aunt were a man, she would be my uncle). There are no facts here to raise the issue of a protective frisk as there is no indication that the police believed Barney was dangerous. *See Michigan v. Long*, 463 U.S. 1032 (1983).

    - **Additional references**: *See* LAFAVE, ISRAEL, KING & KERR, CRIMINAL PROCEDURE § 3.7 (6th ed. 2017); WHITEBREAD & SLOBOGIN, CRIMINAL PROCEDURE: AN ANALYSIS OF CASES AND CONCEPTS § 6.04(c) (7th ed. 2020).

22. **The correct answer is (a).** The rule of *Arizona v. Gant*, 556 U.S. 332 (2009), which permits the police to search the interior of a vehicle as a search incident to arrest provided certain conditions are satisfied, does not include the trunk. Of course, the police are permitted to argue that, in the particular circumstances of an individual case, the trunk *could be*

within the arrestee's grab or reach area. The Court in *Gant* did recognize that there might be "rare circumstances" where police could not secure an arrestee. But that strategy is unavailing here since Barney was apparently infirm, sitting in the police car, and handcuffed. The marijuana will be excluded. **Answer (d) misses the limitation of *Gant* and is wrong.** The premise of the search incident to arrest doctrine is that it is necessary to protect law enforcement officials and/or prevent evidence from being destroyed. *Chimel v. California*, 395 U.S. 752 (1969). If there is no realistic possibility of the contents of the trunk posing a danger or being destroyed, there is no reason for the police to rifle through the trunk's contents. **Answer (b) is a three dimensional loser.** First, there is no evidence of weapons or a fear of weapons and thus, no basis to invoke a protective frisk rationale. Second, the frisk idea, even if it were applicable, would not ordinarily extend to the trunk. *Michigan v. Long*, 463 U.S. 1032 (1983). And third, if the frisk were justified and if there were some exceptional circumstances permitting it to extend to the trunk, the police *could* examine any containers that might contain a weapon. **There is no factual basis for (c), and it is wrong.** There is no evidence to give rise to probable cause to think that either weapons or alcohol were in the car. All we know is that Barney had been drinking at a party. **Answer (e) is an overstatement.** Inventory searches of cars may indeed be a legal windfall for the police if a person is arrested in an automobile. However, the police must be acting pursuant to a pre-existing policy of the department that provides standards for constraining officer discretion as to whether and how to conduct such searches. *Florida v. Wells*, 495 U.S. 1 (1990). Thus, police may not "always" be able to conduct such a search. *See, e.g., United States v. Proctor*, 489 F.3d 1348 (D.C. Cir. 2007) ("Because the officers failed to follow the MPD standard procedure, the impoundment of Proctor's vehicle was unreasonable and thus violated the Fourth Amendment.").

- **Additional references**: *See* LAFAVE, ISRAEL, KING & KERR, CRIMINAL PROCEDURE §§ 3.5(e), 3.7 (6th ed. 2017); WHITEBREAD & SLOBOGIN, CRIMINAL PROCEDURE: AN ANALYSIS OF CASES AND CONCEPTS §§ 6.04(c), 13.07 (7th ed. 2020).

23. **Answer (e) is correct.** Barney was properly ordered out of the car. *Pennsylvania v. Mimms*, 434 U.S. 106 (1977) (it is reasonable to order persons out of car since the intrusion on a driver already stopped is *de minimus*, and the danger to officers in traffic stops is significant). Moreover, the *Mimms* rule is categorical and police need not take the age or physical condition of the driver into account. Consequently, the police were in a lawful position to observe the securities which fell out of Barney's pocket. Thus, the police testimony is based on lawful, plain view observations and will be admissible. **Answer (a) is contrary to the rule announced in *Pennsylvania v. Mimms* and is wrong. Answers (b), (c), and (d) are, each in a different way, kind of silly.** Answer (b) suggests that there is some sort of grace period before police are allowed to look at dropped papers, an odd idea indeed. Answer (c) goes in the other direction and suggests that if one drops his papers, he must pick them up

immediately or they will be considered abandoned, a similarly odd idea. Abandonment requires something hardier than that, namely, an intent to abandon and to lay no further claim. Answer (d) calls securities "public documents," but they are no more public, if not exposed to public view, than other information about one's financial holdings.

- **Additional references**: *See* LAFAVE, ISRAEL, KING & KERR, CRIMINAL PROCEDURE § 3.2(b), (f), (h) (6th ed. 2017); WHITEBREAD & SLOBOGIN, CRIMINAL PROCEDURE: AN ANALYSIS OF CASES AND CONCEPTS §§ 10.03, 11.03(b) (7th ed. 2020).

24. **The right answer is (b).** The facts state that Barney was already under arrest for reckless driving at the time Officer Kojak asked him if he had been drinking. Being placed under arrest is custody for purposes of Miranda as Barney was deprived of his freedom of action and movement. *See Orozco v. Texas*, 394 U.S. 324 (1969). Furthermore, the question about whether Barney had been drinking was reasonably likely to elicit an incriminating response, and was thus interrogation. *See Rhode Island v. Innis*, 446 U.S. 291 (1980). As such, **answer (c), which asserts that there was no custody and answer (a), which denies the question was interrogation, are both wrong**. The elicited statement is inadmissible. **Answer (d) is incorrect** because it mistakenly assumes there was an illegal arrest. Barney was arrested for reckless driving. The officer had probable cause based on his personal observations of Barney's excessive speed and erratic motion. Under *Atwater v. City of Lago Vista*, 532 U.S. 318 (2001), the arrest was reasonable under the Fourth Amendment. **Answer (e) is wrong** because threshold or clarifying questions are questions which are natural and immediate responses to volunteered admissions. For example, a person in custody for a bad check charge is sitting in the station house and suddenly starts hollering, "I killed him, I killed him." An officer may naturally ask, "what are you talking about?" The defendant's answers are still considered volunteered because the officer's questions were simply an attempt to clarify what the defendant was saying. In such circumstances, there would be no Miranda violation, assuming of course, that the questioning did not exceed a permissible attempt simply to clarify what was being said. That is not the case in this question. Barney did not offer any volunteered statements, much less any that would naturally spark clarifying or threshold questions.

- **Additional references**: *See* LAFAVE, ISRAEL, KING & KERR, CRIMINAL PROCEDURE §§ 6.6–6.7 (6th ed. 2017); WHITEBREAD & SLOBOGIN, CRIMINAL PROCEDURE: AN ANALYSIS OF CASES AND CONCEPTS § 16.03 (7th ed. 2020).

25. **The right answer is (d).** Officer Magnum had probable cause to stop Barney based on her personal observations of Barney's driving behavior. Thus the stop was lawful. When Officer Magnum looked through the windshield of Barney's car, she was outside of the vehicle in a place she was lawfully entitled to be, and she made her observations of the betting slips while they were in plain view. There was no entry into the vehicle

and no additional Fourth Amendment intrusion that needed to be justified. Thus, **answer (a) is wrong** because it assumes the stop was illegal and **answers (c) and (e) are incorrect** because they assume that some Fourth Amendment justification, either reasonable suspicion, as in (c), or probable cause as in (e), was necessary to observe the slips and record the numbers that were visible to the naked eye. Neither is the case because the slips were in plain view from a legal vantage point, and no additional Fourth Amendment intrusion was necessary to acquire the information. **Answer (b) is mistaken** because the seizure of intangibles like information about a person or his affairs is protected by the Fourth Amendment. *See Katz v. United States*, 389 U.S. 347 (1967) (seizure of a phone conversation).

- **Additional references**: *See* LAFAVE, ISRAEL, KING & KERR, CRIMINAL PROCEDURE § 3.2(b) (6th ed. 2017); WHITEBREAD & SLOBOGIN, CRIMINAL PROCEDURE: AN ANALYSIS OF CASES AND CONCEPTS § 10.02 (7th ed. 2020).

26. **The correct answer is (d).** This is an administrative search used as a pretext by the police to search for evidence of a crime. An administrative search can dispense with the ordinary requirements of probable cause and a warrant precisely because it is not an ordinary law enforcement search for evidence of a crime. This is true even if the ultimate purpose of the regulatory statute is the same as that of the penal laws (in other words, if a search discloses not only violations of the regulation but also of the criminal laws) and it is also true even if police officers conduct or attend the administrative search. *New York v. Burger*, 482 U.S. 691 (1987). But if the administrative search is in fact an ordinary law enforcement search for evidence of a crime, ordinary Fourth Amendment requirements apply. *Ferguson v. City of Charleston*, 532 U.S. 67 (2001); *cf. Bruce v. Beary*, 498 F.3d 1232 (11th Cir. 2007) (an administrative inspection is a "sham" where it is "a pretext solely to gather evidence of criminal activity" (citation omitted)). Recall that the *Burger* Court upheld the inspection of Burger's automobile junkyard, in part, because there was "no reason to believe that the instant inspection was actually a 'pretext' for obtaining evidence of respondent's violation of the penal laws." Thus, the rule is that in the limited contexts of inventory searches and administrative inspections, an officer's motive can invalidate objectively justifiable behavior under the Fourth Amendment. *Whren v. United States*, 517 U.S. 806 (1996). Here, Officer Friendly was clearly motivated by her desire to search for evidence of marijuana. It is important to understand how this example is distinguishable from other kinds of pretext searches. In *Whren*, the Court held that if an officer has reasonable suspicion or probable cause to stop or search, that stop or search is objectively reasonable and thus comports with the requirements of the Fourth Amendment. Phrased differently, the stop or search is valid even if the real reason the officer acted was to investigate a different or more serious crime. The facts of *Whren* are illustrative: the police conducted a lawful traffic stop, but their real motive was to investigate the defendant for illegal drug activity. The Court dismissed the officers' underlying motive

as irrelevant. So long as the officers' conduct was objectively reasonable, it did not matter that they were using the lawful stop as a pretext. Here, to be valid, the conduct must be justified as an administrative search because Officer Friendly had no probable cause ("nothing reliable to go on") and no warrant. The police must be using administrative methods and pursuing administrative goals, such as inspecting records and business standards and conditions. If, in the course of a lawful administrative search, the police come across evidence of a crime, of course they may use it. Here, however, the police used ordinary law enforcement methods, pursued ordinary law enforcement goals, and acted outside the scope of the administrative reach of the Maple Syrup Board. **Answers (b) and (c) are wrong** because, in different formulations, they assume that the "inspection" was lawful. **Answer (a) is irrelevant**. Either this is a proper administrative search of the farm, in which case it might appropriately include the garage whether or not part of the curtilage, or it is not a proper administrative search, in which case it doesn't matter whether the garage is or is not part of the cartilage. **Answer (e) sounds like a creative way to negate this as an administrative search, but this tactic was rejected** in *New York v. Burger, supra*. In *Burger*, a junkyard dealer claimed that he was not subject to an administrative regime subjecting dealers in automobile parts to inspections. He argued that because he was an unlicensed dealer, no administrative action could be taken against him. The Court appropriately rejected this argument since the law applied to those "in the business." The Court further noted that exempting Burger for his failure to register would frustrate the objectives of the law and invite non-registration.

- **Additional references**: *See* LaFave, Israel, King & Kerr, Criminal Procedure § 3.9(a)–(c) (6th ed. 2017); Whitebread & Slobogin, Criminal Procedure: An Analysis of Cases and Concepts §§ 13.01, 13.03 (7th ed. 2020).

27. **The correct answer is (a).** The facts of this question track, in part, the circumstances of *California v. Hodari D.*, 499 U.S. 621 (1991). There officers chased some youths who ran as the police approached. One of the youths, Hodari D., discarded a packet of drugs during the chase, which the police later recovered. If the drugs were discarded while Hodari was under arrest or otherwise seized by the officers, then he could argue that the drugs were a product of an illegal seizure. The Supreme Court held, however, that a seizure requires not only a show of authority but also actual *submission* to that show of authority. Since Hodari discarded his contraband before he submitted to the police, his act was simple abandonment. There was no Fourth Amendment seizure until Hodari was actually restrained or yielded to the officers. So, too, here. The drugs thrown away by Linus will be admissible against him because, at the time he threw them away, he had not been seized for the purposes of the Fourth Amendment. **Answer (b) is only partly right and, therefore, an incorrect choice.** Following the Supreme Court's opinion in *Illinois v. Wardlow*, 528 U.S. 119 (2000), there is a good argument that Linus's flight

on seeing the officers and his presence in a high crime neighborhood would be enough to give reasonable grounds to stop, but answer (b) incorrectly calls the chase a seizure, which it was not. **Answer (c) is wrong** because it assumes that the police needed a justification to chase Linus. They didn't since the chase, without submission, does not count as a Fourth Amendment intrusion and, therefore, no justification is needed. Moreover, even if a justification were needed, it would not be sufficient to say that Linus was in close proximity to the person described by the tipster. The tip itself is too weak to give rise to reasonable suspicion to stop. *Florida v. J.L.*, 529 U.S. 266 (2000) (anonymous tip stating that young black male standing at a particular bus stop and wearing a plaid shirt was carrying a gun lacked sufficient indicia of reliability to establish reasonable suspicion). Linus's proximity to the subject of the tip is even weaker still. **Answer (d) is wrong** both in assuming reasonable suspicion was needed to commence the chase and in asserting that it was lacking. **Answer (e) is irrelevant** because subsequent facts, like flight at the sight of the police and the ensuing chase and ultimate arrest, control the analysis of this question.

- **Additional references**: *See* LAFAVE, ISRAEL, KING & KERR, CRIMINAL PROCEDURE § 3.8(c) (6th ed. 2017); WHITEBREAD & SLOBOGIN, CRIMINAL PROCEDURE: AN ANALYSIS OF CASES AND CONCEPTS § 11.02(a) (7th ed. 2020).

28. **The best answer, in a close question, is (b).** To analyze this question, it is important to keep your eyes focused on the facts as they relate to Charlie. The tip, which itself is inadequate to give reasonable suspicion to stop the subject of the tip (Schroeder), *Florida v. J.L.*, 529 U.S. 266 (2000), provides nothing to implicate Charlie. He is simply someone talking to two men on a street corner. The police have no basis to stop *him*, even if they have a basis to stop Schroeder or to chase Linus. There has been an unreliable tip, unrelated to him, it is a high crime area, and one of the men takes off running. But Charlie does not flee; he simply sits on a park bench and ignores the officer. Although the Court in *Illinois v. Wardlow*, 528 U.S. 119 (2000), said that headlong flight from officers in a high crime area was enough to create reasonable suspicion to stop, that opinion also emphasized that reasonable suspicion requires particularized facts giving rise to an objective suspicion that *the person stopped* is engaged in criminal activity. The opinion also stressed that "when an officer, without reasonable suspicion or probable cause, approaches an individual, the individual has a right to ignore the police" and refusal to cooperate doesn't furnish the basis for reasonable suspicion. This is still good law after *Hiibel v. Sixth Judicial District Court*, 542 U.S. 177 (2004), which upheld a Nevada law making it a crime not to provide identification after police have stopped a person *based on reasonable suspicion*. Here the question is whether the police had reasonable suspicion to believe Charlie was engaged in criminal activity at the time they first approached him. It's not free from doubt, but on balance, the answer should be no. (And there is also no basis for the frisk since there is no evidence to suggest the presence of weapons on Charlie). **Answers (a), (d), and (e) all assume that there**

was a sufficient basis, on these facts, to stop Charlie, and are, therefore, not the preferred picks. Answer (c) is incomplete and, therefore, not the best choice. Even if an encounter starts off inadequately, facts might develop to give the police a basis to stop an individual. The key question here is whether those subsequent facts were or were not enough. Answer (c) doesn't help us resolve that question.

- **Additional references**: *See* LaFave, Israel, King & Kerr, Criminal Procedure § 3.8(d) (6th ed. 2017); Whitebread & Slobogin, Criminal Procedure: An Analysis of Cases and Concepts § 11.03 (7th ed. 2020).

29. **The right answer is (d).** The police stopped Schroeder based on an anonymous tip that he possessed narcotics. The tipster provided only generally observable facts, no predictive information, and no basis for assessing the allegation of criminality. Such a tip was found insufficient in *Florida v. J.L.*, 529 U.S. 266 (2000). And it is insufficient here too, not because the tipster provided too little to identify a particular individual **(this is the predicate of answer (e), which is wrong)**, but because there was no way to judge the claim of criminal behavior from an unknown, unaccountable informant who neither explained how he knew about the cocaine nor supplied any basis for believing he had inside information about the suspect. Answer (d) also correctly states that, in any event, the frisk was more than a pat down of the outer clothing and exceeded the proper scope of a frisk. Under *Terry v. Ohio*, 392 U.S. 1 (1968), the police may frisk an individual they believe is armed and dangerous. Such frisks are strictly circumscribed by the purpose allowing them in the first place, namely, to determine whether the individual possesses a weapon that could be used against the police or the public. If the frisk goes beyond what is necessary to determine whether the suspect is armed, it is no longer valid. Although an officer may retrieve nonthreatening contraband discovered during the course of an otherwise valid *Terry* frisk, *Minnesota v. Dickerson*, 508 U.S. 366 (1993) (discussing the plain touch doctrine by drawing an analogy to the plain view doctrine), the frisk here exceeded permissible bounds. Two things are important to note here. First, *Terry* made clear that the frisk may not be used to discover evidence of a crime. Second, the plain view doctrine, and by analogy the plain touch doctrine, serves to supplement the prior justification for the search or seizure; that is, the police must have a prior justification for an intrusion during the course of which he or she came across incriminating evidence. *Coolidge v. New Hampshire*, 403 U.S. 443 (1971), *abrogated on other grounds by Horton v. California*, 496 U.S. 128 (1990). In the facts described here, the police had no justification for frisking Schroeder; there was no reasonable suspicion and the police never had a reasonable belief that Schroeder was armed and dangerous. Furthermore, as in *Dickerson*, the officer conducting the frisk did not claim that he thought the item in Schroeder's pocket was a weapon. The officer only determined that the object was contraband after feeling and turning the object several times, and we know from *Dickerson* that the manipulation of an item from the outside is beyond a proper frisk. In sum,

not only was the officer not lawfully in a position to feel the lump in Schroeder's pocket, the facts establish that the incriminating character of the object was not immediately apparent and was only discovered after conducting a further search, one not authorized by *Terry. Minnesota v. Dickerson, supra*; *see also Arizona v. Hicks*, 480 U.S. 321 (1987) (seizure of stereo equipment was not justified because its incriminating character was not immediately apparent). **Answer (a) is wrong.** The police only corroborated the completely neutral and innocent fact that Schroeder was in a particular place with certain pants and shirt. This is not enough to establish reasonable suspicion of criminal activity. **Answer (b) erroneously imports the concept of a public safety exception into Fourth Amendment analysis and is wrong**. A similar, and even stronger, attempt was made in *Florida v. J.L., supra*, where the government argued that, even if the tip was otherwise inadequate and unreliable, there should be a softer rule, an exception, for tips alleging possession of firearms. The Court, acknowledging that guns are dangerous, nevertheless rebuffed the idea because the potential for harassment would be too great, and the exception could not logically be confined to firearms. **Answer (c) is a definite no.** The police may never justify an intrusion by what they ultimately find. The reasonableness of police action must be measured by what officers knew before they conducted their search or seizure. If it were otherwise, the law would be an open invitation to police to act on any hunch or impulse.

- **Additional references**: *See* LAFAVE, ISRAEL, KING & KERR, CRIMINAL PROCEDURE § 3.8 (6th ed. 2017); WHITEBREAD & SLOBOGIN, CRIMINAL PROCEDURE: AN ANALYSIS OF CASES AND CONCEPTS §§ 11.03, 11.04, 11.06 (7th ed. 2020).

30. **The best answer is (b).** Citing prior cases, the Supreme Court in *Colorado v. Connelly*, 479 U.S. 157 (1986), observed, "The most outrageous behavior by a private party seeking to secure evidence against a defendant does not make that evidence inadmissible under the Due Process Clause." Here there is outrageous conduct by Thelma and Louise, but it is their conduct and not governmental conduct. Nor is there sufficient evidence to suggest that the officer had made Thelma and Louise his agents, encouraged or endorsed their behavior, or exploited it in any way. The officer came upon the commotion, asked what was going on, and Kenny poured out his confession. In Due Process terms, this is a voluntary statement. Miranda requirements are not applicable because Kenny was not in custody. Although the site of the ruckus was the police station, this scenario is equivalent to an on-the-scene investigation. The Sixth Amendment has no bearing on the problem whatsoever because Kenny was not even under arrest when he made his confession, much less an "accused" against whom a criminal prosecution had begun. **Consequently (a), (c), and (d) which raise a Due Process, Miranda, or Sixth Amendment issue are all in error. Answer (e) may have some validity, but is not the best of the choices given.** It may be that the question asked by Officer Jones was not interrogation in the Miranda sense because it was not an authoritative demand for an answer,

but, rather, an impulsive question prompted by the surprising circumstances that presented themselves. But courts are not uniform in either accepting a spontaneous question exception for Miranda or in defining one if it is recognized. The stronger answer to the Miranda claim here is that there is no custody. More to the point, however, is the fact that the best and most complete answer is (b) which correctly states that none of Kenny's constitutional rights were violated.

- **Additional references**: *See* LaFave, Israel, King & Kerr, Criminal Procedure § 6.2(b) (6th ed. 2017); Whitebread & Slobogin, Criminal Procedure: An Analysis of Cases and Concepts § 16.02(a) (7th ed. 2020).

31. **The best-answer is (c).** The key to this question is seeing that the police, having climbed onto Nina's back deck ("attached to the back of the house" and equivalent to a back porch), are within the protected curtilage of the home. In *United States v. Dunn*, 480 U.S. 294 (1987), the Court noted that, while not a definitive test, "curtilage questions should be resolved with particular reference to four factors: [1] the proximity of the area to be curtilage to the home, [2] whether the area is included within an enclosure surrounding the home, [3] the nature of the uses to which the area is put, and [4] the steps taken by the resident to protect the area from observation by people passing by." Places appurtenant to the home and which are restricted from public access are protected places, or extensions of the home. *See Oliver v. United States*, 466 U.S. 170 (1984). Looking at the factors here, it is clear that once the police stepped on the back deck, they were no longer in an open field or a place where Nina had no reasonable expectation of privacy. Thus, to be in that protected place, the police needed probable cause and a warrant. They had neither, and there is no indication from the facts that any of the exceptions to the warrant requirement, such as exigent circumstances, applied. As a result, the readings they got from the thermal imaging device and the visual observations of the marijuana plants were derivative of the illegal presence on the back deck and inadmissible. **Answers (a) and (b) are faulty** because they fail to account for the fact that the police gained their vantage point for the thermal readings and their visual observations from a place, the back deck, where they were not authorized to be. Indeed answer (a) is doubly wrong because use of a thermal imaging device directed at the home is itself a search requiring probable cause and a search warrant. In *Kyllo v. United States*, 533 U.S. 27 (2001), the Court held that "[w]here, as here, the Government uses a device that is not in general use, to explore details of the home that would previously have been unknowable without physical intrusion, the surveillance is a 'search' and is presumptively unreasonable without a warrant." Cameras, binoculars, flashlights, and other items in general use may be used by police officers because they merely enhance the natural sensory perception of the police officers. **The issue of consent raised in answers (d) and (e) is irrelevant** because the officers were not in a position to secure valid consent. And so, the issue of consent, whether

given or not, gives way to the prior question of how the police gained their vantage point.

- **Additional references**: *See* LaFave, Israel, King & Kerr, Criminal Procedure §§ 3.2(b)–3.2(d) (6th ed. 2017); Whitebread & Slobogin, Criminal Procedure: An Analysis of Cases and Concepts §§ 4.03(c), 4.03(f), 14.06 (7th ed. 2020).

32. **The right answer is (d).** This question is based on *Moran v. Burbine*, 475 U.S. 412 (1986). There, upon learning that her brother was arrested and being held in police custody, the defendant's sister retained counsel on her brother's behalf. The attorney called the police to inquire after him and said she wanted to be present if the defendant was interrogated. The police told the lawyer that the defendant would not be interrogated, but, in fact, shortly after the call, the defendant received Miranda warnings and was questioned. The police deliberately failed to tell the defendant that a lawyer was waiting in the wings. Nevertheless, the Court held that the defendant's waiver was valid under Miranda and that the police did not have to advise him that a lawyer sought to assist him. Requiring such a new warning, the Court said, would strike a new and more costly balance between the rights of suspects and the need to obtain confessions and punish wrongdoers. It would also muddy Miranda's "relatively clear waters" by spawning all sorts of questions of how and under what circumstances police should be held accountable for knowing the suspect has counsel. A third party, even a lawyer, cannot invoke the Miranda right to counsel on the suspect's behalf. **Answer (b) is wrong** because Detective Dano's deception did not amount to an affirmative misrepresentation to Hilde; he simply failed to provide information beyond the bare Miranda warnings. And, because "[e]vents occurring outside of the presence of the suspect and entirely unknown" to her were not necessary to her "capacity to comprehend and knowingly relinquish a constitutional right," such a failure did not undercut her waiver. It would have been different if Detective Dano affirmatively misrepresented the situation to Hilde, saying, for example, that "of course, no lawyer would take this case, or offer to help you because this crime is really awful . . . " That would be a misrepresentation *actually in the room*, and it could certainly undercut the validity of her waiver. **Answer (a) presents a strong claim, but it was rejected in** *Moran v. Burbine, supra.* The Court did not rule out that especially egregious misconduct by the police could amount to a Due Process violation, but under the circumstances, it did not find that the actions so awful that they met the extreme test of shocking the conscience. The Court said, "the challenged conduct falls short of the kind of misbehavior that so shocks the sensibilities of civilized society as to warrant a federal intrusion into the criminal processes of the state." The conduct in this problem is no more egregious than that in *Moran*. **Answer (c) also presents a strong claim but it, too, was rejected in** *Moran v. Burbine, supra.* There the Court said that the Sixth Amendment, by its very terms, comes into play only when the right has attached, that is, only upon formal charge. Only then are the parties in an adversary relationship with the state committed to using its powers to

prosecute, and only then is the defendant entitled to counsel to help steer him through the intricacies of the law. "[I]t makes little sense to say that the Sixth Amendment right to counsel attaches at different times depending on the fortuity of whether the suspect or his family happens to have retained counsel prior to interrogation. More importantly, [such an approach] misconceives the underlying purposes of the right to counsel . . . [which is not] to wrap a protective cloak around the attorney-client relationship for its own sake" but to protect the defendant once formal charges have been laid. Here Hilde is only under arrest on the murder charge, she has not yet been indicted or otherwise formally charged. The Sixth Amendment cannot be violated because it has not yet attached. **Answer (e) is wrong** because the voluntariness of Hilde's confession is not in issue. The issue is whether the conduct of the police or the defendant's ignorance of the attorney's efforts to reach her taints the validity of her waiver.

- **Additional references**: *See* LaFave, Israel, King & Kerr, Criminal Procedure §§ 6.4(e), 6.9(b) (6th ed. 2017); Whitebread & Slobogin, Criminal Procedure: An Analysis of Cases and Concepts §§ 16.03(d)(2), 16.04(a) (7th ed. 2020).

33. **The best answer is (e).** The officers' initial encounter with Fred on the bus, similar to the DEA officers' encounter with defendant Bostick in *Florida v. Bostick,* 501 U.S. 429 (1991), was not a seizure. Although the confines of a bus are narrow and although a passenger on an intermediate stop may not feel free to leave, the officers did not behave in a way that conveyed the message that compliance with their requests was required. However, the officers' actions thereafter became more intrusive. They asked Fred to accompany them to a bus station office. He departed the bus as other passengers were reboarding, signaling that the bus was about to depart and that he would miss it. The room he was taken to was small, and the officers closed the door and began to question him. They asked to search his bag. Much like the facts of *Florida v. Royer,* 460 U.S. 491 (1983), Fred's strongest argument is that he was under arrest at that point. Police had already acquired enough information to give them reasonable suspicion—traveling from a source drug city to a drug market city, discrepancy between Fred's identification and the name on his bag, Fred's vague answers about his itinerary, and his nervousness. But this same evidence does not add up to probable cause to arrest. The police may not seek to verify their suspicions by means that approach the conditions of arrest, which looks like the situation here. *Royer, supra* (citing *Dunaway v. New York*, 442 U.S. 200 (1979)). So, Fred's best argument is to characterize his confinement as an arrest and exclude the drugs as derived from consent which was the product of an illegal arrest. **Answers (c) and (d) mistake the rules of *Bostick*.** The officers' encounter on the bus was not a seizure, and, so, no reasonable suspicion was needed to approach Fred. The fact that Fred was not "free to leave" is not relevant if his freedom to leave is constrained by circumstances and not by the police. **Answer (a) goes too far.** Although the police failure to have drug sniffing dogs available can be a factor in assessing whether a stop

exceeded its bounds (it shows that the police were not necessarily proceeding with their investigative stop in a reasonably efficient manner, *United States v. Place,* 462 U.S. 696 (1983)), it is an overstatement to say that the police could not engage in *any* investigative actions without having arranged for dogs to be available. **Answer (b) is not the best choice** because it is quite arguable whether Fred's behavior amounted to consent. It is true, as answer (e) explains, that consent resulting from an illegal arrest is invalid. But if Fred doesn't make the argument that there was an arrest without probable cause, his compliance (by handing over the bag) to the police officers' request to search could support the State's contention that the consent was freely and voluntarily given. Although *Royer* says that the government's burden of proving consent "is not satisfied by showing a mere submission to a claim of lawful authority," under the totality of the circumstances valid consent can be express or implied. *See, e.g., United States v. Lakoskey,* 462 F.3d 965 (8th Cir. 2006). The "precise question is not whether [the defendant] consented subjectively, but whether his conduct would have caused a reasonable person to believe that he consented." *United States v. Williams,* 521 F.3d 902 (8th Cir. 2008). Under the facts presented, Fred's actions in handing the bag over could be interpreted as implied consent. Because answer (e) is stronger, answer (b) is not the most appropriate.

- **Additional references**: *See* LaFave, Israel, King & Kerr, Criminal Procedure § 3.8 (6th ed. 2017); Whitebread & Slobogin, Criminal Procedure: An Analysis of Cases and Concepts § 11.02 (7th ed. 2020).

34. **The right answer is (a).** The police have reliable, eyewitness information that Maggie is storing drugs in her house in a specifically described suitcase. This creates probable cause to search, but the police do not have a warrant to enter the house, or any warrant for that matter. Nevertheless, they legally obtain entry into the home by consent. Thus, they are in a place they are lawfully entitled to be and, from that place, observe the item which they have probable cause to believe contains evidence of a crime, namely, the specifically described suitcase. They have probable cause to seize it. But they still have no warrant. Absent some emergency, they may seize the item and apply for a search warrant, but they may not search the item without a warrant. *United States v. Chadwick,* 433 U.S. 1 (1977) (absent emergency or some other exception to the warrant clause, people retain a reasonable expectation of privacy in personal items and, therefore, a search of such items requires probable cause *and* a warrant). **Since the opposite conclusion is the basis of answer (c), it is, accordingly, incorrect. Answer (b) is wrong** because the tip was reliable and based on the informant's personal knowledge that drugs were being stored in Maggie's home in a particular container. This adds up to probable cause. **Answer (d) is incorrect** because, although it is unclear whether Maggie's statement actually amounted to consent to search, it is especially doubtful that she had sufficient authority over the suitcase to give consent. If a person is given control over another person's property, she may consent to a search of that

property. For example, if Maggie and Jake were joint users of the luggage, her consent to search would be sufficient. *Frazier v. Cupp*, 394 U.S. 731 (1969). However, Jake left the suitcase with Maggie for temporary safekeeping, and it would not be reasonable to construe that as control or access to the contents. The fact that the suitcase was not locked is not dispositive because the luggage was closed and as such, the contents were shielded from public view. The expectation of privacy in one's luggage is not lessened by the mere fact that it has been stored on the premises of a third-party. *United States v. Waller*, 426 F.3d 838 (6th Cir. 2005) (holding that defendant had a legitimate expectation of privacy in luggage left at a friend's apartment). Moreover it would not be reasonable for police to believe otherwise since Maggie told them the circumstances. *See United States v. Basinski*, 226 F.3d 829 (7th Cir. 2000) (stating that "it is less reasonable for a police officer to believe that a third party has full access to a defendants purse or briefcase than, say, an open crate"). (Note: Why the police did not arrest Maggie and search the bag as a search incident to an arrest is not the subject of this question, so do not think about it.) **Answer (e) is wrong** because, although Maggie's consent to enter the house excused the need to have a warrant to enter the house, her consent did not extend to the personal property of Jake.

- **Additional references**: *See* LaFave, Israel, King & Kerr, Criminal Procedure §§ 3.5(e), 3.10(d) (6th ed. 2017); Whitebread & Slobogin, Criminal Procedure: An Analysis of Cases and Concepts § 12.04 (7th ed. 2020).

35. **The correct answer is (c).** This question is loosely drawn from *United States v. Sandoval*, 20 F.3d 134 (5th Cir. 1994) (finding entrapment where government engaged in significant and persistent inducement, but provided insufficient evidence of defendant's predisposition). A successful entrapment defense proves two elements: (1) government inducement of a crime and (2) a lack of predisposition on the part of the defendant to engage in the criminal conduct. *Mathews v. United States*, 485 U.S. 58 (1988). Where significant and persistent government encouragement is required to induce the crime, the government needs to show more than the defendant's eager acceptance of a criminal opportunity to establish predisposition, and thus overcome an entrapment defense. *Compare Jacobson v. United States*, 503 U.S. 540 (1992) ("In their zeal to enforce the law, government agents may not originate a criminal design, implant in an innocent person's mind the disposition to commit a criminal act, and then induce commission of the crime so that the Government may prosecute.") *with United States v. Wilder*, 597 F.3d 936 (8th Cir. 2010) ("Where agents simply offer a subject the opportunity to commit a crime, and the subject promptly avails himself of the criminal opportunity, an entrapment defense typically does not warrant a jury instruction."). Other than Sandoval's ultimate acceptance of Hernandez's proposal, the facts here reveal little to establish predisposition. Mr. Sandoval initially and repeatedly tried to engage in a lawful transaction. **Answer (a) is incorrect.** The Supreme Court has stated, "evidence that merely indicates a generic inclination to act within a broad range, not all of which

is criminal, is of little probative value in establishing predisposition." *Jacobson v. United States, supra.* Here, Sandoval only exhibited an inclination to trade information for a monetary reward or, perhaps, prosecutorial lenience—a legal and widespread activity. **Answer (b) is incorrect.** The Supreme Court rejected "eager acceptance" as being sufficient to establish predisposition where persistent government encouragement was required to induce the crime. *See Jacobson v. United States, supra.* The amount of time the government spent persuading the defendant is not as important as the degree of pressure applied. *See United States v. Sandoval, supra. Jacobson* involved repeated mailings from the government, whereas here, agent Hernandez applied the pressure in person, reminded Sandoval of the amount of his tax liability, and repeatedly tried to steer Sandoval away from his intention of making a "lawful" deal. Furthermore, Sandoval did not eagerly accept the opportunity. He consistently and repeatedly tried to act legally and hesitated when he finally realized that Hernandez was asking for a bribe. **Answer (d) is wrong.** Ignorance of the law will not exonerate the defendant and is not relevant to the entrapment defense. *See Jacobson v. United States, supra* ("[D]efendant must be presumed to know the law."). **Answer (e) is also the wrong choice.** Even if we assume that Sandoval's statement is true, the government may prove predisposition with other evidence. A person who has not previously bribed a public official may still be considered predisposed to commit bribery. *Cf. United States v. Lakhani*, 480 F.3d 171 (3d Cir. 2007) (lack of a prior criminal record does not alone establish lack of predisposition); *United States v. Nguyen*, 413 F.3d 1170 (10th Cir. 2005) ("Predisposition to commit a criminal act may be shown by evidence of similar prior illegal acts or it may be 'inferred from defendant's desire for profit, his eagerness to participate in the transaction, his ready response to the government's inducement offer, or his demonstrated knowledge or experience in the criminal activity.' ").

- **Additional references**: *See* LAFAVE, ISRAEL, KING & KERR, CRIMINAL PROCEDURE §§ 5.1, 5.3 (6th ed. 2017); WHITEBREAD & SLOBOGIN, CRIMINAL PROCEDURE: AN ANALYSIS OF CASES AND CONCEPTS § 19.02 (7th ed. 2020).

36. **The best answer is (d).** The question is based on a similar jury instruction approved in *United States v. Hernandez*, 92 F.3d 309 (5th Cir. 1996) (holding jury instruction proper in light of *Jacobson v. United States*, 503 U.S. 540 (1992)). The government does bear the burden of proof of predisposition, and it is proper to rely on all relevant evidence, including prior criminal convictions. *United States v. Nguyen*, 413 F.3d 1170 (10th Cir. 2005) ("Predisposition to commit a criminal act may be shown by evidence of similar prior illegal acts."). A defendant with prior criminal convictions is thus put at some disadvantage in claiming this defense since otherwise inadmissible and prejudicial evidence may be used. **Answer (a) is incorrect.** The Supreme Court has stated that, "[w]here the Government has induced an individual to break the law and the defense of entrapment is at issue . . . the prosecution must prove

beyond a reasonable doubt that the defendant was disposed to commit the criminal act prior to first being approached by Government agents," *Jacobson v. United States, supra; United States v. Holmes,* 421 F.3d 683 (8th Cir. 2005). **Answer (b) should be rejected.** The Supreme Court has held that the factual issue of entrapment, including predisposition, should be decided by the jury, unless it can be decided as a matter of law. *See Sherman v. United States,* 356 U.S. 369 (1958); *United States v. Nguyen, supra* ("Entrapment exists as a matter of law only if the evidence of entrapment is uncontradicted." (citation omitted)). Here, the judge did not find entrapment as a matter of law, so the question was properly sent to the jury. **Answer (e) is incorrect.** As stated above, the jury must determine that Sandoval was predisposed *before* the government approached him and offered him a criminal opportunity. *See Jacobson v. United States, supra.* Otherwise, the entrapment defense is rendered useless; the government could establish predisposition any time a defendant yields to government inducement. **Answer (c) is wrong.** A defendant may not be convicted of an offense if the government cannot negate the defense of entrapment. Under the majority view of entrapment, a jury may not return a guilty verdict against the defendant if she was induced to commit a crime by the government and had no predisposition to do so. The theory is that the legislature could not have intended to criminalize acts committed in such circumstances. But this view of legislative intention is abandoned if the defendant commits an act of violence because the legislature will not be presumed to permit the acquittal of someone importuned to engage in violent acts. *Sorrells v. United States,* 287 U.S. 435 (1932).

- **Additional references**: *See* LaFave, Israel, King & Kerr, Criminal Procedure § 5.3 (6th ed. 2017); Whitebread & Slobogin, Criminal Procedure: An Analysis of Cases and Concepts §§ 19.02, 19.03 (7th ed. 2020).

37. **The best answer is (e).** Ordinarily the grand jury is given wide latitude to subpoena physical evidence, and the usual Fourth Amendment requirement of probable cause does not apply. As the Supreme Court stated in *United States v. R. Enterprises,* 498 U.S. 292 (1991), "The Government cannot be required to justify the issuance of a grand jury subpoena by presenting evidence sufficient to establish probable cause because the very purpose of requesting the information is to ascertain whether probable cause exists." To operate effectively, to investigate criminal activities and preserve secrecy, the grand jury must be free to consider all relevant evidence and not be saddled by preliminary showings and procedural delays. So, ordinarily, the only Fourth Amendment limitation on a grand jury subpoena of evidence is that there be a reasonable possibility that the materials sought will provide information relevant to the general subject of the grand jury's investigation. But these rules arise with ordinary subpoenas for documents. When the grand jury is seeking physical evidence from an individual, the calculus of what is reasonable may vary. At one end of the spectrum are requests for the mere display of a person's physical characteristics, such as voice or fingerprints.

As to that sort of evidence, the Supreme Court has ruled that there is no Fourth Amendment interest at stake. The subpoena to appear is not a seizure in the Fourth Amendment sense, and the nature and acquisition of the evidence involves no invasion of human dignity, privacy, or physical integrity. *United States v. Dionisio,* 410 U.S. 1 (1973)(summons to appear and make a voice recording did not infringe on any interest protected by the Fourth Amendment). But at the other end of the spectrum are cases where the grand jury is seeking physical evidence that involves a greater invasion into the person's privacy and physical integrity, such as giving blood, or at the extreme end, as here, invasive and perhaps risky surgery. As to that sort of evidence, the Fourth Amendment does apply, and it protects against unreasonable intrusions. Although the Supreme Court has not directly confronted the issue, several lower courts have held that a grand jury subpoena for a blood sample, involving as it does the penetration of the skin and seizure of bodily fluids, requires either reasonable suspicion or probable cause. Neither ground can be established here since the facts say that the police are acting on rumors and a hunch. They have neither reasonable suspicion nor probable cause. In *Dionisio* the Court distinguished voice prints from bodily intrusions like blood samples by saying, "The required disclosure of a person's voice is thus immeasurably further removed from the Fourth Amendment protection than was the intrusion into the body effected by the blood extraction in *Schmerber.* The interests in human dignity and privacy which the Fourth Amendment protects forbid any such intrusions on the mere chance that desired evidence might be obtained." quoting *Schmerber v. California,* 384 U.S. 757 (1966) (although the case involved a blood sample sought by the police and not the grand jury, the Court there stressed that intrusions into the human body are particularly offensive and may require a showing stronger than probable cause). Court-ordered surgery may be allowed if, on a balancing test, the evidence is relevant, can be obtained in no other way, probable cause exists, and the surgery is minor and presents minimal risk. *Schmerber, Winston v. Lee,* 470 U.S. 753 (1985)(Fourth Amendment would not permit surgery on defendant to remove a bullet where procedure was an extensive intrusion and state's need for the evidence was not high). **Answer (a) would be correct if we were talking about garden variety grand jury subpoenas, but we are not, so it's incorrect. Answer (b) is wrong and silly.** The fact that a person has seen a doctor about a medical condition does not destroy his or her reasonable expectation of privacy concerning that matter. Be careful not to confuse absolute secrecy with privacy. Moreover, the person also retains a Fourth Amendment protection against bodily invasions. **Answer (c) is simply a policy statement, which you may or may not agree with, but it offers no *legal* basis for enforcing the subpoena and should be rejected. Answer (d) has some appeal, but (e) is better.** In *Rochin v. California,* 342 U.S. 165 (1952), the Supreme Court relied on the Due Process clause to suppress illegal substances obtained from the defendant after the police forced their way into his home, forcibly tried to recover capsules he swallowed, and brought him to a hospital where a doctor put a tube down his throat and induced vomiting. This entire episode "shocked the conscience" of the Court and violated Due Process of law. Here, the order to submit to surgery is subject to judicial review and lacks the strong-arm and flagrantly offensive characteristics of *Rochin*. Reasonableness and the approach of *Winston v. Lee, supra* (decided after *Rochin*) are the more apt standards to apply in this case. **Answer (d) mistakenly invokes the Fifth Amendment and is wrong.** Physical evidence, even though it may turn out to be highly incriminatory, is non-testimonial.

- **Additional references**: *See* LaFave, Israel, King & Kerr, Criminal Procedure § 8.12(d) (6th ed. 2017); Whitebread & Slobogin, Criminal Procedure: An Analysis of Cases and Concepts §§ 5.06(c), 23.05(a) (7th ed. 2020).

38. **The best answer is (a).** Be alert. You are asked for the *strongest* argument that the police activity here, constant surveillance and obtaining phone company records of the telephone numbers you've dialed, is unlawful. Such activity, in general, *may be lawful.* Still, you are asked for the best argument to the contrary-even though it may not be a winning argument. Answer (a) is best because it is plausible and the other alternatives are worse. In terms of visual surveillance, the Supreme Court has said that you have no Fourth Amendment protection from government observation when you go out into public places, and it has even held that the police may use electronic devices, like beepers, to track your movements from one place to another. *United States v. Knotts,* 460 U.S. 276 (1983). The idea is that you have exposed your movements to the public and the police do not have to avert their eyes. Of course, this is quite ridiculous in terms of ordinary expectations of privacy since most people might expect that others could observe their public place behavior, but would not expect to be followed around incessantly, particularly by persons using electronic tracking equipment. Although there is no expectation of privacy in public movements, extended surveillance seems different and the *Knotts* decision itself reserved the question of whether a warrant would be required in a case involving 24-hour surveillance over an extended period of time: "If such dragnet-type law enforcement practices . . . should eventually occur, there will be time enough then to determine whether different constitutional principles apply." In other words, there remains uncertainty about extended surveillance. That is, if a search is sufficiently extended in duration, it *could* alter the rule regarding public observation. And in *United States v. Jones*, 565 U.S. 400 (2012) and *Carpenter v. U.S.*, 585 U.S. ___, 138 S.Ct. 2206 (2018), this was the essential message which is changing the law involving electronic surveillance and is worth an extended discussion here. In *Jones*, a unanimous Supreme Court held that the attachment of a GPS tracking device to a vehicle and monitoring the movement of the vehicle on public streets for four weeks constituted a search under the Fourth Amendment. The opinion for the Court was written by Justice Scalia who relied on a trespass theory to reach that result. For him the reasonable expectation of privacy test for determining whether a police intrusion was or was not

a search did not eliminate the common law trespass basis for Fourth Amendment protections and that a physical occupation of property for the purpose of obtaining information was a search. However five justices, writing separately, did not want to rely exclusively on trespass theory and noted that the GPS tracking in the case was just a fortuitous circumstance. Tracking and other forms of electronic surveillance can and do occur without any physical intrusion. But to find that such tracking and surveillance constituted a search, these justices had to confront well developed Fourth Amendment notions that anything one exposes to the public may be equally observed by the police. Justice Sotomayor put the matter most directly when she said: "More fundamentally, it may be necessary to reconsider the premise that an individual has no reasonable expectation of privacy in information voluntarily disclosed to third parties." But the challenge for these justices was to provide a standard to determine when tracking or surveillance without physical trespass is a Fourth Amendment search. Justice Sotomayor said that the Court will have to take into account the amount of information the government can acquire via GPS tracking, its permanence in storage files, its manipulation via data mining, and the length of time it continues. She offered this general guidance: "I would ask whether people reasonably expect that their movements will be recorded and aggregated in a manner that enables the Government to ascertain, more or less at will, their political and religious beliefs, sexual habits, and so on." The separate opinion by Justice Alito, joined by Justices Ginsburg, Breyer, and Kagan, said, "The best that we can do in this case is to apply existing Fourth Amendment doctrine and to ask whether the use of GPS tracking in a particular case involved a degree of intrusion that a reasonable person would not have anticipated." He said that relatively short term monitoring might be ok but longer term monitoring, at least for most offenses would not. What precisely would separate the two was left undetermined and which offenses would allow different rules was unstated. Justice Alito said, however, that the four week monitoring in this case amounted to a search. These formulations are quite imprecise and may potentially unsettle Fourth Amendment doctrine in many areas like overhead flights or trash searches. And even if just confined to GPS tracking cases, the concurring opinions gave little guidance to the police as to what is or is not permissible. More recently and following *Jones*, the Court added that police acquisition over many days of historic cell-site location information of a suspect's phone was a Fourth Amendment search generally requiring a warrant. Individuals have a reasonable expectation of privacy in the whole of their physical movements, and the extensive information acquired from cell-site location information took the case out of the general third party doctrine cases like *U.S. v. Miller*, 425 U.S. 435 (1976) (no Fourth Amendment interest in one's cancelled checks, deposit slips, and so on held by a third party bank). But neither *Jones* nor *Carpenter* reached the kind of surveillance in this question, and so this question and answer are still correct. Further note that the Fourth Amendment also protects against fright and embarrassment, and depending upon *how* the government conducts its surveillance, a violation might be claimed. If the government, for example, used a large gang of heavily armed officers to trail after you, or if they approached in a way calculated to cause fear, or if their efforts operated to obstruct you from carrying out your ordinary and routine activities, the Fourth Amendment could offer a shield. **Answer (b) offers little promise** since the Supreme Court has specifically ruled that it is not a Fourth Amendment search for the telephone company to record all telephone numbers dialed from a particular phone and furnish them to the police. *Smith v. Maryland,* 442 U.S. 735 (1979). The Supreme Court reasoned that, since you know the phone company has this information, you "assume the risk" that it will turn it over to the police. Again, this may strike the ordinary citizen as ridiculous, but the matter is considered settled. **Answer (c) gains nothing by invoking the federal wiretap statute** since the same rule applies, that is, you have assumed the risk that information that you furnished to the phone company could be turned over to the police. **Answer (d) is not the best** because the Court has not qualified or even hinted at qualifying the ability of the police to monitor your movements simply because you were on the inside of a public building. The touchstone is not whether a person is inside or outside; the touchstone is whether he or she is in a public place, like a street, a bank, a restaurant, or whether, instead, he or she is in a private place inaccessible to the general public, like an apartment or the "off limits" part of the convenience store. **Answer (e) is also not the best choice.** There is simply no barrier to police continuing to investigate a case against someone simply because a grand jury is also hot on the trail. The scenario of the police continuing to investigate a matter even while the grand jury is also investigating should, however, be distinguished from a grand jury continuing to issue subpoenas where indictments have already been handed up and the sole purpose is to gather more information to prepare for trial. This is regarded as an abuse of the grand jury's powers.

- **Additional references**: *See* LAFAVE, ISRAEL, KING & KERR, CRIMINAL PROCEDURE § 3.2(j) (6th ed. 2017 & Supp. 2019); WHITEBREAD & SLOBOGIN, CRIMINAL PROCEDURE: AN ANALYSIS OF CASES AND CONCEPTS § 14.04 (7th ed. 2020).

39. **The right answer is (c) although in the last edition of this book, the opposite of (c), or answer (a) was the best answer.** What changed was the Court's ruling in the recent case of *Heien v. North Carolina,* 574 U.S. 54 (2014). To explain, reasonable suspicion must be based on specific articulable facts; an officer is permitted to rely on her training and experience to assess the facts and draw inferences from the facts. *Kansas v. Glover,* ___ U.S. ___, 140 S.Ct. 1183 (2020) (officer reasonably stopped vehicle after learning registered owner had a revoked license even in the absence of any information that the owner was not the driver). And a factual belief that a person is engaging in unlawful conduct may be reasonable even if it is mistaken. *United States v. Cortez,* 449 U.S. 411 (1981); *Arizona v. Evans,* 514 U.S. 1 (1995) (exclusionary rule would not apply to evidence uncovered incident to arrest even though arrest

based on an outstanding warrant that had in fact been quashed). However lower courts routinely held that reasonable suspicion must be objectively grounded in governing law. *Cortez.* The idea was that, if what an officer reasonably believes is a violation of the law is not a violation of the law, the stop is not and cannot be objectively reasonable. *United States v. Tibbetts*, 396 F.3d 1132 (10th Cir. 2005) (reasoning that "the failure to understand the law by the very person charged with enforcing it is not objectively reasonable"). In *Michigan v. DePhillippo*, 443 U.S. 31 (1979), however, the Supreme Court gave officers some latitude to be in compliance with the Fourth Amendment despite a mistake of law. There police made an arrest under a law later declared unconstitutional, but the Court held that the officers' reasonable assumption that the law was valid gave them "abundant probable cause" to make the arrest. *Heien* went further. There the police officer stopped a motorist because one of his brake lights was out. But under North Carolina law, it was not actually a violation of the law to have only one light working. Nevertheless the Court held that, given the substantial ambiguity in the law concerning whether one or both brake lights must be working, the officer's mistake of law was objectively reasonable and there was, therefore, reasonable suspicion to make the stop and no violation of the Fourth Amendment. The Court said that its decision would not discourage officers from learning the law or permit them to be sloppy about their understandings. Any mistake of law must be objectively reasonable and not based on the subjective understanding of the individual officer. In this question the officer relied on the specific training he received at the Police Academy to the effect that registration stickers must appear on the back window of a vehicle. As such the mistake of law was objectively reasonable, and the stop was legal. **Answer (a) which is the opposite of answer (c) is now wrong. Answer (d) misstates the standing doctrine and is wrong.** Vaughn, as owner of the car, has standing to complain of the illegal stop. Moreover, even if Vaughn did not own the vehicle, he was seized for Fourth Amendment purposes upon being pulled over, and could therefore challenge the constitutionality of the stop under *Brendlin v. California*, 551 U.S. 249 (2007) (explaining that no "reasonable passenger" would "feel free to depart without police permission"). **Answer (e) muddles the fact pattern and is a bad choice.** The officer first stopped Vaughn and the driver. That stop was the beginning of the cascading events and if it was improper, all subsequent, derivative actions were also improper because there was no attenuation. **Answer (b) draws a faulty inference from the fact that the defendant did not stop immediately upon being ordered to do so.** Obviously a suspect cannot erase the justification for a stop simply by refusing to comply. However, as with answer (e), because the initial stop was not reasonable, neither was the subsequent action.

- **Additional references**: *See* LaFave, Israel, King & Kerr, Criminal Procedure §§ 3.3(b), 3.8(d) (6th ed. 2017); Whitebread & Slobogin, Criminal Procedure: An Analysis of Cases and Concepts §§ 3.03(c), 11.03 (7th ed. 2020).

40. The right answer is (a). This question is based on *United States v. Duguay*, 93 F.3d 346 (7th Cir. 1996). When analyzing the propriety of an inventory search of a vehicle, the threshold question is whether the impoundment itself was proper. Thus, the police decision to impound (or seize) a vehicle must be kept separate from the decision to inventory (or search) a vehicle after it is in police custody. The underlying consideration when confronted with an impoundment issue is to determine if it was conducted pursuant to the "community caretaking function" described in *Cady v. Dombrowski*, 413 U.S. 433 (1973). The community caretaking doctrine recognizes that the police perform a multitude of community functions apart from investigating crime and encourages police to act in order to preserve and protect public safety. Illustrations include assisting drunk or injured citizens, taking control of vehicles left on a highway after an accident, or entering a house in response to calls for help. If the police are performing a valid and reasonable caretaking function, they may search and seize things and persons without probable cause or a warrant provided (1) they truly act in response to a safety need, (2) they adhere to established rules or sound policies, (3) their actions are reasonable, and (4) their specific acts are consistent with and within the scope of their caretaking justification. In the vast majority of impoundment cases, the actions will be upheld because, as the Supreme Court has indicated, "[t]he authority of the police to seize and remove from the streets vehicles impeding traffic or threatening public safety and convenience is beyond challenge." *South Dakota v. Opperman*, 428 U.S. 364 (1976). However, when impoundment is not responsive to the needs underlying the community caretaking doctrine, courts will find the impoundment (and the subsequent inventory search) unreasonable. *See, e.g., Miranda v. City of Cornelius*, 429 F.3d 858 (9th Cir. 2005) ("An officer cannot reasonably order an impoundment in situations where the location of the vehicle does not create any need for the police to protect the vehicle or to avoid a hazard to other drivers."). In the instant case, the police defend the impoundment by asserting that it was "for the protection of the owner of the vehicle and to protect the police department against liability." But the facts render this justification untenable. The car was off the highway, legally parked, and the driver, who lived at the complex along with the arrestee's brother, was available to take control of it (Gold was not arrested until she refused to turn over the keys *after* the police claimed authority to impound the vehicle). There is simply no safety justification whatsoever to support the impoundment, therefore rendering it unreasonable. **Answer (b) is attractive but it is not better than (a).** The Supreme Court has said that "standardized criteria or established routine must regulate . . . inventory searches," *Florida v. Wells*, 495 U.S. 1 (1990). While, the Court, in *Colorado v. Bertine*, 479 U.S. 367 (1987), indicated that police may use discretion pursuant to an impoundment policy, it never categorically stated that such a protocol determined the legality of impoundment. Some circuits require the existence of standardized criteria or an established routine before finding police decisions to impound reasonable, others rely on the underlying reasonableness of the action. *Compare United States v.*

Petty, 367 F.3d 1009 (8th Cir. 2004) ("Some degree of 'standardized criteria' or 'established routine' must regulate [impoundments]" but "an impoundment policy may allow some 'latitude' and 'exercise of judgment' by a police officer when those decisions are based on concerns related to the purposes of an impoundment."), *and United States v. Duguay, supra*, (" '[S]tandardized criteria or established routine must regulate' inventory searches."), *with United States v. Smith*, 522 F.3d 305 (3d Cir. 2008) (decision to impound a vehicle in the absence of a standardized procedure is not a per se violation of the Fourth Amendment provided it is reasonable and comports with the community caretaking function), *and United States v. Coccia*, 446 F.3d 233 (1st Cir. 2006) (rejecting contention that the absence of standardized criteria invalidates impoundment so long as the impoundment decision is reasonable under the circumstances. Among those criteria which must be standardized are the circumstances in which a car may be impounded.). Keep in mind that the existence of standardized criteria may be proven by reference to either written rules and regulations or testimony regarding standard practices. *See, e.g., United States v. Matthews*, 591 F.3d 230 (4th Cir. 2009). The point is to have a standardized practice that eliminates the discretion of the officer in the field and eliminates arbitrary action. This is possible even without written policies. **Answer (d) is also appealing but, again, is not better than (a)**. The caretaking function must not be used as a subterfuge to conduct a criminal investigation. But here, although the police acted to impound the car only after Vaughn told Gold not to surrender the keys, the facts are equivocal in terms of the officers' reasons for acting. Indeed, even though the Supreme Court's opinion in *Whren v. United States*, 517 U.S. 806 (1996) notes that an officer's motivation for acting is a consideration in evaluating the legality of inventory searches (and administrative inspections), some lower courts have concluded that "[t]he presence of an investigative motive does not invalidate an otherwise valid inventory search." *United States v. Kanatzar*, 370 F.3d 810 (8th Cir. 2004). So, the better answer remains (a). **Answer (c) is somewhat nonsensical and should be rejected**. The legality of an impoundment does not depend on who the driver of the vehicle was. **Answer (e) is not consistent with the facts.** Gold was not arrested until she refused to cooperate with the impoundment, and the police did know she was available to take control of the safely and legally parked car.

- **Additional references**: *See* LaFave, Israel, King & Kerr, Criminal Procedure § 3.7(e) (6th ed. 2017); Whitebread & Slobogin, Criminal Procedure: An Analysis of Cases and Concepts § 13.07 (7th ed. 2020).

41. **Answer (d) is the best choice.** This question is based on the facts of *Doe v. Little Rock School District*, 380 F.3d 349 (8th Cir. 2004), and, like other school search cases, is analyzed under the "special needs" line of Fourth Amendment jurisprudence. Although students have a *reduced* expectation of privacy in the items they carry to school, students do not completely lose their constitutional rights at the schoolhouse gate. **Answer (c) is wrong** because schoolchildren do retain an expectation of

privacy, albeit a reduced one, in the belongings they carry to school. *See, e.g., Safford Unified School Dist. No. 1 v. Redding*, 557 U.S. 364 (2009). This reduced expectation of privacy means that backpacks, etc., may be searched without a warrant and with a degree of individualized suspicion less demanding than the normal requirement of probable cause. In other words, reasonable suspicion is sufficient. *New Jersey v. T.L.O.*, 469 U.S. 325 (1985). (Keep in mind that this is *not* a drug testing case. In those cases, the Court has appeared to reject the requirement of individualized suspicion in favor of a general reasonableness balancing test that finds the state's interest in protecting student athletes or others voluntarily involved in extracurricular activities to outweigh the minimal intrusion of a urine test. *See, e.g., Board of Educ. v. Earls*, 536 U.S. 822 (2002). Furthermore, unlike the search here, a student's failure to pass a drug test in *Earls* did not result in the subsequent involvement of law enforcement authorities, as a finding of contraband did here.) While the *Doe* Court recognized that "schools surely have an interest in minimizing the harm that the existence of weapons and controlled substances might visit upon a student population," it noted that "public schools have never been entitled to conduct random, full-scale searches of students' personal belongings because of a mere apprehension." The Court hinted that had there been a demonstration of a "drug problem," as in *Earls* and *Vernonia School District 47j v. Acton*, 515 U.S. 646 (1995), or an indication that student safety was in immediate jeopardy, the suspicionless searches would have been upheld. Because there were no such facts, the Court held that the searches were unreasonable. **Answer (a) therefore errs** in asserting the generalized concerns described by the New Amsterdam administrators sufficiently justified the search. **Answer (b) draws a faulty analogy and is therefore incorrect.** The use of metal detectors and canine sniffs are permissible because they, unlike the practice here, do not amount to general rummaging. Recall that the Supreme Court has indicated that canine sniffs are not even searches because they do not disturb the privacy interests in non-contraband. *United States v. Place*, 462 U.S. 696 (1983). The use of metal detectors, like the use of dogs, is limited to identifying the presence of contraband and therefore does not threaten to reveal other personal or private items. **Answer (e) is wrong** because the Fourth Amendment does not have a least intrusive alternative component. *See, e.g., Earls, supra* ("[R]easonableness . . . does not require employing the least intrusive means, because the logic of such . . . arguments could raise insuperable barriers to the exercise of virtually all search-and-seizure powers."). The question is not whether the search was the least intrusive means of enforcing the state interest; rather, the question is whether the search, as conducted, was reasonable under the circumstances (considering the State's interest, the individual's privacy interest, and the degree of intrusion). Although *Safford Unified v. Redding, supra*, did indicate that the reasonableness of a student search would depend on the degree of intrusion in light of the age and sex of the student and the nature of the infraction, this should not be interpreted as imposing a least intrusive alternative requirement. Rather, it is the type of totality of the circumstances language the Supreme Court often uses when assessing the reasonableness of a search.

- **Additional references**: *See* LAFAVE, ISRAEL, KING & KERR, CRIMINAL PROCEDURE § 3.9(k) (6th ed. 2017); WHITEBREAD & SLOBOGIN, CRIMINAL PROCEDURE: AN ANALYSIS OF CASES AND CONCEPTS § 13.08 (7th ed. 2020).

42. **Although a close call, the strongest answer is (c).** That Martha was subjected to interrogation is beyond question (which, means that **answer (e) is irrelevant**). The only issue is whether Martha was in custody. If so, the statement will be excluded for lack of Miranda warnings. If, on the other hand, Martha was not in custody, then there was no custodial interrogation triggering Miranda and the statements may be properly used in the prosecution's case in chief. An interrogation is custodial when "a person has been taken into custody or otherwise deprived of his freedom of action in any significant way." *Miranda v. Arizona*, 384 U.S. 436 (1966). The high court has said that a court performing a Miranda custody analysis should "examine all of the circumstances surrounding the interrogation," *Stansbury v. California*, 511 U.S. 318 (1994) (*per curiam*), but should not consider the "actual mindset" of the particular suspect involved, *Yarborough v. Alvarado*, 541 U.S. 652 (2004). The Court has also said that a child's age is properly considered in the Miranda totality of the circumstances custody analysis. *J.D.B. v. North Carolina*, 564 U.S. 261 (2011). These rules may seem inconsistent with one another but the *J.D.B.* Court explained that a child's age "does not involve a determination of how youth affects a particular child's subjective state of mind." Rather, "childhood yields objective conclusions," including the common sense fact that "children will often feel bound to submit to police questioning when an adult in the same circumstances would feel free to leave." *J.D.B.* Accordingly, if an officer knows or has reason to know a suspect's age at the time of interrogation, the officer must take that into account in deciding whether to give Miranda warnings. Age will not necessarily be determinative or significant in every case and youth, standing alone, does not necessarily mean Miranda warnings have to be given. But, "children cannot be viewed simply as miniature adults." The totality of the circumstances in the instant case supports a finding of custody. The police and school officials knew or had reason to know Martha's age. Moreover, Martha was escorted to the office, the door was closed and the blinds were shut, there is no indication Martha was allowed to call her parents or guardian or that one was summoned on her behalf, and Martha was subjected to very real pressures to confess. *Cf. A.M. v. Butler*, 360 F.3d 787 (7th Cir. 2004) (eleven-year-old, who had no prior experience with criminal justice system, questioned for almost two hours in closed interrogation room with no parent, guardian, lawyer, or anyone at his side, who had no way of leaving police station and was never told he was free to go or that he was not under arrest, was "in custody" and entitled to *Miranda* warnings). It is highly unlikely a young girl would feel free to terminate the closed-door session, even if she wasn't told she was under arrest and it lasted under an hour. Therefore, **answer (d)**,

although appealing, is incorrect. Answer (a) is wrong. The false statements and encouragement to be honest here are not characteristic of the types of deception and trickery that worries courts. **Answer (b) overstates the idea underlying the less stringent requirements for school searches under the Fourth Amendment.**

- **Additional references**: *See* LaFave, Israel, King & Kerr, Criminal Procedure § 6.6(c) (6th ed. 2017); Whitebread & Slobogin, Criminal Procedure: An Analysis of Cases and Concepts § 16.03(a) (7th ed. 2020).

ANSWER KEY EXAM III
CRIMINAL PROCEDURE MULTIPLE CHOICE QUESTIONS ANSWER KEY AND EXPLANATIONS

1.   **Answer (a) is the best answer.** With some modification, questions 1 and 2 are based on *Tankleff v. Senkowski*, 135 F.3d 235 (3d Cir. 1998). The questions have been modified because, after over a decade of appeals, Tankleff's convictions were vacated. The charges were vacated because in the real case, Tankleff recanted his confession immediately after giving it, and the State never followed up on the man who the son said really committed the crimes—a man who owed Tankleff's father a large sum of money and staged his own death shortly after the murders. These facts do not exist in this version of the case. Question 1 poses the issue of when custody arises for the purposes of giving Miranda warnings. Miranda rules apply only if a suspect is interrogated while in police custody. *Oregon v. Mathiason*, 429 U.S. 492 (1977) (*per curiam*) (noting that an officer's obligation to administer *Miranda* warnings attaches "only where there has been such a restriction on a person's freedom as to render him 'in custody' "). Here, there is no question that Martin was interrogated as he was subjected to police questioning. *See Rhode Island v. Innis*, 446 U.S. 291 (1980). There is similarly no question that he did not receive Miranda warnings until after the detective's phone call ruse, two hours after questioning began at the station house. To determine whether a suspect was in custody, courts look at the totality of the circumstances of the interrogation and ask whether, from an objective point of view, a reasonable person would have understood himself to be under arrest. *Stansbury v. California*, 511 U.S. 318 (1994) (*per curiam*). Ultimately, the "inquiry is simply whether there [was] a 'formal arrest or restraint on freedom of movement' of the degree associated with a formal arrest." *California v. Beheler*, 463 U.S. 1121 (1983) (*per curiam*) (citation omitted). Stated differently, an accused is in custody when, even in the absence of a formal arrest, law enforcement officials act or speak in a manner that conveys the message that they will not permit the suspect to leave. Important factors include (1) the place of interrogation, (2) the length and nature of questioning, and (3) the demeanor of the officers. *See United States v. Bassignani*, 560 F.3d 989 (9th Cir. 2009) for an example of one circuit's custody factors. Lengthy and hostile interrogation in a police station interrogation room is highly indicative of custody. That was the case here. Martin voluntarily went to the police station, which normally cuts against a finding of custody, but, once there, he faced hostile questioning for two hours, the detectives accused him of showing insufficient grief, called his denials unbelievable, and said they could not

accept his story. They used the phone call ploy to trick him into making a statement and flatly accused him of the attack. As the decision noted, no reasonable person in Martin's position would have felt that he was free or would soon be free to leave. **Answer (b) is incorrect** because even though formal arrest or telling the suspect that he is under arrest is sufficient to create custody, and is indeed generally dispositive, such action is not necessary to find custody. **Answer (c) could be correct if other facts were not present.** Again, custody must be determined from all of the facts and circumstances that exist at the time the suspect is subject to questioning. Voluntarily going to the police station and voluntarily answering questions are important facts, and without more, might lead to a finding of no custody. But the facts develop further. Martin is subject to two hours of sharp questioning, accusation, and stratagems by the police. The fact that the incident began with a voluntary trip to the station house is only the beginning of the analysis. **Answer (d) is wrong** because it assumes that the police officer's subjective determination to take a suspect into custody is determinative. It is not. *Stansbury v. California, supra.* Custody is determined from the perspective of what a reasonable suspect would have thought in the circumstances—not what the police were thinking. Any thoughts of the officers which are not communicated to the suspect are irrelevant to the question of custody. This, of course, makes sense in light of the premise of Miranda that in-custody interrogation exerts an inherent compulsion on the suspect to speak. A suspect is not influenced by factors which are not known to him or perceived by him. **Answer (e) is incorrect** because it assumes that transporting a suspect in a police car is custody *per se*, which is not the case. Placing a suspect in a squad car could, in different circumstances, lead to a finding of custody. But here Martin willingly took the ride, and no custody would arise from that fact.

- **Additional references**: *See* LAFAVE, ISRAEL, KING & KERR, CRIMINAL PROCEDURE § 6.6 (6th ed. 2017); WHITEBREAD & SLOBOGIN, CRIMINAL PROCEDURE: AN ANALYSIS OF CASES AND CONCEPTS § 16.03(a) (7th ed. 2020).

2.   **Answer (b) is the best answer.** Question 2 requires the student to know the rules of both *Oregon v. Elstad,* 470 U.S. 298 (1985) and *Missouri v. Seibert,* 542 U.S. 600 (2004). In *Elstad* the police went to Elstad's home and, in circumstances later considered custodial, briefly talked to Elstad about a robbery. Elstad, who was not read his Miranda rights, gave incriminating answers. The police then transported Elstad to the police station where, about one hour later, he received Miranda warnings and gave a full confession. The Supreme Court held that the post-warning, police station statements were admissible so long as the in-home statements were voluntary and the police station statements were voluntary. The Court viewed the failure to give warnings in the home as a "mere Miranda" violation, not true compulsion within the meaning of the Fifth Amendment. Therefore, there was no direct violation of constitutional rights, only a violation of Miranda's prophylactic rules, and the usual derivative evidence rules applicable to involuntary confessions

or unreasonable searches and seizures would not apply. *Elstad* did suggest (and some lower courts agreed) that its rule might not apply if police deliberately evaded Miranda to secure an incriminating statement. That was the case in *Missouri v. Seibert, supra,* where police arrested Seibert at 3am and proceeded to question her for thirty to forty minutes. They obtained incriminating statements. After a short break, the police then administered Miranda warnings and continued the interrogation. The failure to give warnings initially was a deliberate technique to get *incriminating* statements, then warn, and then simply have the suspect repeat what was already disclosed. Indeed, after Seibert received the warnings, the police confronted her with her pre-warnings statements ("didn't you [already] tell me that he was supposed to die in his sleep?") Under these circumstances, a plurality of the Court concluded that deliberate questioning in successive phases before and after warnings required exclusion of the warned statement, absent curative measures. According to the plurality, giving a suspect warnings in the middle of an essentially continuous interrogation and after incriminating statements have already been secured, could not possibly be effective: "when Miranda warnings are inserted in the midst of coordinated and continuing interrogation, they are likely to mislead and deprive a defendant of knowledge essential to his ability to understand the nature of his rights and the consequences of abandoning them." *Oregon v. Elstad* was distinguished as a "short, earlier admission, obtained in arguably innocent neglect of Miranda." The plurality was joined by Justices Breyer and Kennedy. Justice Breyer believed the two-step approach required exclusion of the post-warning statements unless the initial failure to warn was in good faith. Justice Kennedy, whose opinion has been oft-cited as controlling, believed that post-warning statements obtained in a two-step approach "used in a calculated way to undermine Miranda" would be inadmissible unless curative measures were taken, such as a substantial break between the two interrogation sessions or an additional warning that the pre-warning statements would be inadmissible. Putting this together, you should approach questions of this nature in the following fashion. First, decide whether police deliberately flouted Miranda in the first round of interrogation. If so, the second confession can still be admitted if curative measures were taken. If, however, the failure to give Miranda warnings was inadvertent, as Justice Kennedy stated in his concurrence, "the admissibility of postwarning statements should continue to be governed by the principles of *Elstad.*" *United States v. Kiam,* 432 F.3d 524 (3d Cir. 2006). In this question, there are three important facts. This was a continuous interrogation and, thus, is unlike the situation in *Elstad.* Yet, it is distinguishable from *Seibert.* There is no apparent *deliberate* evasion of Miranda and little basis to argue that the police planned to exploit the initial failure to give warnings. Rather, it appears that they finally concluded that the voluntary interview had evolved into a true custodial interrogation. Moreover, Detective McCready gave an additional, curative warning that Martin's earlier, pre-warning statements could not be used against him. Thus answer (b) states the right result in this case. **Answer (a) goes too far and is wrong.** This answer states the rule of *Elstad* before it is modified by the Court's ruling in *Seibert*. Not all statements given after warnings will be admissible. That now depends on whether the questioning was a deliberate, two-step evasion of the Miranda rules and whether curative measures were taken. **Answer (c) similarly goes too far and is wrong.** Not all answers will be inadmissible even in a continuous session. If Miranda warnings are given at some point and if the failure to warn previously was in good faith and a curative warning is added, then the post-warnings statements could be admissible. **Answer (d) is wrong** because the facts do not support a finding that the questioning was coercive and amounted to an involuntary confession. Of course, if the initial statements were involuntarily obtained, or if the post-Miranda statements were involuntarily obtained, neither *Elstad* nor *Seibert* apply. **Answer (e) is wrong** because *Elstad* explicitly rejected the idea that the psychological impact of having already given a Miranda-violative statement ("letting the cat out of the bag") constituted compulsion within the meaning of the Fifth Amendment.

- **Additional references**: *See* LaFave, Israel, King & Kerr, Criminal Procedure § 9.5 (6th ed. 2017); Whitebread & Slobogin, Criminal Procedure: An Analysis of Cases and Concepts § 16.05(c) (7th ed. 2020).

3. **The right answer is (d).** Two principles are in play in this question which tracks *United States v. Ortiz,* 177 F.3d 108 (1st Cir. 1999). First, under *Edwards v. Arizona,* 451 U.S. 477 (1981), when a suspect in custody asserts his right to counsel, the police must cease questioning and not reinterrogate until counsel is present. Second, under *Oregon v. Bradshaw,* 462 U.S. 1039 (1989), after a suspect has invoked his right to counsel, the police may reinterrogate without a lawyer present *if* the *suspect* initiates a conversation with police concerning the charges against him. The police may then rewarn and seek a voluntary waiver of rights. Here the *police* took the initiative and approached Ortiz. That violates the *Edwards* rule, and *Oregon v. Bradshaw* is not applicable. The police may not reinitiate the questioning. **Answer (a) is incorrect** because, although Ortiz did ask about the charges against him, he did not initiate the conversation with the police. The officers approached him with an additional two sets of warnings and a question about whether he wanted to cooperate. **Answer (b) is wrong** because it relies on a faulty view of the law. For the purpose of Miranda and its progeny, it does not matter whether Officers O'Neil and Navarro knew of Ortiz's invocation of his right to have a lawyer. The idea is to protect the suspect, not relieve officers of the consequences of their ignorance. **Answer (c) is flatly contradicted** by *Edwards*. In this context, the Court has chosen a bright line and very suspect-protective rule: once a suspect invokes his right to counsel, all questioning is prohibited unless the lawyer is present or unless the suspect initiates discussion about the investigation. **Answer (e) is flatly contradicted** by *Oregon v. Bradshaw* which does permit some reinterrogation, even after invocation of a right to a lawyer, if the

defendant initiates the conversation and if warnings are repeated and waivers secured. The *Edwards* rule is not absolute.

- **Additional references**: *See* LAFAVE, ISRAEL, KING & KERR, CRIMINAL PROCEDURE § 6.9(f) (6th ed. 2017); WHITEBREAD & SLOBOGIN, CRIMINAL PROCEDURE: AN ANALYSIS OF CASES AND CONCEPTS § 16.03(e) (7th ed. 2020).

4. **The correct answer is (d).** This question requires the student to recognize a proper invocation of counsel in the Miranda context and to know the limits of the "initiation" exception to the rule prohibiting further questioning of a suspect who invokes the right to counsel. Once a suspect has waived his rights and questioning is underway, invocation of counsel must be "unambiguous." *Davis v. United States,* 512 U.S. 452 (1994). In *Davis* the Supreme Court ruled that a suspect's statement, "maybe I should talk to a lawyer," was an equivocal statement and not invocation. Here, however, although Glover's statement included a conditional element, "if you are going to continue talking about this," and although one could argue he was reacting to the officers' raised voices, he clearly said, "I want an attorney." Indeed, even though a request for counsel will be deemed clear or ambiguous without regard to the particular officers' views of the matter, it is telling that, here, the detectives immediately recognized the invocation as unequivocal and promptly ended the interrogation. Once there was invocation of the right to counsel, the police were not permitted to reinterrogate without counsel present. *Minnick v. Mississippi,* 498 U.S. 146 (1990). But if the suspect himself initiates a conversation with the police about the investigation, *Oregon v. Bradshaw,* 462 U.S. 1039 (1983), the police may seek a waiver of Miranda rights and begin questioning again without an attorney present. And *Bradshaw* took that very far indeed as the suspect simply asked, "what is going to happen to me now." However, not every comment equals initiation. Some comments are just observations about routine aspects of the custodial relationship, and they cannot fairly be said to evince a desire to open up a general discussion related to the investigation. Such was the case here. Glover's comments were an aside, or a reflection about the way the interrogation was conducted. As such they were more akin to "statements relating to routine incidents of the custodial relationship" or akin to asking for a glass of water or inquiring about when one could use the telephone. **Answers (a) and (b)** are wrong because they reach opposite results on the questions of invocation and initiation, respectively. **Answer (c) misunderstands the meaning of interrogation.** Interrogation is not only express questioning but also the functional equivalent of questioning. Any tactics which the police knew or should have known were reasonably likely to elicit an incriminating response, *Rhode Island v. Innis,* 446 U.S. 291 (1980), equal interrogation. Detective Rich's appeals to tell the truth and the accusation that he believed Glover was somehow involved are classic strategies viewed as interrogation. **Answer (e) is incorrect** because it assumes that the police shouting, without more, created a coercive environment, indeed so coercive that the influence of that encounter necessarily continued to Glover's second interrogation.

The facts do not support the conclusion that the police tactics, in the totality of the circumstances, were sufficiently coercive as to overcome the defendant's will or disable his ability to make a rational choice to speak.

- **Additional references**: *See* LaFave, Israel, King & Kerr, Criminal Procedure § 6.9(f) (6th ed. 2017); Whitebread & Slobogin, Criminal Procedure: An Analysis of Cases and Concepts § 16.03(e) (7th ed. 2020).

5. **The correct answer is (a).** This question is based on *United States v. Montgomery,* 150 F.3d 983 (9th Cir. 1998). Pretrial identification procedures may be so unreliable that they fatally taint, and thus render inadmissible, an in-court identification. The rationale is that use of woefully unreliable identification is fundamentally unfair and violates a defendant's right of Due Process of law. However, defendants face strong headwinds in proving a Due Process violation. To exclude evidence of a pretrial identification, or to exclude an in-court identification tainted thereby, a defendant must first show that the identification was unnecessary and suggestive, and if so, he must then show that it was also unreliable. *Manson v. Brathwaite,* 432 U.S. 98 (1977). An identification is suggestive when it "emphasize[s] the focus upon a single individual" thereby increasing the likelihood of misidentification. *But see Perry v. New Hampshire*, 565 U.S. 228 (2012) (holding that the Due Process Clause was not violated when an officer responding to a call asked the eyewitness to describe the suspect, who then pointed out her kitchen window and identified a man standing next to a police officer, because the unnecessarily suggestive circumstances were not arranged by law enforcement). Showing a single photo or placing the defendant in a line-up with persons of obviously different appearance are examples of suggestive procedures. A procedure is unnecessary when its use is not compelled by exigent circumstances, or it is not an on-the-scene show-up. The pretrial identification procedures used in this problem—the initial photo display and the faxed photo—were both suggestive (a display of one) and unnecessary (there was ample time to put together an array). However, even an unnecessarily suggestive identification is still admissible unless the defendant proves that, under the totality of the circumstances, it was unreliable. Relevant factors include: (1) the witness's opportunity to view the defendant at the time of the incident; (2) the witness's degree of attention; (3) the accuracy of the witness's prior description of the defendant; (4) the level of certainty demonstrated by the witness at the time of the identification procedure; and, (5) the length of time between the incident and the identification. *Manson v. Brathwaite,* 432 U.S. 98 (1977). Here, all of the factors point to a good and reliable identification, and answer (a) captures that conclusion and properly places the burden of proving unreliability on the defendant. **Answer (d) is incorrect** precisely because it places the burden of proving reliability on the government. **Answer (b) is wrong** because the Court has concluded that a truly unreliable identification creates a substantial likelihood of *irreparable* misidentification and, thus, requires complete exclusion, not just challenge via cross examination. **Answer (c)**

[handwritten margin note: Defendant carries the burden in Step 2.]

misapprehends the meaning of suggestive. An identification procedure can be suggestive without police coaching. It is enough if the procedure emphasized a single individual, such as here, where the police used the photograph of just one person. **Answer (e) goes too far.** There is no automatic requirement that a separate hearing be held, particularly here, where all of the facts emerged from the defendant's cross examination of the identifying witness. Of course, holding a separate hearing prior to trial is the better, and more usual, practice.

- **Additional references**: *See* LaFave, Israel, King & Kerr, Criminal Procedure § 7.4 (6th ed. 2017); Whitebread & Slobogin, Criminal Procedure: An Analysis of Cases and Concepts § 17.03 (7th ed. 2020).

6. **The best answer is (c).** The defendant enjoys a Sixth Amendment right to counsel at trial and at any confrontations with the state "where the accused [is] confronted with both the intricacies of the law and the advocacy of the public prosecutor." *United States v. Ash,* 413 U.S. 300 (1973). "The Court consistently has applied a historical interpretation of the [Sixth Amendment] guarantee, and has expanded the constitutional right to counsel only when new contexts appear presenting the same dangers that gave birth initially to the right itself." The surreptitious viewing of the defendant, as here, was not a trial-like confrontation like an arraignment, a preliminary hearing, or an actual line-up. It involved no adversarial confrontation, no opportunities for prosecuting authorities to take advantage of the accused, and no need for a lawyer's skills of defense. It was not, in other words, a "critical stage." **Answer (d) takes the contrary view and is not correct.** Unlike a true line-up, there were no opportunities for the prosecutor to take advantage of the accused, no special disabilities imposed on the defendant if left to fend for himself, and no inability to reconstruct events at trial. **Answer (e) states a correct rationale but offers the wrong conclusion.** There was no impairment of defense counsel's ability to have a full and fair opportunity to cross examine witnesses or for the defendant to receive a fair trial. **Answer (a) is wrong** because if the defendant's right to counsel applied here (but it didn't), no invocation would have been necessary. Blondin viewed the defendant surreptitiously. The defendant would have had no opportunity to invoke his right to counsel. **Answer (b) is incorrect.** There is state action here. The government arranged the circumstances and provided the opportunity for Blondin's observations. And the defendant is "available" to the witness precisely because of the state's proceedings against him.

- **Additional references**: *See* LaFave, Israel, King & Kerr, Criminal Procedure § 7.3 (6th ed. 2017); Whitebread & Slobogin, Criminal Procedure: An Analysis of Cases and Concepts § 17.02 (7th ed. 2020).

7. **The best answer is (e).** This question is a variation on the case of *United States v. Chadwick*, 433 U.S. 1 (1977). In *Chadwick*, the police seized a footlocker which they had probable cause to believe contained drugs, as is

the case here. The police did not search it at the scene, and therefore, could make no argument that it was a search incident to arrest, as is also the case here. Not only did a different officer take the defendant to the station before the search, but the station house search here was conducted at a time when the defendant could not access the bag. *Cf. United States v. Shakir*, 616 F.3d 315 (3d Cir. 2010) (reading *Arizona v. Gant*, 556 U.S. 332 (2009) "as refocusing our attention on a suspect's ability (or inability) to access weapons or destroy evidence at the time a search incident to arrest is conducted"). In the instant case, like in *Chadwick*, the bag had been removed from the trunk of the car. In *Chadwick*, the government did not argue that the connection to the vehicle eliminated the need for a warrant. Although containers in cars may be searched without a warrant, *see, e.g., California v. Acevedo, supra,* a principal rationale for the exception is the diminished expectation of privacy in a vehicle. Once a personal container or package is removed from a vehicle, however, that rationale is lost. As the Court stated in *Chadwick*, "The factors which diminish the privacy aspects of an automobile do not apply to respondent's footlocker." Footlockers, luggage, duffel bags, and other such items are "intended as a repository of personal effects," *Chadwick,* and designed for maintaining privacy whereas a car is a means of transportation that can be peered into and is subject to extensive inspection and regulation. **Thus, answer (c) is wrong** because the duffel bag, having been taken from the car to the porch, and left there until the next day, is no longer within the automobile exception, and a warrant was necessary for the search. **Answer (a) is incorrect** because, again, Skip had already been removed from the scene, time had elapsed, and police could no longer claim that the search was *incident* to the arrest, temporally or geographically. **Answer (b) is an attractive answer but is ultimately wrong** because it overstates the scope of the inventory search. Although items taken by the police and impounded are subject to inventory search, those searches, which may be conducted without probable cause or a warrant, must be pursuant to pre-established regulations or routinely followed procedures that constrain the discretion of the officers, and the officers must act in accordance with those regulations. *Florida v. Wells*, 495 U.S. 1 (1990). There are no facts to establish a valid inventory search here, and thus, the statement that "any search at police headquarters is a valid inventory search" covers too much ground. Note, however, that *Illinois v. Lafayette*, 462 U.S. 640 (1983), expressly permits inventory searches of personal items upon arrest if conducted pursuant to standardized procedures. (Note further that this is not a question about inevitable discovery. If the police department had a policy of inventorying, as most do, the officer's warrantless search here would have been excused by inevitable discovery.) **Answer (d) is wrong** because it suggests that Officer Chang lacked probable cause to arrest or search. That is incorrect. The informant was reliable, the information of criminality was based on firsthand observation, and the predicted behavior proved accurate. This easily meets the "fair probability" test set out in *Illinois v. Gates*, 462 U.S. 213 (1983).

- **Additional references**: *See* LaFave, Israel, King & Kerr, Criminal Procedure §§ 3.5(e), 3.7(c) (6th ed. 2017); Whitebread & Slobogin, Criminal Procedure: An Analysis of Cases and Concepts §§ 4.03(d), 6.03, 7.02–7.04 (7th ed. 2020).

8. **The best answer is (c).** Picking the correct answer to this question requires that you know the permissible scope of the actions police may take while lawfully arresting a dangerous felon inside a home. Police are entitled to ensure their own safety by looking into those spaces, including closets, which immediately adjoin the place of arrest and from which an attack upon them could be immediately launched. They need no probable cause or reasonable suspicion for this safety initiative. In addition, police may conduct a protective sweep through the rest of the premises and look anywhere another person could be hiding *if* they have reasonable suspicion based on articulable facts, that the area swept harbors an individual posing a danger to the officer or others. This is a quick, cursory inspection only. These rules were developed in *Maryland v. Buie,* 494 U.S. 325 (1990). **Answer (a) is wrong** because it eliminates the need for reasonable suspicion for the protective sweep of the premises, and **answer (b) is wrong** because it adds reasonable suspicion to the protective sweep of the immediate area of the arrestee. **Answers (d) and (e) miss the mark** by introducing the requirement of probable cause either to both protective actions (answer (d)) or to a sweep of the premises. Answer (e) is also wrong for introducing the requirement of reasonable suspicion to the sweep of the area immediately adjoining the arrest.

- **Additional references**: *See* LaFave, Israel, King & Kerr, Criminal Procedure § 3.6(d) (6th ed. 2017); Whitebread & Slobogin, Criminal Procedure: An Analysis of Cases and Concepts § 6.04(b) (7th ed. 2020).

9. **The right answer is (e).** As with most Fourth Amendment questions, the best strategy is to break down the fact pattern into smaller pieces— what did the police do, to whom, with what justification, and to what extent? Here the police properly stopped Potter for speeding. So far, so good. But, then, the officer, on rather flimsy suspicion, believes Potter possesses drugs and conducts a search (not a pat down/frisk) of his person. This was illegal, but only as to Potter. As a result of the search, the officer discovers a crack pipe and Potter candidly admits that he smokes crack. This is illegally obtained derivative evidence because there was no attenuation, *Wong Sun v. United States*, 371 U.S. 471 (1963), but, again, it is only illegally obtained as to Potter. The evidence gave the officer probable cause to believe there was cocaine in the vehicle. Accordingly, the officer was free to conduct a warrantless search of every place in the car where cocaine might be found, including containers, such as the handbag, belonging to a passenger provided the container was capable of concealing the evidence sought. *Wyoming v. Houghton*, 526 U.S. 295 (1999). **Answer (a) is incorrect.** The characterization of the search of Mr. Potter as a search incident to arrest is mistaken because nothing in the facts indicates an arrest occurred prior to searching the handbag.

Answer (b) is wrong because it fails to take account of the fact that Ms. Lambert has no standing to complain of the illegal search of Mr. Potter. For questions raising issues of standing, ask if the person seeking exclusion had her Fourth Amendment rights infringed *and* whether the disputed search and/or seizure infringed an interest that the Fourth Amendment was designed to protect. *Rakas v. Illinois*, 439 U.S. 128 (1978). *Rakas* rejected the idea that a third party could vicariously assert the Fourth Amendment rights of another. Remember, however, to keep this separate from the rule of *Brendlin v. California*, 551 U.S. 249 (2007), which provides that passengers have standing when challenging the legality of an initial vehicle *stop* (because when a car is stopped, all passengers in the car are effectively *seized*). *See also United States v. Grant*, 349 F.3d 192 (5th Cir. 2003) (while "the *search* of an automobile does not implicate a passenger's Fourth Amendment rights, a *stop* results in the seizure of the passenger and driver alike" (citation omitted)). But here the stop was valid. **Answer (d) is wrong** because it makes too much of the standing problem. Ms. Lambert has a reasonable expectation of privacy in her own possessions, such as her handbag, and would have standing to complain of that search. Of course, on the merits, she will lose. **Answer (c) errs** because it asserts that Officer Jenkins had probable cause to search Mr. Potter prior to finding the pipe and hearing Mr. Potter's admission when, at best, she had reasonable suspicion to investigate further.

- **Additional references**: *See* LaFave, Israel, King & Kerr, Criminal Procedure § 3.7(c) (6th ed. 2017); Whitebread & Slobogin, Criminal Procedure: An Analysis of Cases and Concepts § 7.04 (7th ed. 2020).

10. **The correct answer is (b).** The platform question here is whether the scope of the search was permissible. The answer is yes. Although the police found the "headquarters" of the obscenity operation in the basement, they were authorized to look everywhere on the premises for evidence of the obscenity operation, including accounts and proceeds. This entitled them to look at the letter. Thus they legally learned of Max as a potential witness. Although it is true that, if Max's name were discovered illegally, the exclusionary rule would not necessarily bar the testimony of a willing witness (the free will of the witness breaks the chain or, at least, fundamentally attenuates the causal connection to the illegality), *United States v. Ceccolini,* 435 U.S. 268 (1978), we don't have to rely on that principle here. Max's identity was discovered legally. **Thus answer (a) is faulty** because it asserts that Max's name was discovered illegally. **Answer (c) is wrong** because the entry into the house was lawful. The police need not wait to execute a warrant until someone is at home. They knocked, announced their presence, and waited. Only then did they gain entry by forcing the door—entirely reasonable conduct under the circumstances. **Answer (d) misstates the legitimate scope of this search.** Police need not stop looking for evidence once they have discovered the likely bulk of what they are looking for; they may continue and search everywhere on the described premises where further evidence

may be found. **Answer (e) sounds wholesome but it's nutty.** A person may have a reasonable expectation of privacy in a letter, but probable cause and a warrant allow that interest to be invaded, and there is nothing to the idea that at least one party to the letter had to consent to its opening.

- **Additional references:** *See* LaFave, Israel King & Kerr, Criminal Procedure § 3.4(j) (6th ed. 2017); Whitebread & Slobogin, Criminal Procedure: An Analysis of Cases and Concepts § 5.05 (7th ed. 2020).

11. **The best answer is (b).** To answer this question correctly, you need to be familiar with the Court's ruling in *New York v. Harris,* 495 U.S. 14 (1990). There the Court said that a probable cause, but warrantless, arrest in the home (even if the warrant was purposefully not sought) operated to exclude only incriminating statements *in the home.* The Court's theory, much criticized, was that the lack of a warrant was a transgression against the sanctity of the home and that, once the police left the home, the transgression was at an end. It did not carry over to subsequent questioning or incriminating statements. However, the Court was careful to point out that its rule applied only to an arrest made *with probable cause.* In contrast, an arrest *without probable cause* is, in effect, a continuing transgression against the liberty of the person to be free of unlawful restraint. So the strongest basis to exclude the statements in the squad car and at headquarters is to pull this case outside of *Harris.* That can be done because the facts say that the police "suspected" that Winchell murdered his brother. A suspicion is not probable cause. That said, it becomes immaterial to argue the close question of whether the comments in the house were the functional equivalent of interrogation and, hence, **answer (a) is wrong. Answers (c) and (d) are inadequate to move the case out of the control of *Harris.*** Therefore, they are not the strongest bases for excluding the later statements. **Answer (e) assumes that the failure to have a warrant carries significance outside of the house and is wrong.** Moreover there is no duty to warn that the incriminating statements made in the home cannot be used. Although a warning is considered good police practice, and would help to ensure the admissibility of the Mirandized statements, it goes too far to describe a warning as a duty.

- **Additional references**: *See* LaFave, Israel, King & Kerr, Criminal Procedure § 9.4(a) (6th ed. 2017); Whitebread & Slobogin, Criminal Procedure: An Analysis of Cases and Concepts § 2.04(b)(3) (7th ed. 2020).

12. **The correct answer is (d).** There are three salient events in this problem: the police encounter with the tavern patrons in the bar, Buffy's request to have a lawyer, and Buffy's agreement to talk about the crime but not put anything in writing. In the tavern encounter, the police discover a homicide and a small group of people, one of whom likely committed it. It is fair to construe the command to "freeze" as a temporary detention to investigate via on-the-scene questions. It would go too far to

characterize the situation as custody since a reasonable person, innocent of any crime, would not consider the circumstances as the functional equivalent of arrest. The police behavior is entirely consistent with a detention to figure out what the situation was, as illustrated by the brief questioning of each patron and the fact that Buffy was readily permitted to leave. The situation is akin to an ordinary traffic stop, which is just that, a stop. *Berkemer v. McCarty,* 468 U.S. 420 (1984). Under the circumstances, the requisite justification for a stop, namely, reasonable suspicion, exists to permit this investigative detention. So far, so good. Next, Buffy's "invocation" of her right to counsel, while clear, is untimely. For this invocation to be effective under Miranda, it must come at the time when she faces actual or imminent custodial interrogation. *McNeil v. Wisconsin,* 501 U.S. 171 (1991). For this invocation to be effective for Sixth Amendment purposes, the right to counsel must have attached (via the commencement of adversary proceedings, i.e., the filing of a formal charge). *Moran v. Burbine,* 475 U.S. 412 (1986). On these facts, neither condition is met. Finally, Buffy's agreement to talk but her unwillingness to put anything in writing is similar the defendant's situation in *Connecticut v. Barrett,* 479 U.S. 523 (1987). Buffy's waiver may signal her ignorance that oral statements can be just as damning as written ones. But, since she received and, by all accounts, understood the basic Miranda warnings, she effectively waived her Miranda rights. This is a sufficiently "knowing and intelligent" waiver for Miranda purposes. **Answer (a) is wrong because, as indicated, Buffy manifested an understanding of the Miranda warnings** *per se,* and that is sufficient. **Answer (b) misfires** because Buffy cannot anticipatorily invoke her Miranda rights; she must be facing interrogation. **Answer (c) is incorrect** because it assumes that the police encounter in the tavern was an arrest thus triggering the need for probable cause. It was, however, no more than a detention. In any event, there is a basis to say that even probable cause existed because there was a fight in the tavern, a homicide resulting therefrom, and a small enough group of suspects to believe there was a fair probability that all of them were implicated in one way or another. This is a stretch, perhaps, but it is an issue that need not be reached. **Answer (e) is doubly faulty** because there were no errors in the tavern, and if there were (e.g., a lack of probable cause, an invocation of the right to counsel), they could not be cured by the giving of Miranda warnings. That cure could work if there were an initial set of inadequate warnings, statements secured, then the giving of proper warnings and a second set of statements secured. That is not this scenario.

- **Additional references**: *See* LaFave, Israel, King & Kerr, Criminal Procedure §§ 6.4(e), 6.6 (6th ed. 2017); Whitebread & Slobogin, Criminal Procedure: An Analysis of Cases and Concepts § 16.03 (7th ed. 2020).

13. **Among the choices, answer (e) is the strongest argument that Marty could make to suppress his confession.** This is because if the Sixth Amendment waiver was not knowing and intelligent, then it was not valid. Here, Marty was given Miranda warnings after his Sixth

Amendment right attached (Marty was indicted). Because Miranda warnings sufficiently apprise defendants of the right to counsel under both the Fifth and Sixth Amendments, a waiver of Miranda rights can also function as a waiver of the Sixth Amendment right to counsel during interrogation. *Montejo v. Louisiana*, 556 U.S. 778 (2009) ("[W]hen a defendant is read his Miranda rights (which include the right to have counsel present during interrogation) and agrees to waive those rights, that typically does the trick."); *Patterson v. Illinois*, 487 U.S. 285 (1988). However, this does not mean "that all Sixth Amendment challenges to the conduct of postindictment questioning will fail whenever the challenged practice would pass constitutional muster under Miranda." *Patterson v. Illinois, supra.* In footnote nine, the *Patterson* Court explained that while the Court permitted a Miranda waiver to stand in the Fifth Amendment context where a suspect was not told that his lawyer was trying to reach him during questioning, *Moran v. Burbine*, 475 U.S. 412 (1986), "in the Sixth Amendment context, this waiver would not be valid." (The Court provided another illustration, pointing to the difference in treatment of statements made to undercover officers by unindicted suspects and the indicted accused.) Although this footnote may stand on shakier ground given the outcome and rationale of *Montejo*, the Court has not directly confronted the issue. As such, answer (e) represents Marty's best chance for getting the confession excluded. **Answer (d) is incorrect** because it mirrors the argument made by the defendant, and explicitly rejected by the Court, in *Moran*. In the context of custodial interrogation, events unknown to a suspect have no bearing on the capacity to comprehend and knowingly relinquish a constitutional right. **Answer (a) may sound logical but it is wrong.** *Patterson* says if a defendant received Miranda warnings, he was sufficiently apprised of his Sixth Amendment rights and the consequences of abandoning those rights. As such, a waiver on this basis will be considered a knowing and intelligent one. Consequently, no special supplementary warnings are required in order to find a valid waiver of Sixth Amendment rights in the context of interrogation. Only one Circuit Court ever imposed an additional indictment warning requirement before a valid Sixth Amendment waiver would be found; however, this approach was abandoned in the wake of *Patterson*. **Answer (b) errs** because even though Marty may have been appointed counsel at the arraignment, the Supreme Court has indicated that there is no reason to assume that a defendant like Marty, who has done nothing at all to express his or her intentions with respect to Sixth Amendment rights, would not be amenable to speaking with police in the absence of counsel. *See Montejo v. Louisiana, supra.* **Answer (c) is incorrect for two reasons.** First, *Berghuis v. Thompkins*, 561 U.S. 1046 (2010), makes it clear that a prolonged silence is not an invocation of a suspect's Miranda rights. Suspects must unambiguously and unequivocally invoke their right to silence. Second, even if the aforementioned rule did not exist, there would still be no violation. After four hours of interrogation, the police gave up for the evening, returning to interrogate Marty again the following morning. This is certainly a sufficient amount of time to satisfy the rule of *Michigan v. Mosley*, 423 U.S. 96 (1975), which requires police officers to "scrupulously honor" a valid invocation of silence. *Cf. United States v. Rambo*, 365 F.3d 906 (10th Cir. 2004) ("Whatever else *Mosley* might require, it is clear that some break in the interrogation must occur.").

- **Additional references**: *See* LAFAVE, ISRAEL, KING & KERR, CRIMINAL PROCEDURE § 6.4(e)–(f) (6th ed. 2017); WHITEBREAD & SLOBOGIN, CRIMINAL PROCEDURE: AN ANALYSIS OF CASES AND CONCEPTS §§ 16.03(c), 16.04(c) (7th ed. 2020).

14. **The right answer is (c).** The police entered McGiver's house without a warrant and, ordinarily, this Fourth Amendment violation of the sanctity of the home would require that statements in the house be excluded from evidence. *New York v. Harris*, 495 U.S. 14 (1990). But, new crimes committed in front of the officer are generally not considered fruits of the antecedent violation. *United States v. Smith*, 7 F.3d 1164 (5th Cir. 1993) (failure to give inmate in psychiatric ward Miranda warnings during interview conducted by warden and Secret Service agent did not prevent prosecution of new crime of threatening President of United States, made during interview). Thus, if a person assaults a police officer or another, as here, or attempts to bribe an officer, evidence of that new crime is admissible. *See, e.g., United States v. Hunt*, 372 F.3d 1010 (8th Cir. 2004) (bribe in response to illegal detention and arrest properly admitted at trial as a new and distinct crime); *United States v. Waupekenay*, 973 F.2d 1533 (10th Cir. 1992) (holding that evidence of a separate, independent crime initiated in police officer's presence after police illegally entered defendant's trailer will not be suppressed under the Fourth Amendment). This is true even if the suspect's acts were a response to illegal police activity. *United States v. Sprinkle*, 106 F.3d 613 (4th Cir. 1997). In these cases, the suspect's own illegal acts are sufficiently attenuated from the initial illegality and are thus not properly excluded under the doctrine of *Wong Sun v. United States*, 371 U.S. 471 (1963). **Answer (a) is wrong** because it would provide too much suspect protection concerning statements in the house. Although the con scheme statements would be inadmissible as products of the illegal entry into the house, the threats were a new crime and will not be excluded. **Answer (b) is wrong** because it would provide too little suspect protection concerning the statements in the house. The new crimes evidence will be admissible, but the con scheme statements would not be. **Answer (d) is incorrect.** There are some constitutional errors involving "rights so basic to a fair trial that their infraction can never be treated as harmless error," *Chapman v. California*, 386 U.S. 18 (1967). But this isn't one of them. Those types of errors are structural errors that are deemed to infect the entire trial process such as a total deprivation of counsel. The type of error here is a trial error, a type of error that can be assessed in the context of all the other evidence. *Arizona v. Fulminante*, 499 U.S. 279 (1991). Answer (d) is also wrong because the police are not attempting to use the statements regarding the fraud. Rather, they are using it in an unrelated prosecution for assault. In assessing whether a defendant committed a crime following

unconstitutional police conduct, circuit courts rely on an objective analysis of the circumstances to determine whether there was probable cause to arrest for a distinct crime. The officers here certainly had probable cause to arrest McGiver for the assault, as it was committed in their presence. The initial subjective intent of the officers is thus irrelevant. **Answer (e) is essentially beside the point.** There are no facts showing that McGiver was subject to interrogation, so the lack of Miranda warnings is irrelevant. But even if there had been interrogation, the new crimes rule would still be the same. That is, even though Miranda violative incriminating statements would not be admissible, evidence of a new crime conducted in the officers' presence would not be considered a fruit of the Miranda violation.

- **Additional references**: *See* LAFAVE, ISRAEL, KING & KERR, CRIMINAL PROCEDURE §§ 9.4(f), 27.6 (6th ed. 2017); WHITEBREAD & SLOBOGIN, CRIMINAL PROCEDURE: AN ANALYSIS OF CASES AND CONCEPTS § 29.05 (7th ed. 2020).

15. **The right answer is (e).** In general, the grand jury is entitled to every person's testimony, and anyone summoned to appear is required to do so. *Branzburg v. Hayes*, 408 U.S. 665 (1972). However, a witness appearing before a grand jury does retain some privileges (explaining why **answer (a) is overbroad and wrong**), including the Fifth Amendment privilege against self-incrimination. *Counselman v. Hitchcock*, 142 U.S. 547 (1892). The burden is on the witness claiming the privilege to invoke it before answering incriminating questions. Some states have, by statute, required that all grand jury witnesses, including targets, receive Miranda-style warnings advising them of their right not to incriminate themselves. But no such right exists as a matter of federal constitutional law and, after the Court's decision in *United States v. Williams*, 504 U.S. 36 (1992), it does not appear that federal courts may prophylactically regulate grand jury procedures via their supervisory power by, for example, imposing a warning requirement. Moreover, most federal courts considering the matter have refused to treat a grand jury appearance as analogous to the inherently coercive setting of in-custody police interrogation. As the Supreme Court has said, "for many witnesses the grand jury room engenders an atmosphere conducive to truthtelling. . . . But it does not offend the guarantees of the Fifth Amendment if in that setting a witness is more likely to tell the truth than in less solemn surroundings." *United States v. Washington*, 431 U.S. 181 (1977). A grand jury appearance is regarded as more akin to an appearance before a judicial tribunal, like a trial or preliminary proceeding, and to extend Miranda warnings "to questioning before a grand jury inquiring into criminal activity under the guidance of a judge is an extravagant expansion never remotely contemplated by this Court in Miranda." *United States v. Mandujano*, 425 U.S. 564 (1976) (noting that the oath requirement puts witnesses on notice). The Supreme Court has also held that a witness need not be informed that he is a target of the grand jury, that is, that he is someone likely to be indicted. *United States v. Washington, supra.* As a matter of practice, however, the United States

Department of Justice polices itself by requiring self-incrimination warnings to be given to potential targets (note, however, that there is no private remedy for a violation of this policy). Of course, the warnings cannot track Miranda precisely because a grand jury witness does not have a general right to remain silent but only a right not to incriminate himself. Similarly, a witness does not have a constitutional right to have a lawyer present in the grand jury room, *Conn v. Gabbert*, 526 U.S. 286 (1999), or a right to have counsel appointed. All of the aforementioned should be enough to conclude that Ferris's incriminating statements could be used against him in this question. But there's more. In *United States v. Wong*, 431 U.S. 174 (1977), the court considered whether a witness (who was also a target) who gave false testimony before a grand jury (and was subsequently indicted for perjury) was entitled to have the false testimony suppressed on the ground that she was not effectively apprised of her Fifth Amendment privilege. The Court held that the Fifth Amendment grants a privilege to remain silent without risking contempt, but it "does not endow the person who testifies with a license to commit perjury." As the Court stated in *Oregon v. Hass*, 420 U.S. 714 (1975): "[T]he shield provided by Miranda is not to be perverted to a license to testify inconsistently, or even perjuriously. . . ." **Answers (b) and (c) are wrong** because there is neither a constitutional requirement of a warning regarding one's right against self-incrimination or about one's target status. **Answer (d) is appealing, but it is not correct.** Given the nature of a grand jury appearance—no lawyer at your side, a secret proceeding, questioning by the prosecutor—one could argue that explicit waiver of one's rights should be required. But the Supreme Court has never recognized such a requirement and, again, even if there were such a rule and it was not adhered to, that behavior would not be a defense to perjury.

- **Additional references**: *See* LAFAVE, ISRAEL, KING & KERR, CRIMINAL PROCEDURE § 8.10 (6th ed. 2017); WHITEBREAD & SLOBOGIN, CRIMINAL PROCEDURE: AN ANALYSIS OF CASES AND CONCEPTS §§ 23.04–23.05 (7th ed. 2020).

16. **The right answer is (c).** Don't be fooled by the failure of the police to finish giving Miranda warnings here. This is a volunteered statement. And volunteered statements, statements offered by a suspect without police questioning on his or her own initiative, *are always admissible*. Miranda itself makes this plain: "volunteered statements of any kind are not barred by the Fifth Amendment and their admissibility is not affected by our holding today." **Answers (a) and (e) are incorrect** because they put emphasis on waiver, but waiver is not in issue. We never get to waiver because the suspect volunteered his statements before warnings were completed. He did not submit to questioning—he simply offered a confession on his own initiative. *See United States v. Maret*, 433 F.2d 1064 (8th Cir. 1970). **Answer (b) is wrong** because the volunteered statements made the Miranda warnings irrelevant. The suspect was not subjected to interrogation. **Answer (d) is really off** because there has

been no invocation of a right to counsel or anything remotely suggesting it.

- **Additional references**: *See* LaFave, Israel, King & Kerr, Criminal Procedure § 6.7(d) (6th ed. 2017); Whitebread & Slobogin, Criminal Procedure: An Analysis of Cases and Concepts § 16.03 (7th ed. 2020).

17. **The correct answer is (a).** The leading case is *Steagald v. United States*, 451 U.S. 204 (1981). Federal agents arrested Lyons in Steagald's home, and while in Steagald's home, found evidence against Steagald. Steagald claimed that the evidence was inadmissible against him because the police had only an arrest warrant for Lyons, but no search warrant to enter his premises. The Supreme Court agreed and explained that an arrest warrant addresses only the interests of the arrestee. A search warrant, carrying the imprimatur of a neutral judicial officer that there exists probable cause to believe that the perpetrator is in a third party's home, is needed to protect the third party's separate interests. That is the situation in this question. **Answer (b) is wrong.** Plain view could offer a basis to establish probable cause to seize evidence of a crime, but a valid plain view must come from a spot *where officers are lawfully entitled to be.* The officers here did not have a search warrant to enter Marge's home and, thus, a plain view justification is unavailable. **Answer (c) is wrong** because police only developed probable cause to arrest Marge after they entered the house and spied the cocaine. It was their entry, however, which was unlawful, and the ensuing discoveries are inadmissible. **Answer (d) misses the mark, too.** Again, it is not what did or did not develop after the police were in the house. It was unlawful to enter the house without a search warrant in the first place. **Answer (e) is incomplete.** In order to secure a search warrant to arrest Flanders in Marge's home, the police would need probable cause to believe that Flanders would be found there. But probable cause, while necessary, is not sufficient. There was no search warrant.

- **Additional references**: *See* LaFave, Israel, King & Kerr, Criminal Procedure § 3.6(a) (6th ed. 2017); Whitebread & Slobogin, Criminal Procedure: An Analysis of Cases and Concepts § 3.04(c) (7th ed. 2020).

18. **The best choice is (e).** In this question, Eleanore is not anonymous. She is an ordinary citizen in the presence of the police. Under these circumstances, she is presumed reliable because she gives a firsthand account and has no motive to lie. Moreover, her eyewitness account and the immediate identification of the perpetrator is a factual basis sufficient to create a "fair probability" (*Illinois v. Gates*, 462 U.S. 213 (1983)) that it was Drummond who robbed her. There is, in other words, probable cause to arrest Drummond. **Answer (a) is incorrect.** Even if police had employed an investigative stop here, it would not have been to obtain a search or arrest warrant. If there was probable cause to arrest, which there was, no warrant would be needed for a public place arrest. If there was a basis to arrest, a search incident could be conducted without a

warrant. **Answer (b) is wrong** because no right to counsel had yet attached. Drummond was not even arrested much less indicted or facing formal charges. **Answer (c) may have some superficial appeal, but it is incorrect.** The answer may lure you into thinking that driving Eleanore around the area was an unnecessarily suggestive identification procedure. And if you've gone that far, you might think that, to avoid a Due Process reliability problem, maybe a lineup would have been preferable. Whoa. First, this was not a one-man show-up as that practice is generally understood. In such a procedure, the police have the suspect in hand and the victim or witness is asked to confirm or deny that he is the offender. Here the police just drove Eleanore around, and she looked at whomever she pleased. But, even if the facts here were equivalent to a show up, an exception to the unnecessarily suggestive line of cases is recognized for show-ups occurring in proximity to and near the time of the crime. Absent unusual circumstances, such prompt identifications are regarded as necessary and likely to lead to accurate identifications. *See, e.g., Brisco v. Ercole,* 565 F.3d 80 (2d Cir. 2009) (show-up immediately after the crime was not unnecessarily suggestive: "If no identification was made at the showup, the officers could resume their search for the offender"); *United States v. Martinez,* 462 F.3d 903 (8th Cir. 2006) ("Police officers need not limit themselves to station house line-ups when an opportunity for a quick, on-the-scene identification arises. Such identifications are essential to free innocent suspects and to inform the police if further investigation is necessary. Absent special elements of unfairness, prompt on-the-scene confrontations do not entail due process violations."). In any event, there is no categorical rule requiring line-ups as the means of identification although they are preferred. **Answer (d) is the next best answer but not better than (e).** Even though, under the circumstances, Eleanore is presumed reliable, and even though her account and subsequent identification "would warrant a prudent [officer] in believing that the [suspect] had committed or was committing an offense," *Beck v. Ohio,* 379 U.S. 89 (1964), a detailed description of the robber would have strengthened the case. But, still, that is not to say that the case for probable cause has *not* been made. It has.

[handwritten margin note: Exception to the unnecessarily suggestive show-up (if there's one)]

- **Additional references**: *See* LaFave, Israel, King & Kerr, Criminal Procedure § 3.3(d) (6th ed. 2017); Whitebread & Slobogin, Criminal Procedure: An Analysis of Cases and Concepts §§ 3.03, 18.03 (7th ed. 2020).

19. **The best choice is (d).** A correct selection depends on reducing these facts to two questions: what level of suspicion did the police have with respect to Moriarity, and what level of suspicion did they have with respect to Pinky. For Moriarity, the police plainly had probable cause to arrest for drug selling since he, in fact, just sold drugs to Detective Watson. He could be arrested and, *a fortiori,* he could be subject to the lesser intrusion of a frisk. For Pinky, however, the situation is different. The detectives have no information about him and have observed no illegal conduct by him. They only know that he is associated with Moriarity and was with him in the apartment just prior to Moriarity's sale

to Watson. This may give rise to reasonable suspicion, but it falls short of probable cause to arrest Pinky for a crime. Thus, answer (d) correctly states that the arrest of Moriarity was lawful but the arrest of Pinky was not. **Answer (a) is wrong** because no warrant was needed for a public place arrest, as here. *United States v. Watson*, 423 U.S. 411 (1976). **Answer (b) is wrong** because, even though the stop and frisk of the duo may have been valid, it is not true that *neither* was subject to arrest since there was probable cause to arrest Moriarity. **Answer (c) is based on a non-existent rule.** There is no obligation for police to obtain a warrant for an arrest as soon as they develop probable cause, and there are no consequences for failure to do so. **Answer (e) falters** because it pronounces the arrest of Pinky as lawful, but there was no probable cause for that intrusion.

- **Additional references**: *See* LaFave, Israel, King & Kerr, Criminal Procedure § 3.3 (6th ed. 2017); Whitebread & Slobogin, Criminal Procedure: An Analysis of Cases and Concepts §§ 3.03, 3.04(a) (7th ed. 2020).

20. **The correct answer is (b).** The fingerprinting of Woody was unlawful because the police forcibly took him to headquarters without probable cause to arrest. This action, though taking only an hour and for the arguably limited purpose of fingerprinting, was a seizure amounting to arrest for Fourth Amendment purposes. That Woody was not told he was under arrest and was not "booked," does not make his seizure even roughly analogous to the narrowly defined intrusions approved in *Terry v. Ohio*, 392 U.S. 1 (1968). *Terry* allows police officers to stop individuals upon a standard of proof less than probable cause because a stop is far less intrusive than an arrest. But, here, the police forcibly moved Woody to the stationhouse, which seems like the type of overly intrusive investigation technique the Fourth Amendment was designed to limit. Although the Supreme Court has hinted that it might consider detention at the stationhouse for fingerprinting, as opposed to interrogation or conventional custody, as something less than an arrest and something, therefore, demanding less than probable cause, *Davis v. Mississippi*, 394 U.S. 721 (1969), it has not so held. In fact, the Court came out the other way in *Hayes v. Florida*, 470 U.S. 811 (1985). Here, as in *Davis* and *Hayes*, there was no probable cause to arrest, no consent to the trip to the police station, and no judicial authorization for such an investigatory detention, even if for the limited purpose of obtaining fingerprints. **Answers (a), (c), and (e) are all similarly flawed** because they assume that only reasonable suspicion was needed to take Woody to headquarters. Answer (a) is additionally off the mark in suggesting that the giving of fingerprints implicates the Fifth Amendment. Fingerprint evidence is "non-testimonial," and the Fifth Amendment does not come into play. *Schmerber v. California*, 384 U.S. 757 (1966) ("Both federal and state courts have usually held that [the privilege] offers no protection against compulsion to submit to fingerprinting, photographing, or other measurements, to write or speak for identification, to appear in court, to stand, to assume a stance, to walk, or to make a particular gesture.").

Answer (c) also raises false issues because it suggests that separate probable cause and a warrant would be needed to take someone's fingerprints. If the police had probable cause to arrest Woody, then taking his fingerprints would work no new intrusion, and no additional probable cause or a warrant would be necessary. (While not relevant to this question, students may be interested to know that DNA testing is gaining prevalence as an identification technique, and the courts are analogizing this technique to fingerprinting. *Maryland v. King*, 569 U.S. 435 (2013) (taking and analyzing cheek swab of arrestee's DNA is like fingerprinting and mug shots, a legitimate booking procedure reasonable under the Fourth Amendment). Similarly, the Third Circuit has held that post arrest, pre-conviction DNA testing, like fingerprinting, conducted with probable cause is a reasonable identification technique under the Fourth Amendment. *United States v. Mitchell*, 652 F.3d 387 (3d Cir. 2011) (*en banc*).) On the facts of this question, the flaw is the lack of probable cause to arrest. **Answer (d) is wrong** because, although consent and a subpoena duces tecum are *alternate* ways of obtaining fingerprints, they are not the *only* ways of doing so.

- **Additional references**: *See* LaFave, Israel, King & Kerr, Criminal Procedure § 3.8(g) (6th ed. 2017); Whitebread & Slobogin, Criminal Procedure: An Analysis of Cases and Concepts § 3.02(a) (7th ed. 2020).

21. **The right answer is (c).** Frequently the government may obtain evidence either via a warrant or a grand jury subpoena. That is the case here. A warrant requires probable cause to think that evidence of a crime may be found in a particular place. The victim described items, including the diary, which she observed first hand. There is no suggestion that the victim is unreliable, or that the information is stale, nor is there any other reason to doubt the existence of probable cause. A subpoena duces tecum issuing from a grand jury may reach any evidence relevant to its investigation. The Fourth Amendment is satisfied so long as the subpoena is reasonable in scope and particularity. All of those ingredients are satisfied on these facts. The only possible wrinkle is whether a "diary," as a very personal document, is entitled to any additional protection under either the Fourth or Fifth Amendments. The answer is no, with an explanation. First, this "diary" is not fairly characterized as conventional diary, i.e., a highly personal record such as one might keep next to the bed and in which write the most personal of information. It is more like a business record. Second, even if it were a true diary, the logic of the Supreme Court's cases, if not the precise holdings, removes the need for any special justification. At one time, the Supreme Court, in the interests of the privacy of the home and personal documents, held that warrants could not reach "mere evidence," that is, evidence which was not contraband, or proceeds, or instrumentalities of crime. *Gouled v. United States*, 255 U.S. 298 (1921). But in *Warden v. Hayden*, 387 U.S. 294 (1967), the Court repudiated this idea. And in *Andresen v. Maryland*, 427 U.S. 463 (1976), the Court said that even "communicative" documents were subject to seizure. The Court found that a warrant to seize documents

involved no Fifth Amendment claim because there was no government compulsion to *create* the documents—they already existed by choice of the defendant. Although *Andresen* involved only business records, its rationale and language appear to apply to all documents. **Answer (d) misfires** because it takes the opposite approach and assumes that the Fifth Amendment would bar both the warrant and the subpoena. **Answer (a) is wrong** because a subpoena *and* a warrant could be used here. **Answer (b) is an overstatement.** It is true that the good faith exception will cover many lapses in getting a warrant. But it will not excuse "any constitutional objection." **Answer (e) is incorrect in two ways.** First, there is no *Fourth Amendment* act of production doctrine. This arises only under the Fifth Amendment and is supported by *Fisher v. United States*, 425 U.S. 391 (1976). Second, the act of production exception protects persons who are compelled to turn over information to a grand jury, via subpoena, not those who have property taken from them by a warrant. In the case of the subpoena, a person forced to bring information to the grand jury is, in effect, forced to testify that she knew of the evidence in question and had custody of it. (For an example of a case in which the rare act of production exception was properly invoked, *see In re Sealed Case*, 832 F.2d 1268 (D.C. Cir. 1987) (simply admitting control over the records was incriminating and therefore, Fifth Amendment privilege applied).) With warrants, the police can obtain the evidence.

- **Additional references**: *See* LAFAVE, ISRAEL, KING & KERR, CRIMINAL PROCEDURE §§ 3.2(i), 3.4, 8.3(c), 8.12–13 (6th ed. 2017); WHITEBREAD & SLOBOGIN, CRIMINAL PROCEDURE: AN ANALYSIS OF CASES AND CONCEPTS §§ 5.03, 5.06(a), 23.05, 24.02(a)(4) (7th ed. 2020).

22. **Answer (d) is the best answer.** All claims of excessive force involving "free" citizens, whether deadly or not, are assessed under Fourth Amendment standards of reasonableness. *Graham v. Connor*, 490 U.S. 386 (1989). (Excessive force claims of prisoners are evaluated under the Eighth Amendment's cruel and unusual punishment clause.) **Answer (c) errs** because due process does not govern excessive force claims. *See, e.g., Bryan v. Macpherson*, 630 F.3d 805 (9th Cir. 2010). When evaluating the appropriateness of force, courts balance the nature and quality of the intrusion on the individual's Fourth Amendment interests against the counterveiling governmental interests at stake. *Scott v. Harris*, 550 U.S. 372 (2007); *Tennessee v. Garner*, 471 U.S. 1 (1985). Stated differently, courts "balance the amount of force applied against the need for that force." *Meredith v. Erath*, 342 F.3d 1057, 1061 (9th Cir. 2003). In some cases that would mean even deadly force could be justified. *Plumhoff v. Rickart*, 572 U.S. 765 (2014). This balancing is objective, viewing the use of force from "the perspective of a reasonable officer on the scene, rather than with the 20/20 vision of hindsight." *Graham v. Connor, supra.* The factors guiding the government interest prong are "[1] the severity of the crime at issue, [2] whether the suspect poses an immediate threat to the safety of the officers or others, and [3] whether he is actively resisting arrest or attempting to evade arrest by flight." *Graham v. Connor, supra;*

see also Davenport v. Causey, 521 F.3d 544 (6th Cir. 2008) (listing other considerations such as "the number of lives at risk, relative culpability of those at risk, the demeanor of the suspect, the relative size and [apparent strength] of the parties involved, and whether the suspect was fighting with police"). Use of these factors demonstrates that the amount of force against Feather was unjustified and thus unreasonable. To begin, Feather had a weighty interest in avoiding the violent seizure and avoiding the serious injuries. On the other hand, the State's interests were not particularly compelling. First, Feather was stopped for speeding, not a violent crime. *See, e.g., Parker v. Gerrish*, 547 F.3d 1 (1st Cir. 2008) ("Though driving while intoxicated is a serious offense, it does not present a risk of danger to the arresting officer that is presented when an officer confronts a suspect engaged in an offense like robbery or assault."). There was no substantial government interest in employing significant force to effect Feather's arrest for a traffic violation, which at most amounts to a misdemeanor. *Bryan v. Macpherson, supra* ("Our sister circuits have likewise concluded that misdemeanors are relatively minor and will generally not support the deployment of significant force."). Second, although Feather was shouting and acting strangely, a reasonable police officer would not think Feather posed an immediate threat. *Bryan v. Macpherson, supra* ("Although [defendant] had shouted expletives . . . and had taken to shouting gibberish, and more expletives, outside his car, at no point did he level a physical or verbal threat against Officer MacPherson."); *Smith v. City of Hemet*, 394 F.3d 689 (9th Cir. 2005) (*en banc*) (although the victim was shouting expletives, there was no threat leveled against the officer). Moreover, Feather was wearing only shorts and shoes. There was no indication he was carrying a weapon, and, his attire suggests that he was not reasonably able to conceal a weapon on his person. Because there was no reasonable perception of risk to Officer Segal, **answer (e) is incorrect.** Third, Feather was not actively resisting arrest or attempting to flee but was standing 20 feet away. Officer Segal did not even warn Feather that he might be shot with a taser if he didn't calm down. In sum, the amount of force used here was excessive in light of the specific facts surrounding the incident. **Answer (a) is wrong** because although tasers are in the non-lethal force category (rendering **answer (b) erroneous as a general matter**), they are still subject to the reasonableness balancing test. That tasers are non-lethal does not mean that their use is automatically non-excessive. *Bryan v. Macpherson, supra* (rejecting argument that because tasers result in "temporary" inflictions of pain, their use is automatically a non-intrusive level of force). Moreover, non-lethal force is not a monolithic category: "A blast of pepper spray and blows from a baton are not necessarily constitutionally equivalent levels of force simply because both are classified as non-lethal." *Bryan v. Macpherson, supra*. While non-lethal force is easier to justify than lethal force ("lethal force" is force that creates a substantial risk of death or serious bodily injury, *Smith v. City of Hemet, supra*), courts must still consider whether the amount of force was justified under the circumstances. Here, it was not.

- **Additional references**: *See* LaFave, Israel, King & Kerr, Criminal Procedure § 3.5(a) (6th ed. 2017); Whitebread & Slobogin, Criminal Procedure: An Analysis of Cases and Concepts § 3.05(b) (7th ed. 2020).

23. **The best answer is (d).** This question is loosely based on *United States v. Groves*, 530 F.3d 506 (7th Cir. 2008) *cert. denied*, 555 U.S. 1176 (2009) and concerns the validity of Mrs. Smith's consent. First, there is the question of whether Mrs. Smith may give consent to search the house, including the bedroom, that she and Mr. Smith share(d). The answer is yes because Mrs. Smith was listed as living at the address and had not yet moved her things out. Technically, Mrs. Smith had actual authority over the house. *United States v. Matlock*, 415 U.S. 164 (1974). Even if she didn't possess actual authority, the police had no reason to question her authority so her consent was valid under the doctrine of apparent authority. *Illinois v. Rodriguez*, 497 U.S. 177 (1990). Under either doctrine, Mr. Smith is deemed to have assumed the risk that Mrs. Smith would consent to a search. Second, given the suggestion in the facts that Mrs. Smith may not have appreciated the fact that she could refuse consent, is her consent valid? Yes, again. Ordinarily a waiver of one's constitutional rights requires knowledge of the right to refuse waiver. Nevertheless, with respect to consent to search, knowledge of one's right to refuse is a relevant but not a necessary ingredient to finding valid consent. The test is whether the consent is voluntary and "the prosecution is not required to demonstrate . . . knowledge [of the right to refuse] as a prerequisite to establishing a voluntary consent." *Schneckloth v. Bustamonte*, 412 U.S. 218 (1973). Consent is voluntary so long as, under the totality of the circumstances, the will of the person consenting is not overborne by the police. Here, Mrs. Smith was not pressured or tricked, and the police told her what they were seeking. The fact that they were rebuffed by Mr. Smith the day before is relevant, but does not render her consent the product of coercion or duress, by implicit or explicit means. Finally, did Mr. Smith's apparent rejection of consent on the previous day invalidate Mrs. Smith's consent? No. The Court in *United States v. Groves*, *supra*, did indicate that the defendant's previous denial to authorize consent, the magistrate's denial of a search warrant, and the officers' subsequent decision to approach the apartment at a time when they knew the defendant would be absent "gave them pause." However, following *Georgia v. Randolph*, 547 U.S. 103 (2006), they found the search constitutional. This was reaffirmed in *Fernandez v. California*, 571 U.S. 292 (2014), where the Court held that defendant's wife's consent to search the premises was valid even though the defendant had objected to the search when the officer initially approached the home. The rationale used to uphold the search as reasonable applies with equal force to the question presented here. First, *Georgia v. Randolph* requires that the objecting co-tenant be physically present at the door in order to render consent involuntary as to him. Mr. Smith was *not* present when Mrs. Smith gave consent, and hence, she did not give consent in the face of his contemporaneous objection. Secondly, there is no evidence that the police

removed the potentially objecting tenant, Mr. Smith, from the entrance for sake of avoiding a possible objection. Because the police did not actively secure Mr. Smith's absence, there is no violation of *Georgia v. Randolph, supra,* and **answer (e) is wrong.** The cocaine will be admissible in Mr. Smith's trial. **Answer (a) is incorrect** because it was sufficient that Mrs. Smith had authority to consent and voluntarily gave it. **Answer (b) is wrong** because Mr. Smith has standing to object to the search. Standing depends on having a reasonable expectation of privacy in the area searched, and Mr. Smith plainly has such an interest in his own home. **Answer (c) misunderstands the consequences of a valid consent to search.** Once valid consent is given, it eliminates the need to establish probable cause.

- • **Additional references**: *See* LaFave, Israel, King & Kerr, Criminal Procedure § 3.10 (6th ed. 2017); Whitebread & Slobogin, Criminal Procedure: An Analysis of Cases and Concepts §§ 12.01–12.05 (7th ed. 2020).

24. **The right answer is (d).** This question is fashioned from the classic derivative evidence case of *Wong Sun v. United States*, 371 U.S. 471 (1963). There the police illegally seized the defendant, Wong Sun. Wong Sun then gave incriminating statements to the police. The defense sought to exclude the statements as derivative of the illegal seizure. The Court, however, refused to apply the exclusionary rule saying that the connection between Wong Sun's illegal arrest and his statements "had become so attenuated as to dissipate the taint" of the original illegality. That is, Wong Sun's decision to speak resulted not from the illegal arrest, but, rather, from an intervening act of free will. He had been arrested, arraigned, and released on his own recognizance. He voluntarily returned to the police station to make his statements. We have a similar case here. The police invaded Rebecca's house without a warrant, and, had she made statements then and there, those would have been excluded. But Rebecca was arraigned and had returned home. The next day, at the prompting of her mother, she "thought it over" and voluntarily returned to the police station to give a statement. Although this is a closer case than *Wong Sun* (because there was an illegal arrest and an illegal search and because only one day, not several, intervened), the facts are strong to conclude that Rebecca's statements were the product of her own decision to speak and not caused by the illegal police action. **Answer (a) reaches the opposite conclusion and is wrong. Answer (b) mistakenly assumes that warnings were necessary for Rebecca's statement to be voluntary.** Rebecca was not in custody, and she spoke on her own initiative, not at the prompting of the police. **Answer (c) is a correct observation but irrelevant.** It is true that Rebecca has no standing to complain of the illegal acts against Tommy, but Rebecca faced her own illegal invasion when the police entered and searched her home without a warrant. **Similarly, answer (e) makes a correct observation but draws a wrong conclusion.** Arraignment is a critical stage for purposes of the Sixth Amendment, and Rebecca's right to counsel had attached, but the confession is not thereby inadmissible. There was no violation of her Sixth

Amendment right because her statement was voluntary and not the product of deliberate elicitation by the state.

- **Additional references**: *See* LaFave, Israel, King & Kerr, Criminal Procedure §§ 9.3(c), 9.4 (6th ed. 2017); Whitebread & Slobogin, Criminal Procedure: An Analysis of Cases and Concepts § 12.04(b) (7th ed. 2020).

25. **The best answer is (d).** Although the Supreme Court in *Camara v. Municipal Court*, 387 U.S. 523 (1967), modified the usual requirements of a warrant and probable cause in connection with regulatory inspections of homes, it did not dispense with them altogether. Rather, the Court held that non-consensual residential inspections were unreasonable without a warrant, but that a warrant need not be based on probable cause that the inspected building contained violations. It would be sufficient if there was "area-wide" probable cause, that is, probable cause to believe that the *area as a whole*, because of the age of the buildings or the time elapsed since previous inspections or other neutral criteria, needed to be inspected. Since there was no warrant here, the non-consensual inspection is unlawful. **Answer (a) is wrong.** There may be probable cause to inspect this particular house, but, in the absence of an emergency (a matter not raised on the facts), a warrant is still needed. **Answer (b) sounds plausible, but there are no facts to support it in the question.** The Court has held, at least with respect to business inspections of "closely regulated businesses," that warrantless inspections may be permissible if there is a demonstrated need to dispense with warrants, if the government has a substantial interest in close regulation of the type of business, (such as arms sales), and if the inspection scheme provides "a constitutionally adequate substitute for a warrant." *Donovan v. Dewey*, 452 U.S. 594 (1981). Here there is a residential inspection, and a warrant is needed. **Answer (e) is just not the law.** Consent is nice, and the Court has assumed that consent will be given in most cases, but inspections may be made pursuant to area-wide warrants if consent is not forthcoming.

- **Additional references**: *See* LaFave, Israel, King & Kerr, Criminal Procedure § 3.9(b)–(c) (6th ed. 2017); Whitebread & Slobogin, Criminal Procedure: An Analysis of Cases and Concepts §§ 13.02, 13.03 (7th ed. 2020).

26. **The correct answer is (a).** Reasonable suspicion cannot be based on hunches or a gut feeling that something "doesn't look right." There must be articulable facts that would warrant an officer of reasonable caution to think that criminal activity is afoot. *Terry v. Ohio*, 392 U.S. 1 (1968). Seeing two men standing together in an alley with one of them unknown to the officer is too flimsy even for the thin requirements of reasonable suspicion. *Brown v. Texas*, 443 U.S. 47 (1979). The pat down here was unwarranted because there is no indication the officer believed that the subject of the frisk was armed or dangerous. *Terry v. Ohio*, *supra*. And the scope of the pat down, involving as it did reaching into the man's pocket and examining the contents of a container, was beyond a permissible frisk because *Terry* frisks cannot be used to search for evidence. The police

officer in this question "overstepped the bounds of the strictly circumscribed search for weapons allowed under *Terry*." *Minnesota v. Dickerson*, 508 U.S. 366 (1993). **Answers (b), (d), and (e) incorrectly assume** that there were grounds for the stop and that the only questions relate to either the frisk (answer (b)), or to the scope of the stop (answers (d) and (e)). But the problem goes deeper; there were no grounds for the stop. **Answer (c) is correct about the stop, but is stumbles in the conclusion that the frisk was proper.**

- **Additional references**: *See* LAFAVE, ISRAEL, KING & KERR, CRIMINAL PROCEDURE § 3.8 (6th ed. 2017); WHITEBREAD & SLOBOGIN, CRIMINAL PROCEDURE: AN ANALYSIS OF CASES AND CONCEPTS §§ 11.03–11.05 (7th ed. 2020).

27. **The correct answer is (e).** Miranda warnings were not given to Smith before he made his incriminating admission about having a couple of drinks. There is interrogation here, but the key question is whether there is custody. The answer is no. An ordinary traffic stop, as here, is non-custodial. *Berkemer v. McCarty*, 468 U.S. 420 (1984); *see also United States v. Vinton*, 594 F.3d 14 (D.C. Cir. 2010); *Wilson v. Sirmons*, 536 F.3d 1064 (10th Cir. 2008). The fact that the officer planned to arrest Smith for drunk driving does not alter that conclusion. Custody is judged from the perspective of the suspect, that is, would a reasonable person, innocent of any crime, *and in the suspect's circumstances*, believe that he was under arrest. An officer's unconveyed intentions or undisclosed assessment of the situation, if not communicated to the suspect, cannot influence the issue of whether the person is in custody for purposes of Miranda. *See Berkemer v. McCarty, supra*; *Stansbury v. California*, 511 U.S. 318 (1994) (*per curiam*). It may seem curious that a traffic stop amounts to a "seizure" under the Fourth Amendment but does not amount to "custody" for the purposes of Miranda and the Fifth Amendment. But recall that the doctrine of *Terry v. Ohio*, 392 U.S. 1 (1968) permits a brief investigative detention (a "stop") in order to investigate a reasonable suspicion of criminal activity. In the context of a traffic stop, "reasonable suspicion" is defined as a particularized and objective basis for believing that the person being stopped is committing or did commit a traffic violation. In other words, if police detain a car and its occupants pending inquiry into an actual vehicular violation (here, reckless driving), the *Terry* condition of a lawful investigatory stop is satisfied. *Arizona v. Johnson*, 555 U.S. 323 (2009). Further recall that *Terry* suggests that the scope of the detention must be related to the purpose for which the detention was initially made. As long as the police conduct during the stop is reasonably related to the circumstances justifying the stop, the officer may investigate the facts on which their reasonable suspicion is based in order determine whether the suspect is engaged in unlawful activity. *Cf. Berkermer v. McCarty, supra* (roadside stop did not become an arrest where the officer asked the suspect a limited number of questions and asked suspect to perform a simple balancing test). Here, the initial stop was to investigate a reasonable suspicion that Smith was driving under the influence of alcohol. Thus, it follows that the officer's use of a

breathalyzer to determine whether Smith was intoxicated did not exceed the scope of the otherwise permissible stop. *See, e.g., Amundsen v. Jones*, 533 F.3d 1192 (10th Cir. 2008); *United States v. Caine*, 517 F. Supp. 2d 586 (D. Mass. 2007) ("Courts have deemed field sobriety tests to be within the scope of the initial stop, when the stop is based on a reasonable suspicion that the driver was under the influence of alcohol."). Accordingly, the fact that the officer here administered a roadside sobriety test did not convert the stop into an arrest. Although a full array of tests or a prolonged and demanding on-the-scene evaluation *could* convert the stop into full-fledged custody, a breath test following consent from the suspect is akin to consent to search a car, and is thus not custody. *See Ohio v. Robinette*, 519 U.S. 33 (1996). **Answer (d) incorrectly states** probable cause was necessary. Probable cause is not necessary for an ordinary traffic stop because it is not an arrest (custody in Miranda terms). It is simply a brief detention, so a standard less than probable cause is all that is required. **Answers (a) and (c) are both wrong** because they assume that there was custody and that Miranda was applicable. **Answer (b) improperly concludes that the roadside sobriety test was an unlawful search.** Although a breathalyzer, like a urine sample, can properly be considered a search, *Skinner v. Railway Labor Executives' Ass'n*, 489 U.S. 602 (1989), a "field sobriety test is a minor intrusion on a driver only requiring a reasonable suspicion of intoxication and an easy opportunity to end a detention before it matures into an arrest," *Wilder v. Turner*, 490 F.3d 810 (10th Cir. 2007). The State's great interest in preventing drunk driving outweighs the minimal the nature and degree of the intrusion. Moreover, it is arguable that Smith consented to the test.

- **Additional references**: *See* LaFave, Israel, King & Kerr, Criminal Procedure § 6.6 (6th ed. 2017); Whitebread & Slobogin, Criminal Procedure: An Analysis of Cases and Concepts § 16.03(a)(1) (7th ed. 2020).

28. **The right answer is (d).** On these facts there is both custody and interrogation. Hence Miranda warnings were necessary, and since not given, the government may not use Harry's incriminating statements against him. Custody arises from the flagrant circumstances and is not affected by the officers' statements that there is no arrest and that Harry could remain free until morning. Four officers made a late-night home invasion, surrounded Harry, and trained their guns on him. A reasonable person in such circumstances, even one innocent of any crime, would believe he was under arrest. It is highly relevant and frequently determinative that police tell a suspect he is not under arrest, but all of the circumstances have to be weighed. Again, on these facts, the flagrancy, fright, and fear associated with the dominating actions of the police dwarf the statement of no arrest. More to the point, though, the no-arrest statement came *after* the incriminating statements were secured, and custody must be measured in the circumstances and at the time the incriminating statements are obtained. There was also interrogation. A demand that a person "come clean" or reveal incriminating information is

the functional equivalent of questioning., Interrogation need not be in the form of express questions; it is enough if the police use words or actions "that the police should know are reasonably likely to elicit an incriminating response from the suspect." *Rhode Island v. Innis*, 446 U.S. 291 (1980). **Answer (a) is wrong** because it asserts that there was no interrogation. **Answer (b) is wrong** because it asserts that there was no custody. **Answer (c) is not factually supportable but,** even if a claim of voluntariness could be successful, Miranda would still foreclose use of Harry's statements. **Answer (e) is incorrect.** Even if the statements were unlawfully obtained from Harry, Bob would have no standing to object to how they were secured. And if the statements amount to probable cause, they can be used to arrest Bob.

- **Additional references**: *See* LAFAVE, ISRAEL, KING & KERR, CRIMINAL PROCEDURE §§ 6.6–6.7 (6th ed. 2017); WHITEBREAD & SLOBOGIN, CRIMINAL PROCEDURE: AN ANALYSIS OF CASES AND CONCEPTS § 16.03(a)–(b) (7th ed. 2020).

29. **The best answer is (c).** This question is loosely based on the facts of *United States v. Flood*, 339 Fed.Appx. 210 (3d Cir. 2009) (unpublished) *cert. denied* 559 U.S. 1055 (2010). The main issue here is whether the warrant was properly supported by probable cause. If not, the warrant was invalid and if it was so deficient in probable cause that a reasonable officer could not rely on it, then even the good faith exception will not save the day. *United States v. Leon*, 468 U.S. 897 (1984). Moreover, if the warrant was invalid then Flood's in-home confession will have to be suppressed as the product of the illegal entry. *New York v. Harris*, 495 U.S. 14 (1990). If, however, the warrant was valid then the motion will be denied. So, how does the warrant fare in the instant case? The warrant issued here is called an anticipatory search warrant. This is so because the facts indicate that the place to be searched was sufficiently described as were the items to be seized. However, the items (the marijuana and other evidence of drug activity) were not at Flood's house when the warrant was issued. This is fine because like regular search warrants, anticipatory warrants require the magistrate to determine (1) that it is now probable that (2) contraband, evidence of a crime, or a fugitive will be on the described premises (3) when the warrant is executed. *United States v. Grubbs*, 547 U.S. 90 (2006). Thus, the fact that the warrant here did not describe the "triggering condition" is not fatal as the Supreme Court stated in *Grubbs*. Implicit in the warrant is that it will not be executed until the trigger, here the delivery of marijuana, occurs. **Answer (a) is wrong** because the contraband did not have to be at the home before the warrant issued, as the law of anticipatory search warrants teaches us, and because it wrongly asserts that Brubaker was unreliable. Anticipatory warrants require two probable cause analyses. The first is that there is a "fair probability that contraband or evidence of a crime will be found in a particular place." *Illinois v. Gates*, 462 U.S. 213 (1983). Here, Brubaker's inside knowledge as a participant in the drug distribution network, in addition to the other information the police presumably gathered about Flood prior to even soliciting Brubaker's assistance in

their investigation, provided a fair probability that the marijuana would be at Flood's house. The second probable cause inquiry is whether there is also probable cause to believe that the triggering condition will occur. For all we know, shipment delays could be a regular occurrence in the drug delivery industry and thus, two delayed shipments do not render Brubaker's information unreliable. Thus, answer (c) is correct because the warrant was supported by probable cause. Furthermore, the police entry occurred only after Brubaker confirmed that the marijuana was in fact in the residence. **Answers (b) and (d) are wrong** because they both make erroneous assertions about the knock and announce requirement. While answer (b) correctly states that the knock and announce requirement is part of the reasonableness equation, a violation of this rule does not result in the exclusion of evidence. *Hudson v. Michigan*, 547 U.S. 586 (2006). This is because the "interests protected by the knock and announce requirement do not include the shielding of potential evidence from the government's eyes." Rather, the requirement protects (1) life and limb, (2) property from being destroyed (e.g., a door), and (3) the elements of privacy and dignity that can be sacrificed by a sudden police entry. Excluding the evidence because of a violation of the knock and announce rule would thus not be responsive to the underlying interests protected by the rule itself. Assuming that the rule was violated, exclusion will not be the remedy. Answer (d) was explicitly rejected by the Court in *Richards v. Wisconsin*, 520 U.S. 385 (1997). **Answer (e) is incorrect** and was specifically rejected in *United States v. White*, 401 U.S. 745 (1971). In that case, the Court held that there is no search when a willing informant wears a wire. The Court reasoned that the law permits the frustration of actual expectations of privacy and, much to the chagrin of the dissenters, endorsed assumption of the risk approach by explaining that one who engages in illegal activities must realize the risk that his companions may be reporting these activities to law enforcement authorities. While not relevant to the correct answer here, students should note that some states such as Alaska and Michigan do not permit the recording of conversations without the consent of all parties.

- **Additional references**: *See* LaFave, Israel, King & Kerr, Criminal Procedure § 3.3 (6th ed. 2017); Whitebread & Slobogin, Criminal Procedure: An Analysis of Cases and Concepts § 5.03 (7th ed. 2020).

30. **The best answer is (e).** The police must have a warrant to arrest a person in his or her home, unless some exigency or emergency excuses this obligation. The usual emergency justifications are hot pursuit, imminent danger to the police or the public, or imminent destruction of evidence. The facts negate any of these possibilities. First, Col. Mustard is quite unaware he is being watched or pursued and seems to have settled in for the night. Most courts say that a suspect must be aware he or she is being pursued for exigent circumstances to apply. *Cf. Welsh v. Wisconsin*, 466 U.S. 740 (1984). This is because hot pursuit is an amalgam of the other exigent circumstances insofar as the underlying premise is that if police do not pursue the suspect, he could continue to be a danger

or could destroy relevant evidence. Here, there is nothing "hot" going on at all. Second, there is no imminent danger to anyone. Again, Col. Mustard is unaware he is being watched, there are no facts suggesting he is armed (and the candlestick has been recovered), and he is apparently alone in the house. Third, there is no threat of imminent destruction of evidence because police seem to have recovered all of the evidence from the house already, including the candlestick, and again, Mustard is unaware he is under surveillance. Since the police arrested Mustard without a warrant, any statements taken from him in the house (had there been any) would be inadmissible as the fruit of the unlawful invasion into the home. *See New York v. Harris*, 495 U.S. 14 (1990). **Answer (a) wrongly assumes** there is an emergency. **Answer (b) is simply contrary to the facts** in asserting there is no probable cause. The facts say that the police have an eyewitness and physical evidence linking Col. Mustard to the crime. **Answer (c) is not a wise choice.** Arrest warrants, unlike search warrants, do not become stale. Unless probable cause evaporates—in which case, there will be no basis to arrest—once there is probable cause to arrest, that justification continues. Moreover, there are no facts suggesting flight. To the contrary, all is in repose. **Answer (d) may sound appealing but resist, because it's wrong.** There is no murder crime scene exception to the warrant requirement. An actual emergency is still a prerequisite to a crime scene search, even if it was a murder crime scene. *Mincey v. Arizona*, 437 U.S. 385 (1978); *Thompson v. Louisiana*, 469 U.S. 17 (1984).

- **Additional references**: *See* LaFave, Israel, King & Kerr, Criminal Procedure § 3.6(a) (6th ed. 2017); Whitebread & Slobogin, Criminal Procedure: An Analysis of Cases and Concepts §§ 3.04(d), 8.03 (7th ed. 2020).

31. **The right answer is (a).** Peacock has been arraigned and, consequently, her Sixth Amendment right to counsel has attached. If the state then surreptitiously tries to elicit incriminating evidence from Peacock, (and, thus, improperly interposes itself between her and her counsel) that evidence will be excluded from her trial. But the state's actions here, although deliberate, were not elicitation. Using a jailhouse plant who merely listens and does not provoke conversation or affirmatively draw out discussions about the crime does not amount to elicitation. *Kuhlmann v. Wilson*, 477 U.S. 436 (1986). If the jail plant had initiated and stimulated conversations about the crime, even if instructed by government agents not to do so, the result would be different. *United States v. Henry*, 447 U.S. 264 (1980). The fact that Peacock was placed in a jail cell which looked in the direction of the crime is an apparently coincidental and lucky circumstance and, again, not deliberate elicitation. **Answers (b), (c), and (d) are all wrong** because they assume that use of an informant under the circumstances amounted to deliberate elicitation and, therefore, a violation of the Sixth Amendment. **Answer (e) is similarly flawed but, in addition, is too sweeping a statement of applicable law.** It is simply not true that, once the right to counsel has attached, that only defendant-initiated statements are admissible.

There are circumstances, not here applicable, where the defendant has been indicted, advised of that fact and given his Miranda warnings, and where *the police* may initiate conversation and seek a waiver of the Sixth Amendment right. *See Patterson v. Illinois*, 487 U.S. 285 (1988).

- **Additional references**: *See* LAFAVE, ISRAEL, KING & KERR, CRIMINAL PROCEDURE § 6.4(g) (6th ed. 2017); WHITEBREAD & SLOBOGIN, CRIMINAL PROCEDURE: AN ANALYSIS OF CASES AND CONCEPTS § 16.04(b) (7th ed. 2020).

32. **The best answer is (b).** Despite feints and irrelevant facts, such as the police having no probable cause and looking into the windows of the farmer's house, the principal focus here is whether the invasion into the shrub-obscured garden was protected by the Fourth Amendment. The answer is no because the area is akin to an open field and society does not recognize privacy interests in such areas. Despite fences, no trespassing signs (or laws), despite the landowner's efforts or desires to keep others away or any other subjective expectation of privacy, areas away from the home and not within the curtilage (that is, structures or areas immediately adjacent to the house or appurtenant to the house; extensions of the house where private and intimate activities take place), are not protected by the Fourth Amendment. Although these unprotected areas are dubbed "open fields," they need not actually be open or actually comprise fields. *Oliver v. United States*, 466 U.S. 170 (1984); *United States v. Dunn*, 480 U.S. 294 (1987). **Answer (a) is radically wrong**. Although canine sniff cases such as *United States v. Place*, 462 U.S. 696 (1983) seem to imply that there is no privacy interest in contraband, if contraband could be pursued by any means so long as it was, in fact, contraband, we would effectively repeal the Fourth Amendment. Police could do what they wished so long as, in the end, they were right about the illicit nature of what they seized. **Answer (c) is not the best choice.** While it is true that observations made from low flying aircraft, where the public would have access, are not searches, *California v. Ciraolo*, 476 U.S. 207 (1986), there is no assurance on these facts that the airspace above the plants, from which the relevant observations could be made, is in fact accessible to the public. *See Florida v. Riley*, 488 U.S. 445 (1989). Answer (b) is the better choice because the area is an open field and that is enough. **Answer (d) erroneously portrays the facts.** The police are acting on an uncorroborated, anonymous tip, which is not enough to provide reasonable suspicion. *Florida v. J.L.*, 529 U.S. 266 (2000) (anonymous tip that a certain person with a plaid shirt and standing at a bus stop had a gun was held insufficient to create reasonable suspicion to stop or frisk). **Answer (e) fumbles** because it bespeaks a much too expansive concept of the curtilage. The area of the curtilage must be determined on a case-by-case basis, but necessary ingredients include the proximity to the home, the nature of the activities conducted there, the sheltered or enclosed quality of the area, and the property owner's efforts to keep the area private. *United States v. Dunn, supra*. We are looking for areas that are effectively extensions of the house and thus within its umbrella of privacy. Here, the area is a quarter of a mile from the home, and it is used

for growing plants. Even though the property owner took steps to conceal the area from others, it was readily accessible to anyone walking in that area, and therefore, the facts do not create an effective platform from which to argue the area is part of the curtilage. Once an area is determined not to be within the curtilage, it is considered "open fields," and open fields are, by definition, outside of Fourth Amendment protection.

- **Additional references**: *See* LaFave, Israel, King & Kerr, Criminal Procedure § 3.2(d) (6th ed. 2017); Whitebread & Slobogin, Criminal Procedure: An Analysis of Cases and Concepts § 4.03(c) (7th ed. 2020).

33. **The best answer is (a).** The essential question here is whether Milhous has actual or apparent authority to give consent to search Bart's boxes. The answer is no. The boxes were owned by Bart and were given to Milhous for storage. First, Bart maintained a legitimate expectation of privacy in his belongings, satisfying the standing standard delineated in *Rakas v. Illinois*, 439 U.S. 128 (1978). Under that standard, Bart retained his expectation of privacy because he sought to preserve the items as private (they were placed in closed boxes, Bart never gave Milhous permission to go into the boxes, and there is no indication Milhous previously opened the boxes) and because society recognizes this expectation as reasonable. *Cf. United States v. Waller*, 426 F.3d 838 (6th Cir. 2005) ("[C]ommon experience of life . . . teaches all of us that the law's 'enclosed spaces' [—] mankind's valises, suitcases, footlockers, strong boxes, etc. [—] are frequently the objects of his highest privacy expectations."). Second, it was not reasonable for the police to believe that Milhous had the power to consent to a search of Bart's private effects, even under the doctrine of apparent authority, since Milhous explained the circumstances of how the boxes came to be in the garage. The police may not simply presume authority to consent. *See Illinois v. Rodriguez*, 497 U.S. 177 (1990) (woman had a key to her boyfriend's apartment, said she had her things there, and otherwise comported herself as a joint occupant of the premises; police acted reasonably in acting on her consent to enter). **Answer (b) travels down an irrelevant path.** Whether Bart was an overnight guest would be important if he were claiming some right of privacy in the home itself. He isn't. Bart owns the items in the garage, left them with Milhous for safekeeping, and insofar as the boxes themselves are concerned, he retains an expectation of privacy whether he is staying over or not. **Answer (c) fails to focus on Milhous's lack of access to the boxes themselves and is wrong.** Milhous may have access to his own garage, but he took Bart's personal items for safekeeping and not for rummaging. While in Milhous's garage, the contents are off limits to Milhous. *Cf. United States v. Waller*, *supra* (rejecting argument that apartment tenants had authority to give consent to search a piece of closed luggage a friend had stored with them for safekeeping); *United States v. Fultz*, 146 F.3d 1102 (9th Cir. 1998) (holding that where defendant stored cardboard boxes in neighbor's garage, neighbor had no authority to consent to search of the boxes; "A person has an expectation of privacy in

his or her private, closed containers" and "does not forfeit that expectation of privacy merely because the container is located in a place that is not controlled exclusively by the container's owner"). **Answer (d) uses a different formulation to say the same thing as answer (c), and it is just as wrong.** Mutual access to an area is not analogous to mutual access to a container stored within that area. As the Supreme Court explained in *United States v. Matlock*, 415 U.S. 164 (1974), "common authority is, of course, not to be implied from the mere property interest a third party has in the property" rather common authority rests "on mutual use of the property by persons generally having *joint access* or control for most purposes" (emphasis added). Accordingly, even though Milhous could effectively consent to search the garage, he could not give his consent to search Bart's items. **Answer (e) misses the point.** If the consent were valid, the lack of probable cause would not matter. As such, the issue of probable cause is irrelevant.

- **Additional references**: *See* LaFave, Israel, King & Kerr, Criminal Procedure § 3.10(d)–(e) (6th ed. 2017); Whitebread & Slobogin, Criminal Procedure: An Analysis of Cases and Concepts § 12.04 (7th ed. 2020).

34. **The best choice is (c).** This question may put you in mind of *Florida v. Bostick*, 501 U.S. 429 (1991), but be careful. The facts are significantly different and so is the outcome. In *Bostick*, the police boarded a bus and for no particular reason, approached Bostick and asked to see his ticket and identification. All was in order, and the documents were returned. The officers then asked Bostick if they could search his luggage, informing him that he need not consent. He agreed and you know the rest of the story: drugs were found and he was prosecuted. A 6–3 majority of the Supreme Court turned back Bostick's argument that the consent was invalid because it was a product of an unlawful detention without reasonable suspicion. The Court rejected the idea that Bostick was detained simply because he was on a cramped bus and did not feel free to leave because the bus was about to depart. The Court stated: "Bostick's freedom of movement was restricted by a factor independent of police conduct—i.e., by his being a passenger on a bus. Accordingly, the 'free to leave' analysis on which Bostick relies is inapplicable. In such a situation, the appropriate inquiry is whether a reasonable person would feel free to decline the officers' requests. . . ." The Court remanded the case with the following guidance: " . . . no seizure occurs when police ask questions of an individual, ask to examine the individual's identification, and request to search his or her luggage—so long as the officers do not convey a message that compliance with their requests is required." That is precisely what occurred here. The officers' instructions, even though prefaced with the words, "with your co-operation," were in the nature of an instruction. The passengers were told to ready their bags for inspection, no one was informed of any alternative, and each passenger, who had to get off the bus anyway, was permitted to go only after the search was completed. The discovery of the object in Scully's bag was a direct product of the illegal search, and all that transpired thereafter was derivative of that illegality.

Answer (a) puts the case too strongly, although it is true that *Bostick* includes some unfortunate language in this regard. In suggesting that the officers there did not convey the message that compliance with their requests were required, the Court cites the following factors: "the officers did not point guns at Bostick or otherwise threaten him and . . . they specifically advised Bostick that he could refuse consent." However, it doesn't follow that an encounter is not a detention simply because the police did not threaten physical harm. They may send the message of compliance in other ways as well, as here. **Answer (b) mistakenly characterizes this as a consensual encounter; it is a detention, as indicated. Answer (d) is wrong.** Scully may have voluntarily admitted she was carrying cocaine, but the admission was a direct product of the illegal detention. That is, after all, how the police discovered the suspicious brick. **Answer (e) makes the test of detention turn on whether the police advised the passengers of the right to refuse consent; this is an error.** It is true that such advice is a factor in determining what message the police conveyed, but it is not necessarily a determinative factor.

- **Additional references**: *See* LAFAVE, ISRAEL, KING & KERR, CRIMINAL PROCEDURE § 3.8 (6th ed. 2017); WHITEBREAD & SLOBOGIN, CRIMINAL PROCEDURE: AN ANALYSIS OF CASES AND CONCEPTS § 11.02 (7th ed. 2020).

35. **The correct answer is (c).** This question is loosely drawn from *United States v. Nolan-Cooper*, 155 F.3d 221 (3d Cir. 1998). Together with the next question, it tests your understanding of the Due Process defense of outrageous government conduct. The defense is based on the idea that a criminal case can be dismissed if the *government's conduct* in gathering information against the defendant is "so outrageous as to shock the conscience of the court." *United States v. Dyess*, 478 F.3d 224 (4th Cir. 2007). The Supreme Court, in dicta, recognized the existence of the defense saying, "We may someday be presented with a situation in which the conduct of law enforcement agents is so outrageous that due process principles would absolutely bar the government from invoking judicial processes to obtain a conviction." *United States v. Russell*, 411 U.S. 423 (1973) (citation omitted). The Court confirmed the theoretical availability of the defense in *Hampton v. United States*, 425 U.S. 484 (1976), but it is only applied in "rare cases," *United States v. Dyess, supra, accord United States v. Santana*, 6 F.3d 1 (1st Cir. 1993) ("The banner of outrageous conduct is often raised but seldom saluted."). To prevail with this defense, the defendant must show government conduct that is not just bad or unsavory, but conduct that is so offensive that it shocks the conscience and renders an ensuing prosecution fundamentally unfair. *United States v. Ciszkowski*, 492 F.3d 1264 (11th Cir. 2007); *United States v. Dyess, supra*. In this regard, the defense stands with such extreme instances of government misbehavior such as using violence to extract evidence from a suspect, securing convictions through known perjury, and conducting sham trials or trials hurried to conclusion by mob domination. *See Brown v. Mississippi*, 297 U.S. 278 (1936) (cataloging examples of shocking

government conduct). These are unmistakably bad things, things that offend our fundamental principles of justice. The use of informants, sting operations, and false friends routinely involves government lying, deception, or preying upon a person's misplaced hope or affections. These actions are perhaps distasteful, but according to the courts, they aren't shocking. *See United States v. Hoffecker*, 530 F.3d 137 (3d Cir. 2008) (a court should not dismiss an indictment each time the government acts deceptively or participates in a crime that it is investigating). In this regard, although the Supreme Court has not set clear standards in this area, lower courts have rejected the idea that sexual intercourse during an investigation constitutes outrageous government conduct. *United States v. Nolan-Cooper, supra* (intimate exchanges were not orchestrated by the government to achieve investigatory advantages; no outrageous government conduct found); *accord United States v. Simpson*, 813 F.2d 1462 (9th Cir. 1987) (with government awareness, FBI informant developed a sexual relationship with the defendant and later asked him to sell drugs to her "friends" who were in fact FBI agents; deceptive use of sex may, as an abstract matter, be morally offense but not shocking in the real world of law enforcement). **Thus, answer (d), which asserts that a sexual relationship with a target is always outrageous conduct, is wrong.** Similarly, **answer (a) is incorrect.** The fact that a government agency does not approve of its agent's behavior does not resolve whether that behavior was so shocking as to violate fundamental fairness under due process of law. The agent is still acting as an agent even if acting contrary to policy. **Answer (b) falls into error** because it confuses the defense of outrageous conduct with the defense of entrapment. The two defenses are often discussed together but are different. Under the majority and federal view, entrapment is a non-constitutional defense resting on the idea (some say "fiction") that the legislature did not intend to criminalize acts induced by government agents and committed by persons with no predisposition to commit the offense. Thus, the focus is on the defendant's predisposition. But with outrageous government conduct, the focus is exclusively on the government and its actions. *See, e.g., United States v. Russell, supra; United States v. Ciszkowski, supra*. The predisposition of the defendant is irrelevant. The reason why outrageous government conduct and entrapment are linked relates to the minority view of entrapment that focuses on whether the government conduct was of a kind likely to induce a reasonable person to commit the crime charged. This so-called objective test focuses on the government's behavior, not on the defendant's predisposition. In that sense, it is similar to the outrageous conduct defense. But the similarity ends there. Even this version of entrapment is a non-constitutional defense, the defense is available even if not shocking so long as it operated to induce criminality, and the government must disprove entrapment beyond a reasonable doubt. Finally, **answer (e) is wrong** because, again, conduct is not necessarily outrageous simply because it violates internal law enforcement policies.

- **Additional references**: *See* LaFave, Israel, King & Kerr, Criminal Procedure § 5.4(c) (6th ed. 2017); Whitebread & Slobogin, Criminal Procedure: An Analysis of Cases and Concepts §§ 19.02, 19.03 (7th ed. 2020).

36. **Only answer (e) correctly states the essence of the defense of outrageous government conduct and the consequences of a violation.** Outrageous government conduct is a Due Process defense which, if proved by the defendant, will lead to a dismissal of the charges. *See United States v. Russell*, 411 U.S. 423 (1973); *United States v. Twigg*, 588 F.2d 373 (3d Cir. 1978); *United States v. Barbosa*, 271 F.3d 438 (3d Cir. 2001) (if defendant had shown that the government unreasonably increased the likelihood of drug mule's swallowing of drugs, case would have been dismissed as outrageous given the inherent risk of death or serious bodily harm in drug trafficking through swallowing). Due process violations always result in dismissal or exclusion (think of other subjects, such as confessions or identifications). **Answers (a), (b), (c), and (d) confuse this constitutional shield with the statutory-based defense of entrapment and should be rejected.** Under the majority view of entrapment, a jury may not return a guilty verdict against the defendant if she was induced to commit a crime by the government and had no predisposition to do so. The theory is that the legislature could not have intended to criminalize acts in such circumstances. But this view of legislative intention is abandoned if the defendant commits an act of violence because the legislature will not be presumed to permit the acquittal of someone importuned to engage in violent acts. *Sorrells v. United States*, 287 U.S. 435 (1932). With outrageous government conduct, the focus is on the government's behavior, not the defendant's, and therefore **answer (a)** is incorrect. **Answer (b) errs** because the government bears the burden of proving that the defendant was not entrapped while the defendant bears the burden of proving outrageous government conduct. *See, e.g., United States v. Dyess*, 478 F.3d 224 (4th Cir. 2007). **Answer (c) incorrectly suggests** that outrageous conduct is a question of fact. Entrapment is a question of fact for the jury; outrageous government conduct rising to the level of a Due Process violation is a conclusion of law for the court. **Answer (d) is flawed.** Entrapment exists as a matter of statutory interpretation; outrageous government conduct is a constitutional defense which, like any other constitutional defense, is immune from mere legislative attempts to negate it. *See Dickerson v. United States*, 530 U.S. 428 (2000) (Miranda rules are constitutionally based and may not be abrogated by Congressional legislation).

- **Additional references**: *See* LaFave, Israel, King & Kerr, Criminal Procedure § 5.4(c) (6th ed. 2017); Whitebread & Slobogin, Criminal Procedure: An Analysis of Cases and Concepts §§ 19.02, 19.03 (7th ed. 2020).

37. **The correct answer is (e).** Ordinarily, the entry into and search of a person's home requires probable cause and a warrant. But Mr. Tee is a parolee, and as the facts suggest, he is released under applicable rules

and regulations, to which he assented, that permit parole officers to make a home visit and conduct searches of his living quarters. Accordingly, the search here was entirely lawful. The Supreme Court, in *Samson v. California*, 547 U.S. 843 (2006), described a continuum of privacy expectations. In other words, a person's reasonable expectation of privacy will differ depending upon one's status as a regular citizen, a probationer, or a parolee. The Court then upheld, for the first time, a status search conducted without any individualized suspicion (which explains why **answer (c) is incorrect**); that is, a search based entirely on one's status as a parolee. Notably, the Court did not rely on the "special needs" doctrine, but rather conducted a "totality of the circumstances" reasonableness analysis balancing the individual and state interests. The *Samson* Court reasoned that no suspicion is required for parolee searches because parolees technically remain in custody—instead of completing a term of incarceration in prison, parolees are permitted to complete their sentence outside prison walls. In exchange for this early release, parolees agree to be bound by certain conditions. Statutes may provide that suspicionless searches are one such condition. So long as the parolee is aware of this condition, a suspicionless search will be reasonable because the governmental interests in rehabilitation and crime prevention far outweigh the diminished privacy expectations of parolees. **Answer (a) errs in two ways.** First, rumors do not amount to reasonable suspicion. Secondly, even *if* there was reasonable suspicion, none was needed for the search here. Note, however, that reasonable suspicion is required for warrantless searches of *probationer's* homes because, based on the continuum described in *Samson*, probationer's retain more privacy than parolees but less than regular citizens. *Griffin v. Wisconsin*, 483 U.S. 868 (1987). **Answer (b) is wrong** because no warrant was necessary. Lastly, **answer (d) is incorrect** because, even though the parole officers brought the police for "back up," this was only to protect them in case Mr. Tee decided to become violent or otherwise uncooperative. The presence of the police did not convert this into a standard law enforcement action. Of course, *if* the police were using the parole officers and their special access as a pretext to investigate criminal activity, then ordinary Fourth Amendment principles would apply. But that's not our case. Finally, with respect to all of the answers, the use of Mr. Tee's statement in the apartment is entirely dependent on the legality of the entry into the apartment. If the parole officers were validly in the apartment, which they were, then the statement is admissible. If they were illegally present, all of the evidence plus the in-house statement would be inadmissible as a fruit of the illegality. *New York v. Harris*, 495 U.S. 14 (1990).

- **Additional references**: *See* LAFAVE, ISRAEL, KING & KERR, CRIMINAL PROCEDURE § 3.9(j) (6th ed. 2017); WHITEBREAD & SLOBOGIN, CRIMINAL PROCEDURE: AN ANALYSIS OF CASES AND CONCEPTS § 13.10 (7th ed. 2020).

38. **The correct answer is (b).** This question is based on *United States v. Simmons*, 560 F.3d 98 (2d Cir. 2009). At first blush, this case sounds like *Florida v. J.L.*, 529 U.S. 266 (2000), where the Supreme Court considered

"whether an anonymous tip that a person is carrying a gun is, without more, sufficient to justify a police officer's stop and frisk of that person." In *J.L.*, an anonymous called reported to police "that a young black male standing at a particular bus stop and wearing a plaid shirt was carrying a gun." Police went to the bus stop, saw three black males, one of whom was wearing a plaid shirt, and arrested the male with the plaid shirt after a frisk revealed a gun. The Court found that the stop and subsequent arrest in *J.L.*, lacked sufficient reliability because the stop was based solely on the "bare report of an unknown, unaccountable informant who neither explained how he knew about the gun nor supplied any basis for believing he had inside information about J.L." Here, however, the anonymous 911 caller in this case reported an assault with a weapon in progress (more than the simple possession reported in *J.L.*). Based on language from *J.L.* which hinted that some situations would be so dangerous as to justify a search even without the same level of reliability, several circuit courts have "distinguished *J.L.* when the tip is not one of general criminality, but of an ongoing emergency." *United States v. Hicks*, 531 F.3d 555 (7th Cir. 2008) (collecting cases); *United States v. Brown*, 496 F.3d 1070 (10th Cir. 2007) (911 call reporting a man who entered an apartment brandishing a gun and threatening the tenant); *United States v. Elston*, 479 F.3d 314 (4th Cir. 2007) (911 call reporting a drunk driver); *United States v. Terry-Crespo*, 356 F.3d 1170 (9th Cir. 2004) (911 caller had been threatened by the suspect with a firearm). As such, several circuits have found that a tip reporting an ongoing emergency, as opposed to general criminality, is entitled to a higher degree of reliability and requires a lesser showing of corroboration than a tip that alleges general criminality. *United States v. Simmons, supra.* Courts are more willing to find that anonymous callers are reliable if the informant indicates that his or her report is based on contemporaneous personal observation of the call's subject. *United States v. Elston*, 479 F.3d 314 (4th Cir. 2007). This is because it is the job of the police to respond to reports of emergency situations without delay. *Navarette v. California*, 572 U.S. 393 (2014) (A recent somewhat related case involving the proof necessary to establish reasonable suspicion is worthy of note here). In *Navarette*, a California Highway Patrol officer stopped a pickup truck because it matched the description of a vehicle that a 911 caller had recently reported as having run her off the road. The Court held that an anonymous 911 caller who claimed that a driver ran her off the road bore the adequate indicia of reliability to provide officers with reasonable suspicion, under the totality of the circumstances, to stop the suspected driver. However, in order to make the stop, the police must still have reasonable suspicion that criminal activity is afoot. *Terry v. Ohio*, 392 U.S. 1 (1968). Here, reasonable suspicion existed. Simmons matched the 911 caller's description, he was wearing sweatpants and a leather jacket in the middle of August, and he began to walk away briskly when he noticed the police officers. Flight, coupled with presence in a high-crime area, is often suggestive of illegal activity. *Cf. Illinois v. Wardlow*, 528 U.S. 119 (2000). Although none of these factors is dispositive, together with the possibility of an ongoing emergency, they gave rise to reasonable suspicion. Moreover, the frisk was permissible given the report that the officers received and because of Simmons' refusal to stop and remove his hands from his pocket. *Adams v. Williams*, 407 U.S. 143 (1972) (noting that a frisk is justified when an officer reasonably believes that a suspect is armed and dangerous because it "allow[s] the officer to pursue his investigation without fear of violence"). **Answer (d) is incorrect.** While a mere "refusal to cooperate, without more, does not furnish the minimal level of objective justification needed for a detention or seizure," *Florida v. Bostick*, 501 U.S. 429 (1991), the factors supporting the stop existed before Simmons refused to remove his hands from his pocket. **Answer (a) is also incorrect** because the officers did not have, and did not need, probable cause to stop Simmons. All they needed was reasonable suspicion. **Answer (c) is wrong** because by the end of the exchange, the police did have probable cause to arrest Simmons. **Answer (e) errs** because it fails to account for the other circumstances that gave rise to reasonable suspicion.

- **Additional references**: *See* LAFAVE, ISRAEL, KING & KERR, CRIMINAL PROCEDURE § 3.8(d)–(e) (6th ed. 2017); WHITEBREAD & SLOBOGIN, CRIMINAL PROCEDURE: AN ANALYSIS OF CASES AND CONCEPTS §§ 11.02, 11.03 (7th ed. 2020).

39. **The right answer is (d).** In this question, Nora is in custody and is subjected to interrogation. Miranda requires that warnings be given. If they aren't, then none of the incriminating statements may be used. And it doesn't matter if the police were acting in good faith. **Hence, answer (b) is incorrect.** And it doesn't matter if, had the warnings been given, Nora would have talked anyway. Miranda announced a bright-line rule, designed to avoid inquiries into what might have, could have, or would have happened if the police acted differently. **Hence, answer (a) is incorrect.** But, what if the statements were truly, honestly, no kidding around, voluntary? Are state judges free to excuse a violation of Miranda if, in the individual case, there was no "real" compulsion placed on the suspect to talk? The answer is no, and Miranda was direct and clear about that. Just as Congress may not by legislation overrule the prophylactic rules of Miranda, neither may state trial judges. *Dickerson v. United States*, 530 U.S. 428 (2000). Moreover, returning to a voluntariness, case-by-case approach is not "equally as effective as Miranda;" to the contrary, it was that approach that Miranda was attempting to replace. **So, answer (c) should be rejected. Answer (e) comes close to being correct, but it is too muscular.** The Miranda warnings are not "constitutionally compelled" requirements. They are, as answer (d) puts it, constitutionally based. They are court-fashioned, prophylactic rules that protect more than the Fifth Amendment protects in order to insure that the Fifth Amendment is protected. But this constitutional foundation is enough to make the Miranda rules legitimately binding on state courts. *United States v. Dickerson, supra*.

- **Additional references**: *See* LaFave, Israel, King & Kerr, Criminal Procedure § 6.5 (6th ed. 2017); Whitebread & Slobogin, Criminal Procedure: An Analysis of Cases and Concepts § 16.02 (7th ed. 2020).

40. **The right answer is (a).** If police have probable cause to search a car, they may do so without a warrant under the so-called "automobile exception" to the warrant clause. *Chambers v. Maroney*, 399 U.S. 42 (1970). And if they have probable cause to search a container and that container is in a car, they may search the container without a warrant under the so-called "automobile exception." *California v. Acevedo*, 500 U.S. 565 (1991). However, the question whether the police may search with or without a warrant is an issue separate from the *scope* of a permissible search. This is a scope question. The police only have probable cause to believe that the briefcase contains evidence of a crime. They have no probable cause to believe that the taxi contains evidence of a crime. There are no facts suggesting that the taxi driver is in league with Dan Couche, no facts suggesting Couche may have hidden evidence of a crime in the interior of the taxi (he was under constant surveillance), and no facts suggesting any separate criminal activity by the taxi driver. The scope of the search was, therefore, limited to the briefcase, and any search beyond that was a violation of the taxi driver's Fourth Amendment rights. Indeed this very scenario was anticipated by the Court in *California v. Acevedo, supra*. Referring to an earlier automobile exception case, *United States v. Ross*, 456 U.S. 798 (1982), the Court said: " 'Probable cause to believe that a container placed in the trunk of a taxi contains contraband or evidence does not justify a search of the entire cab.' We reaffirm that principle. In the case before us, the police had probable cause to believe that the paper bag in the automobile's trunk contained marijuana. That probable cause now allows a warrantless search of the paper bag. The facts in the record reveal that the police did not have probable cause to believe that contraband was hidden in any other part of the automobile and a search of the entire vehicle would have been without probable cause and unreasonable under the Fourth Amendment." **Answer (d) misses the scope limitation entirely and is wrong.** Yes, there was probable cause to believe that illicit drugs were in the briefcase which was in the taxi, but the probable cause started and ended there. **Answer (b) is incorrect** because it focuses on the lack of a warrant, which because of the automobile exception, is not at issue in this question. **Answer (c) can't be taken seriously.** If a person has a reasonable expectation of privacy in the place or thing searched or seized, he has standing. *Rakas v. Illinois*, 439 U.S. 128 (1978). The taxi driver was the person detained by the police. He is the owner/lawful custodian of the car. He has a reasonable expectation of privacy in his own freedom of movement and in property he owns or controls. At one time, there was an argument that, *in addition* to persons who would otherwise have standing to object to a search, the courts should also recognize standing of a target (e.g., the police invading a house of a third party in order to obtain evidence against you). *Rakas v. Illinois, supra* (idea raised and rejected); *Alderman v.*

United States, 394 U.S. 165 (1969) (Justice Fortas argues for target standing in a separate opinion; majority implicitly rejects it). But there is no support for the idea that a person cannot complain of police intrusions into her property or person *unless* she was a target. Obviously that would be an invitation to considerable mischief. **Answer (e) sounds appealing, but it's not a good choice.** Whatever might be said about administrative searches and the rules and regulations that could govern taxi operations, there are no facts here establishing the existence of such rules and regulations. In the absence of such rules and regulations, a taxi driver, no less than any other owner/operator of an automobile retains a reasonable expectation of privacy in personal property kept within the car.

- **Additional references**: *See* LAFAVE, ISRAEL, KING & KERR, CRIMINAL PROCEDURE § 3.7(c) (6th ed. 2017); WHITEBREAD & SLOBOGIN, CRIMINAL PROCEDURE: AN ANALYSIS OF CASES AND CONCEPTS § 7.04 (7th ed. 2020).

41. **The best answer is (e).** This question is modeled after *United States v. Briasco*, 640 F.3d 857 (8th Cir. 2011). (*See United States v. Branch*, 537 F.3d 328 (4th Cir. 2008) *cert. denied*, 555 U.S. 1118 (2009) for another case discussing reasonable suspicion in a similar situation.) To begin, Officer Parson plainly had probable cause to make the initial traffic stop as John was driving 20 miles per over the speed limit. During the course of this otherwise lawful traffic stop, Officer Parson observed the following facts: the trunk was sagging, both John and Marybeth were vague in describing their travel plans, John grew increasingly anxious, John had a criminal record of narcotics distribution, and the air freshener appeared to be used in order to cover something up. Do these facts amount to reasonable suspicion of an offense other than the traffic violation? While in isolation each fact seems innocent enough, reasonable suspicion is a commonsense inquiry that asks if police officers, based on the totality of the circumstances, possessed specific and articulable facts giving rise to a fair possibility of criminal activity. *United States v. Arvizu*, 534 U.S. 266 (2002). This inquiry allows police to draw upon their experience in making the reasonable suspicion assessment. The Supreme Court has recognized that factors consistent with innocent travel can, when taken together, give rise to reasonable suspicion. *United States v. Sokolow*, 490 U.S. 1 (1989) ("Any one of these factors is not by itself proof of any illegal conduct and is quite consistent with innocent travel. But we think taken together they amount to reasonable suspicion."). Here, all of the facts amount to reasonable suspicion that criminal activity was afoot and therefore **answer (b) is wrong**. This reasonable suspicion provided the justification necessary for the ensuing investigatory detention. Note that it was only after establishing an articulable reasonable suspicion that Officer Parson expanded the scope of the detention and sought consent to search the trunk. *See Arizona v. Johnson*, 555 U.S. 323 (2009) ("An officer's inquiries into matters unrelated to the justification for the traffic stop . . . do not convert the encounter into something other than a lawful seizure, so long as those inquiries do not measurably extend the duration

of the stop."). At the time Officer Parson sought John's consent, a mere 10 minutes had passed. This short extension of the stop was not unreasonable. Now, the question remains whether the remaining 42 minutes was unreasonable. To answer this, recall that traffic stops are analogous to investigatory *"Terry* stops." *Berkemer v. McCarty*, 468 U.S. 420 (1984). Accordingly, the investigatory activity conducted pursuant to a traffic stop is limited in duration and it "must be reasonably related in scope to the circumstances which justified the interference in the first place." *Terry v. Ohio*, 392 U.S. 1 (1968). While there is not a strict time limit on a permissible stop, at some point, a stop becomes an arrest (and therefore, must be supported by probable cause). *United States v. Sharpe*, 470 U.S. 675 (1985). Here, Officer Parson was justified in continuing the detention because he was unable to confirm or dispel his reasonable suspicion that criminal activity was underway. While 42 minutes may seem like a long time, Officer Parson gave John the opportunity to put a quick end to the stop (by consenting to the search) and when John refused to take this offer, Officer Parson diligently pursued a canine to conduct the search. Accordingly, the 42 minute detention was a reasonable extension of the initial stop and **answer (c) incorrect**. *United States v. Sharpe, supra*. **Answer (d) is not the best choice** because if the canine was not diligently pursued, the mere fact Officer Parson gave John an "out" would not be sufficient to render the 42 minute wait reasonable. (Note: Although refusal to consent cannot ordinarily give rise to the justification to search, the justification here existed independent of John's refusal. If Officer Parson had used the refusal to "ratchet up" the level of suspicion, probable cause would have arisen and because of the automobile exception, *Chambers v. Maroney*, 399 U.S. 42 (1970), Officer Parson would have been able to conduct a search right then and there as opposed to waiting for Officer Larson to bring Dante to the scene.) Now, let's discuss the canine sniff. We know that canine sniffs are not searches because they only detect the presence or absence of contraband. *United States v. Place*, 462 U.S. 696 (1983). Therefore, a canine sniff does not require additional justification provided that the detention leading up to the sniff was not offensive to the Fourth Amendment. *Illinois v. Caballes*, 543 U.S. 405 (2005) (canine sniff of vehicle permissible because investigative technique did not unreasonably prolong the detention). Once a trained narcotics dog alerts officers to the presence of contraband, probable cause arises. *United States v. Branch, supra*; *United States v. Perez*, 440 F.3d 363 (6th Cir. 2006). **Answer (a) misses the mark** because once Dante gave a positive signal, the officers had the requisite cause to search the trunk of the car, including any containers that were capable of concealing the object of the search. *California v. Acevedo*, 500 U.S. 565 (1991). John's motion to exclude the evidence will be denied.

- **Additional references**: *See* LaFave, Israel, King & Kerr, Criminal Procedure § 3.8(d) (6th ed. 2017); Whitebread & Slobogin, Criminal Procedure: An Analysis of Cases and Concepts §§ 11.02, 11.03, 11.06 (7th ed. 2020).

42. The best answer is (d). The police watched Mark and Hernan engage in a drug transaction with a known dealer and therefore, they had probable cause to arrest the men. They also had probable cause to seize any drugs in the vehicle, even if those drugs were in the trunk of the car, as well as any evidence that was in plain view while they were lawfully in a place to see and access the evidence. Just because the police had probable cause to arrest as soon as the initial transaction was completed, the police were not required to seek a warrant immediately nor were they required to make an arrest on the spot. **Answer (a) and (c) are incorrect** because, as the Supreme Court declared in *Kentucky v. King*, 563 U.S. 452 (2011), "[l]aw enforcement officers are under no constitutional duty to call a halt to criminal investigation the moment they have the minimum evidence to establish probable cause." Answer (a) is correct about the fate of the evidence inside of the home as it applies to Hernan's trial. Although Mark's sister owned the home, there is no evidence that Hernan was there for anything other than illicit activity, that is, dropping off drugs and manufacturing other drugs. *Cf. Minnesota v. Carter*, 525 U.S. 83 (1998). Perhaps if there was some evidence that Hernan was a regular and welcome guest, the analysis would be different. Answer (c) is incorrect in categorizing the home entry and search as falling under the protective sweep doctrine. Hernan ran into the home and thus, the police were not conducting a protective sweep. Rather, the police here were engaged in hot pursuit and were fully justified in entering the home without a warrant under the exigent circumstances doctrine. *United States v. Santana*, 427 U.S. 38 (1976). This explains why **answer (b) is wrong**. Even if the police were engaged in a protective sweep, that doctrine allows the police to enter the home and conduct a limited cursory investigation of any place where individuals may be hiding. *Maryland v. Buie*, 494 U.S. 325 (1990). Because a person could have been hiding behind the meth lab door, the police would not have exceeded the bounds of a permissible *Buie* sweep. Because the police learned the information about the meth lab while legally inside of the home (due to the exigent circumstances), everything the police learned while inside was properly used to obtain a warrant. Moreover, the police acted properly in not investigating further without a warrant. Thus, **answer (e) is plainly incorrect**.

- **Additional references**: *See* LaFave, Israel, King & Kerr, Criminal Procedure §§ 3.2(c), 3.6(e) (6th ed. 2017); Whitebread & Slobogin, Criminal Procedure: An Analysis of Cases and Concepts § 9.03 (7th ed. 2020).